Cousteau

Cousteau

THE CAPTAIN AND HIS WORLD

Richard Munson

PARAGON HOUSE
NEW YORK

First Paperback edition, 1991

Published in the United States by

Paragon House
90 Fifth Avenue
New York, NY 10011

Reprinted by arrangement with William Morrow & Company, Inc.

Library of Congress Cataloging-in-Publication Data

Munson, Richard.
    Cousteau, the captain and his world / Richard Munson. —1st pbk. ed.
      p.   cm.
    Reprint. Originally published : New York : W. Morrow, © 1989.
    Includes bibliographical references and index.
    ISBN 1-55778-415-9 : $12.95
    1. Cousteau, Jacques Yves.   2. Oceanographers—France—Biography.
I. Title.
GC30.C68M86   1991
551.46'0092—dc20
   [B]   90-36476
                                       CIP

Manufactured in the United States of America

10 9 8 7 6 5 4 3 2 1

To Diane

Contents

Cousteau

Introduction

The Captain was late. His camera crew, weary after two hours of small talk with the park ranger, began to worry that the rising morning sun would cast shadows on the star's face. An officious young volunteer, obviously trained in pacifying officials forced to wait for Jacques-Yves Cousteau, walked to his car to retrieve presents for the ranger, including a colorful picture book, a T-shirt, and other Cousteau Society paraphernalia.

Cabrillo Beach showcased an ideal September morning in Southern California. Schools had reopened, so only a few wet-suited surfers ventured into the calm water. As the morning warmed up and wore on, the crew abandoned their flannel jackets and donned dark sunglasses.

Suggesting that the Captain might have gone directly to the beach, the volunteer walked under the coast highway that separated the ranger's headquarters from the shore. Half an hour later he scurried back, urgently announcing, "He's arrived!" The crew scrambled to their cars and followed the ranger to special parking spaces near the beach.

Cousteau was taller and more slender than his films suggest. He appeared frail and tired. His son Jean-Michel, casually dressed in a Mediterranean-style blousy white shirt open to the middle of his chest, tried to take charge. Two new assistants looked frazzled from a hectic morning of adjusting to the Captain's changing schedule.

No apologies. No one assumed they were needed. We later learned that the Captain had been making complex financial arrangements for

13

Jan, widow of Philippe, his beloved son who had died in a plane accident in 1979.

The volunteer introduced Cousteau to the park ranger, explaining how the official had arranged for the day's filming at the state facility. The Captain became animated for a moment, flashed his famous smile, signed an autograph, and headed for the shade behind a lifeguard station that overlooks the cove.

Jean-Michel and the crew discussed filming strategies for the television advertisements intended to boost membership in the Cousteau Society. The heir apparent immediately rejected the proposed arrangements, declaring that his father was weary and would stand for only one location shot. The crew adjusted their plans, descended the steep stairs to the cove, and set up the camera next to the water.

The sound man, not a Cousteau regular, argued that the breaking waves would overpower the Captain's speech. Jean-Michel dismissed the complaint with the smug confidence that Cousteau filmmakers, having won countless awards, are the world's best.

Zheek (the familiar nickname that comes from pronouncing Cousteau's acronym, JYC, with a French accent) and his son reviewed the script, written in large letters on white cue cards. The two fluctuated between English and French, moving to their native tongue to express emotion or to argue.

Finally satisfied and ready for action, Captain Cousteau came alive. Disregarding his seventy-six years, he scampered across the beach and to the surf to wet down his hair. Clearly here was a pro who knew what he needed to look good for the camera. But his effort to capture a bit of the ocean spray said something more about him. As he bent to the water and moved with the waves, he became the ocean's conductor, directing the sea to lap up gently before him.

The cameras rolled, and the celebrated Cousteau persona emerged. The lyrical French accent became animated and sincere, and from deep within the gaunt face glistened the sharp blue eyes of the world's most famous living adventurer.

The two assistants tried to hush the small crowd that had gathered to watch Jacques Cousteau make a "movie." Slight variations in the text and the delivery were suggested. The Captain reluctantly agreed to one more reading.

The producer, another Cousteau Society newcomer, tried to remove the multicolored set of pens protruding obviously from a pocket on the star's left shoulder. But the Captain would not hear of abandoning his "trademark," and he delivered a short lecture on the symbolism of the colors he carried with him on his voyages.

The crew and the crowd applauded Cousteau's last take. The Captain turned to talk with the sea, throwing his arms open to engulf the scene. He ran up the beach, stopped, and declared to his son in French that it was time to go. Jean-Michel, however, had lines to deliver for his own series of ads. The Captain sulked back to the protective shade of the lifeguard station, and the young volunteer stood guard to protect his privacy.

With filming complete, the two Cousteaus posed for photographs with the producer, the radioman, the ranger, and a few bystanders. The impatient Captain rapidly reviewed his plans for the rest of the day with his assistants. One remained to make editing arrangements for the television spots. The other shuttled the living legend into a waiting car, and Jacques-Yves Cousteau was off to another appointment.

CHAPTER ONE

The Living Legend

"Divers are true spacemen," began the announcer. On the screen, five undersea explorers descended into the dark waters, each holding a bright torch that sent a thick trail of silver bubbles perking back up toward the surface. Sixty-five feet below them, Jacques Cousteau floated in liquid space, recording the underwater flight of this torch team in order to reveal, for the first time to a large audience, the ocean's exquisite and colorful beauty. To thousands of theatergoers this opening spectacle of *The Silent World,* a 1956 film that won an Oscar and the Grand Prize at the Cannes Film Festival, ignited their imagination and sense of wonder as never before.

In the ensuing thirty-three years, despite some notable lapses, Captain Cousteau has continued to amaze the public. While traveling aboard the *Calypso,* he has touched giant whales, befriended shy octopuses, and confronted frenzied sharks. He has produced and starred in almost a hundred films shown in scores of countries and has hosted the most popular documentary series in television history. The author or coauthor of more than eighty books, Cousteau also has taken at least a million photographs, directed a major museum, and founded environmental organizations in the United States, Canada, and France.

As the Wright brothers conquered the skies, so the Captain opened the undersea world to humans. In addition to co-inventing the Aqua Lung,℠ which enables divers to breathe and move about freely, Cousteau helped perfect underwater photography with new cameras and lights. He launched the science of undersea archaeology, discovered petroleum beneath the ocean floor in the Persian Gulf, and constructed undersea stations and small submarines for oceanographic research. For his accomplishments, the French explorer-inventor-filmmaker has received many prizes, including tne Medal of Freedom, the United States' highest award for civilians.

These achievements alone, however, have not made Cousteau one of the world's most admired humans. He's revered more for his unique zest for life, his irrepressible curiosity, his youthful sense of wonder. I've spent my life, he exclaims, "amazed by nature and dazzled by the experiences of life."

The lithe and lean adventurer is a product of the media age, having appeared longer on television than almost any actor or actress. He began filming his exploits at the age of thirteen, and he has orchestrated a lifetime of activities to be recorded by his cameras and set down by his pen.

Beyond the television persona, however, the public knows little about Jacques-Yves Cousteau. And that's just the way he has wanted it. Out of the camera's focus, Cousteau has suffered, struggled, and prospered. He endured chronic anemia as a child and almost lost his left arm in an automobile accident at the age of twenty-six. His older brother was sentenced to death by the French government for collaborating with the Nazis during World War II. His younger son died in a plane crash.

Cousteau denies he's wealthy, having mortgaged his own home three times to raise funds for early films, but he has come to manage an international empire of prosperous businesses. He chairs U.S. Divers of Santa Ana, California, which manufactures half the diving gear sold in the United States. Similar companies operate in Japan, Italy, and France, while other Cousteau ventures market wind turbines and design marine structures. Cousteau has spent much of the personal fortune accumulated from his successful television and film productions and business dealings on elaborate equipment for future voyages. Frequently he suggests that "the ideal is to own nothing," but he travels first class and is a connoisseur of fine French wine.

The Captain and his staff have worked hard to promote and protect the Cousteau legend. Not a modest man, he has cultivated an image of himself as "the world's greatest explorer," the ingenious inventor of undersea equipment, and the ocean's best champion. But scores of colleagues and experts see things differently. Cousteau, for instance, claims to have made earthshaking discoveries, but leading oceanographers complain that he focuses more on showmanship than on science. And although the Captain boasts that he has "rescued countless endangered species and exposed the ecological dangers which are making mankind an equally endangered species," key ecologists argue that he fails to use his substantial political clout to protect the environment.

Cousteau begins nearly every day at an airport. On his way to inspect various branches of his international empire, he uses the commercial planes on which he travels as an office. When in the air, he says, "I warn the hostess: no drinks, no food, just bring me tea repeatedly and without request. Then I tear through stacks of magazines and books, ripping out things I can use and writing memos. It's a fantastic chewing process where I try to keep up with the whole world: engineering, politics, religion, stupidities, films, and plays, which I never go to see, but I want to know what the critics say anyway."

While the Captain flies from project to project, his wife, Simone, usually remains aboard the *Calypso*. In fact, she's spent more time on the ship than her husband and sons combined. Descended from a prominent French military family, Simone is a strong-willed protector of her husband and his staff. While adamant about remaining off camera and behind the scenes, she provides continuity, direction, and support to the crew, who call her *la bergère,* or the Shepherdess.

Jacques and Simone have owned the same large apartment in Monaco for more than twenty years, but neither spends many hours overlooking the Mediterranean. They also maintain a three-room apartment in Paris, near the Arc de Triomphe. On the rare occasions when the Captain has an hour alone, he seals off the world to enjoy his vast library of records. Trained as a classical pianist, he infrequently sits at the keyboard or picks up an accordion. On impulse, he also writes poems, although he throws them away, and he paints surrealistic landscapes.

Cousteau avoids discussions of his often strained family life. His brother died blaming Jacques for not having done more to free him from French prisons. And the immediate family has not been as close-knit as photo albums suggest. Philippe, the dashing adventurer who drowned in a seaplane accident in 1979, tended to take after his imaginative and creative father, while Jean-Michel adopted many of his mother's industrious habits. The two boys rarely got along, and when it was apparent that the younger Philippe would inherit his father's businesses, Jean-Michel went off to architecture school and later started his Ocean Search tourist center, initially headquartered in Hilton Head, South Carolina.

Cousteau Society staff members found Philippe to be a daring and handsome man who, like Errol Flynn, conveyed an adventuresome spirit on film, but they complained of his arrogance and mismanagement. Jean-Michel, they say, is less charismatic but more systematic and easier to deal with. While women swooned over Philippe, they call Jean-Michel a "sweetie."

The Captain stops by the society's New York office for about three days every few months. If his schedule is not overloaded, he holds court in the conference room, thrilling the staff with stories of his adventures, his reactions to recent articles, and his views on topics ranging from pollution to sex.

Staffers claim that "it's hard to work for a living legend." While they praise the Captain for his constant creativity, they admit that many of his ideas are "absolutely outrageous." For instance, Cousteau recommended that *The Cousteau Almanac,* a large collection of respectable articles on resource and population issues, include a special chapter on "making love." The editors, embarrassed by the suggestion, could not muster the courage to challenge Cousteau's suggestion directly, but they quietly ignored the segment and never mentioned it again to the Captain, who had quickly gone on to other ideas.

Cousteau may be a master of self-promotion, but teamwork dominates life aboard the *Calypso.* Unlike many captains, who maintain their own dining rooms, Cousteau, when he is present, eats all his food with the crew. More than a dozen bottles of French wine are consumed every day during the lively and jovial meals, which serve as occasions for the group to plan its next activities. Several team members have worked as part of the *Calypso* community for more than twenty years. Albert Falco, who dived alongside Cousteau on early expeditions in the Mediterranean, now commands the fabled vessel.

Though the Captain cherishes his privacy, he manages a public life. He celebrated his seventy-fifth birthday in 1985 with several hundred fans, including celebrities Jack Lemmon, John Denver, Stephanie Powers, Jose Ferrer, Loretta Swit, and Ted Turner. The world-famous explorer can easily arrange meetings with almost any head of state, even Fidel Castro, whom he interviewed for a 1986 television segment on Cuba. He says he knew Ronald Reagan "very well" as governor of California, and "I told him, 'You are going to be President of the United States.' He remembered that and invited me to dinner at the White House.'' Cousteau claims to own only one tie, which he saves for meals with world leaders.

The Captain's favorite audiences, however, are children, perhaps because, like him, they still marvel at everything. Adults, Cousteau says, ''have lost the ability to see what they're looking at,'' abandoning their spontaneity to reason and logic. But children, he declares approvingly, ''jump around, pick up flowers, throw inkpots at walls. It's wonderful.''

To comprehend Jacques-Yves Cousteau requires more than a recounting of inventions, adventures, or even behind-the-camera exploits. His is a story of changes, of alterations to his sense of mission made in response to problems, opportunities, and societal developments. An automobile accident forced him to abandon flying. The donning of a pair of goggles opened his eyes and imagination to the world beneath the surface of the sea. A lucrative television contract led him to abandon oceanographic experiments. And after witnessing the destruction of his beloved diving sites, the Captain supplanted his quest for industrial development with a concern for the environment.

Understanding Cousteau provides insight into more than a talented and charismatic man. It is to appreciate an entire generation's quest to explore the unknown. It is to help perceive the impact of movies and television on twentieth-century culture. And it is to trace the advance of the environmental movement, which Cousteau could have led to significant victories if he had only chosen to do so.

CHAPTER TWO

On the Road

St.-André-de-Cubzac lies along the Dordogne River in the Bordeaux region of France, about a day's train ride south of Paris. At the turn of the twentieth century the small market town of thirty-eight hundred people continued the medieval traditions of the wine trade. Surrounding vineyards supplied some of the world's most treasured grapes, and merchants expressed little interest in the technological advances—from the light bulb to the X ray and the automobile—that were revolutionizing life in France's major cities.

Jacques Cousteau's grandfather was a leader among St.-André's businessmen. A *notaire,* he executed real estate sales, deeds, and marriage contracts. Living a comfortable middle-class life, he planned to pass on his practice to one of his four sons. Daniel, clearly the brightest, had been encouraged to complete law school.

The vibrant young Daniel, entranced by the inventions and experiences of Thomas Edison, Wilhelm Röntgen, and Henry Ford, dreamed of a faster life outside his quiet town. But he did not move quickly. He did become a lawyer and spent several years notarizing documents with his father and dabbling in the stock market. Only at the age of thirty-one did the stocky, athletic, optimistic attorney venture to Paris, and only after he had married Elizabeth Duranthon, thirteen years his junior.

Elizabeth, one of five daughters, grew up in St.-André-de-Cubzac's wealthiest family. Her forebears had long been successful wine exporters, and she was comfortable with the provincial traditions that accompanied that success. Quiet and reserved, she seemed a perfect foil to the vivacious and outgoing Daniel. Though the dramatic differences in their temperaments, ages, and social backgrounds cast an odd tilt on their marriage, Daniel's enthusiasm for the future and his desire to conquer faraway places enchanted the sheltered Elizabeth, and her sense of security and strength gave him the courage he needed to explore the world.

In early 1906 the young couple moved to Paris, where Daniel had gained employment as a legal adviser to and traveling companion for James Hazen Hyde, the thirty-one-year-old son of the founder of the Equitable Life Assurance Society in the United States. Hyde, a fervent Francophile and president of Harvard University's Le Cercle Français, had been vice-president of Equitable and a director of forty-eight different corporations, including banks, trust companies, and railroads. But in response to allegations that he used stockholder money to finance his lavish life-style, he quit Equitable and sold his shares at a significant loss. Still, he maintained enough wealth to pursue his expensive habits in Paris.

As 1906 came to a close, Elizabeth gave birth to a son, whom she named Pierre-Antoine. While Daniel traveled with James Hyde, his wife and the baby spent several months with relatives in St.-André-de-Cubzac.

When Elizabeth became pregnant again, the couple journeyed together from Paris to her family's country home, where Jacques-Yves was born on June 11, 1910. Initial baby pictures show a plump and cheerful infant with a full head of black hair. No sooner did the young Cousteau enter the world than he was bundled up to accompany his itinerant family. Jacques's earliest memory is of being rocked to sleep in a train hammock.

The First World War restricted most of Hyde's travels and put a damper on his pleasures. German forces delivered annihilating blows against France, particularly on the country's northeastern frontier with Belgium. In fact, the German Army advanced to within twenty-five miles of Paris, causing the French government to retreat to Bordeaux. But in early September 1914 French forces halted the German drive in a weeklong battle on the Marne River. For most of the following four years, the western front, stretching along the Marne from Verdun to the English Channel, was to be the site of bloody trench warfare. Though Paris was no longer under siege, the "City of Lights" did not recapture its prewar luxury for many years.

Before the United States entered the conflict, Hyde quarreled with his legal adviser and fired him. The Cousteaus, forced to rely upon Elizabeth's family wealth, struggled to make ends meet in Paris. Their predicament was exacerbated by the suffering Jacques experienced from chronic enteritis, a painful inflammation of the intestines, during the first seven years of his life. Family photographs reveal that the plump baby had become a delicate and gaunt lad with long, curly locks falling over each ear.

The 1918 armistice marked the return of color and commerce to the French capital, attracting a new generation of American millionaires, including Eugene Higgins, an energetic bachelor who hired Daniel Cousteau as his legal adviser and companion. Higgins's father had built a New York carpet manufacturing firm valued at more than fifty million dollars. Although Eugene had nothing to do with the prosperous business, eventually he inherited his father's fortune.

A contemporary newspaper story ranked Higgins as the wealthiest of New York bachelors: "Mr. Higgins is not only the richest, but the handsomest unmarried New Yorker. He is a devoted golfer, an expert cross-country rider, a good gun, a skillful fisherman, and a yachtsman of no mean seamanship. Sartorially, he is all that can be desired." Other journalistic accounts reported Higgins's lavish parties and expeditions to entertain the idle rich. It was said that he mapped out "sumptuous pleasure campaigns" in advance by the season, with no refinement overlooked.

In addition to his Fifth Avenue house and New Jersey estate, Higgins bought a large town house on the Place d'Iena in Paris and an imposing yacht, which he moored at Deauville. In his early sixties when he hired Cousteau, however, the millionaire spent most of his time traveling to resorts, where he demanded that Daniel match him in tennis, golf, and other sports. Recalls Jacques: "My parents were moving a lot at a time when it was difficult to move a lot."

The few memories Cousteau enjoys recounting about his childhood focus on water. "When I was four or five years old," he says, "I loved touching water. Physically. Sensually." Young Jacques also spent many hours at the ocean watching ships pass, wondering why they didn't sink under their heavy weight. These early experiences, he maintains, foretold his undersea expeditions. "They triggered my mind to become a naval officer, and from then on, I wondered what was underneath my keel. It's a very simple story."

Young Jacques, too weak to participate in most sports, read a great many books. The stories that impressed him most were those that featured the sea. He particularly enjoyed Henri de Montfreid's tales of Red Sea pearl divers, pirates, slaves, and hashish smugglers, adventures that the sedentary Cousteau craved but could barely imagine.

Against advice from the Cousteau family doctor, the athletic Higgins pushed young Jacques to learn how to swim. Despite the odds, the sickly child, who contracted anemia not long after recovering from enteritis, slowly mastered the exercise.

In 1920 the family sailed with Higgins across the Atlantic to live in New York City for two years. Settled in an apartment on Ninety-fifth Street, ten-year-old Jacques (who briefly called himself "Jack") enrolled in Manhattan's Holy Name School, and Pierre attended DeWitt High School. They learned street stickball from their friends, while introducing New Yorkers to two-wheeled European roller skates. As Jacques's anemia gradually subsided, he grew more energetic, joining his brother in mischievous adventures and dangling from fire escapes. The pair spent the summer at a camp on Lake Harvey in Vermont, where Jacques first dived under the water.

Cousteau's oft-told diving story centers on the demands of Mr. Boetz, a German teacher, who, as Jacques remembers, "didn't like me very much, and I didn't like him at all. He forced me to ride horses, and I fell a lot. I still hate horses."

It seems that Mr. Boetz, angry at Jacques's persistent pranks, also ordered the young Cousteau to clear the fallen branches and dead trees from the bottom of the lake under the springboard so that the campers could dive without danger. "I worked very hard," Cousteau recalls, "diving in that murk without goggles, without a mask, and that's where I learned to dive."

The actual experience of diving contradicted the stories Cousteau had read. In one fictional account, a hero hid from villains by sitting on the river bottom and breathing through a hollow reed. Jacques tried to replicate the experiment by placing a garden hose through a block of cork on the surface and descending to the lake's bottom with the other end of the hose and a stone weight. He could suck no air, however, and was forced to return frantically to the surface. "Boys thereby gather cynical impressions about storybooks," Cousteau recounted several years later. "The author of my book, like others who write diving yarns, had never been on a river bottom with a straw in his mouth."

Jacques demonstrated diverse talents early. In 1921, at the age of eleven, he borrowed the blueprints for a two-hundred-ton floating crane and built a four-foot electric-powered model, devising unique features which engineers later added to the larger structure. Two years later, after a family trip, he wrote, illustrated, typeset, and bound a book entitled *An Adventure in Mexico*.

Cousteau used his allowance to purchase one of the first movie cameras to be sold in France. The young tinkerer frequently disassembled the Pathé and put it back together again. "I was fascinated by the hardware," he states. "That's how I got started—the cameras, how to process the film and devise chemicals."

At the age of thirteen he shot his first movie at a cousin's wedding. By sixteen he had photographed and directed homemade melodramas. Even at this early stage Cousteau placed himself in front of the camera. One early film had Jacques, sporting a dark suit and a black-painted mustache, push a fair damsel into his convertible. A white-suited gentleman pursued and pulled Cousteau away from the heroine, over the rumble seat, and onto the ground. The hero and the lady drove off into the sunset. Cousteau, self-cast as the villain, sat dejectedly in the dust.

In another clip Cousteau, appearing again to be the lecherous scoundrel, begged a lovely woman to come with him. She scorned his advances and pushed him, fully clothed, into the lake. Jacques labeled his production company Société Zix, and he made sure that the film credits clearly announced that he, J. Cousteau, was producer, director, and chief cameraman.

"My early movies weren't much good," Cousteau later stated. "What I liked was taking the camera apart and developing my own film."

Despite his early inventions and productions, Cousteau was a bored and indolent student, and many of his experiments created little more than trouble. As a sophomore at a French lycée, for instance, he decided to test his theory that a strongly thrown stone makes only a small hole in glass. Seventeen broken school windows later, Jacques was expelled.

"I was a misfit," Cousteau concedes. Such mischievousness, he now maintains, demonstrated an early proclivity for adventure.

Daniel and Elizabeth shipped their teenage prankster to Alsace on the French-German border, where a strict German teacher governed a rigorous academy. The discipline and academic challenge quickly converted Cousteau into a successful and inspired scholar. "I even studied with a flashlight in bed," he declares.

Cousteau was graduated in 1929, confused about whether to become a film director, a radiologist, or a naval officer. He turned to the military to fulfill his yearning to travel. In 1930 he passed the difficult entrance examination and entered the École Navale in Brest, the national naval academy of France.

Cousteau's class was the first allowed a one-year cruise around the world on the school ship *Jeanne d'Arc*. Camera in hand, Jacques produced a rough documentary of the adventure that illustrated the crew's encounters with the sultan of Oman, Douglas Fairbanks in Hollywood (a classmate filmed Fairbanks offering a cigarette and a light to Cousteau), dancers in Bali, and geishas of Japan.

While in Vietnam conducting a hydrological exercise in the Bay of Port Dayot, Cousteau caught an early glimpse of the wonders within the sea. The midshipman watched carefully as a local fisherman, stripped naked and without gear or goggles of any kind, slipped beneath the boat during the dead calm of midday. Cousteau noted in his diary: "He surfaced a minute later with a marvelous fish wriggling in each hand and explained with a mischievous smile: 'They nap at this time of day.' "

In 1933 Cousteau was graduated second in his class, promoted to second lieutenant, and assigned to the French base in Shanghai. Again, he brought along his camera, and while participating in official map-making surveys, he shot rare footage of public life in China and Siberia. On his way home from the Far East, Cousteau boarded the Trans-Siberian Express and recorded his travels across Russia, only to have Soviet authorities, reflecting the rise of totalitarianism, confiscate most of his film.

The changing political environment throughout Europe and Asia had little additional impact on Jacques Cousteau. Not so for his brother. Pierre, a quick-witted debater and acerbic writer, throve on political argument, and France after the Great War was rife with factions.

For several years following the stock market crashes in the United States and most of Europe, the French economy, bolstered by a huge gold reserve and a high degree of self-sufficiency, remained an island of prosperity in a sea of economic misery. But when disaster arrived in 1932, it struck quickly. Industrial production fell almost one third, exports plummeted, and investors, fearing possible devaluation, fled the country at an alarming rate.

The war had drawn the country together, but the government's inability to cope with the financial crisis created political chaos and heightened the century-old divisions between the republican left and the royalist right. Bitter debates pitted the workers of the republican faction against the wealthy business leaders and conservative peasants.

A coalition of Radicals, Socialists, and Communists vigorously decried the plight of French laborers relative to those in other industrialized countries. With the election of Socialist Premier Léon Blum in the mid-1930's, France finally adopted a forty-hour workweek, compulsory arbitration of labor disputes, paid vacations for employees, and many other welfare measures.

Businessmen and bankers refused to cooperate with the mandated reforms, arguing that shorter hours and higher wages increased French production costs. At the same time, members of various Fascist leagues, right-wing groups, and royalist organizations staged riots in Paris and throughout the country, declaring that they would "cut the throat" of the republic. In response, left-leaning workers organized successive waves of sit-down strikes that brought industry to a virtual standstill. The democratic government proved itself powerless to create unity.

Pierre Cousteau, convinced of the need for fundamental reforms, initially sided with the left. But experiences in the disorganized and defeatist French Army made him yearn for order, and a brief stint as a political reporter on the daily *Le Journal* persuaded him of democracy's inability to impose social controls. He soon began to write short columns about the need for forceful leadership.

While completing his political conversion, Pierre fell in love with Fernande Semaille, secretary for Tatiana, a celebrated journalist whom he had interviewed for an article. Although Fernande was married, Pierre's political respect for tradition did not retard his love affair. The petite Parisienne eventually filed for divorce, married Pierre, and delivered a baby girl named Françoise. In 1934 the young family moved into the large Paris apartment owned by Pierre's parents. While Daniel traveled with Higgins, Elizabeth enjoyed the company of a grandchild, and Pierre and Fernande became energetic participants in the far right's social circle.

Pierre Gaxotte, editor of the ultraright *Je Suis Partout,* recruited the talented thirty-one-year-old Pierre. Financed by wealthy perfumer René Coty and publisher Arthème Fayard, the weekly magazine (translated as "I Am Everywhere") targeted military officers, some of whom were losing faith in the democratic process. PAC, as Pierre-Antoine

Cousteau liked to be referred to, enflamed the totalitarian passions and increasingly idolized the authoritarianism being enforced by Francisco Franco's rebels in Spain, Benito Mussolini in Italy, and Adolf Hitler in Germany.

Captain Cousteau refuses to discuss his brother. Family members, however, suggest that Jacques, particularly as a boy, admired his clever and aggressive sibling. Early photographs show the young brothers smiling together in the woods and at swimming holes. The pair relied upon each other for companionship while their parents traveled.

As the Second World War approached, Jacques expressed little interest in Pierre's political machinations. The young officer, searching for adventure, entered the fleet aviation academy at Hourtin, an Atlantic coast town west of Bordeaux, where he focused his ever-present camera from the cockpit on staged dogfights. Preferring aerobatics to political debate, Jacques and his colleagues argued only over airplane performances, cars, and women.

The gay times, however, would not last forever. Just before graduation, in early 1936, Cousteau borrowed his father's Salmson sports car to attend a friend's wedding in the Vosges Mountains. As evening fell and fog settled over the foothills, he climbed the road's hairpin turns. Suddenly the headlights failed, and the open car hurtled off the road and rolled over several times. Cousteau laid unconscious in the woods for several hours. He awakened with his head jammed into the ground. "It was two o'clock in the morning," he remembers, "and I thought I was going to die. I was losing my blood."

The accident crushed several ribs and perforated his lungs. The bones of Cousteau's left forearm stuck out through the skin. His right arm would not move. Doctors wanted to amputate the fractured left limb because of massive nerve injuries and extensive infection, but Cousteau adamantly refused. He endured eight frustrating months of whirlpool baths and painful therapy before willing himself to move one finger. Several months later he had all the fingers working again.

Cousteau often recalls the accident. "It was a test for me," he claims. "Every morning, every night, I wonder at how lucky I am to still be alive, to have seen so many things, and to carry on, being eager to see more."

Ironically, Cousteau's auto crash saved him from the war-related death that befell every other cadet in his flying class. The accident actually opened dramatic new vistas for the twenty-six-year-old. To recuperate, the navy sent him to Toulon on the Mediterranean coast, where he met Philippe Tailliez, a navy lieutenant, and Frédéric Dumas, a champion spearfisherman—two men who would long remain his partners in adventure.

Tailliez encouraged Cousteau to strengthen his arm by swimming daily in the sea. After supervising the exercise for several months, Tailliez introduced a pair of Fernez goggles, similar to those used by Japanese pearl fishermen.

"Sometimes we are lucky enough to know that our lives have been changed," Cousteau recalls. "It happened to me that summer's day when my eyes opened to the world beneath the surface of the sea." Cousteau stuck his face under the clear Mediterranean water and witnessed a new environment of fish and flora, unlike the blurred experience in murky Lake Harvey. One minute he was looking at the urban landscape of La Mourillon in the south of France, the next he saw "wildlife untouched, a jungle at the border of the sea, never seen by those who floated on the opaque roof."

In the same year, 1936, Cousteau also encountered Simone Melchior, a seventeen-year-old lycée student living in Paris. Visiting his parents in Paris while recuperating from the automobile accident, Jacques attended a party, accompanied, as usual, by his camera. Surviving film clips portray an attractive, slim green-eyed girl with a demure smile, sitting among friends and calling out her name shyly to the cameraman. Cousteau still comments on the girl's youthful beauty.

Simone, like Cousteau's mother, enjoyed the benefits of a wealthy family. Three generations of Melchiors had been French admirals. Her father had recently retired from the military to become a senior executive at Air Liquide, the multinational producer of industrial gases. Her mother descended from Irish aristocracy, and her cousin later became chairman of the giant British Petroleum.

Simone spent much of her childhood in Japan, where her father was stationed and she attended a convent school. She proved to be an intelligent, headstrong, if somewhat reserved scholar.

The young couple maintained a long-distance courtship for almost a year. Because Simone's parents forced her to finish school, Cousteau traveled to Paris from Toulon during each furlough. She found Jacques to be a glib, energetic, and entertaining suitor; of equal importance, he was a naval officer whose career, as the Melchior family discovered, appeared promising. He found someone who loved the sea, dismissed convention, and longed for adventure.

The formal wedding occurred on July 12, 1937. Cousteau, then twenty-seven years old, wore his gala uniform. Eighteen-year-old Simone shone in a full-length white gown, highlighted with a strand of organdy. The couple, captured on camera, marched under the unsheathed swords of the groom's colleagues.

Jacques and Simone moved into a modest house at Sanary, the officers' community near the Toulon naval base. Simone quickly joined her husband, Tailliez, and Dumas in the water at La Mourillon Bay or below the Sanary cliffs.

Pierre, Fernande, and baby Françoise visited the newlyweds frequently. Pierre discussed politics, while Jacques outlined the engineering problems he was grappling with as he tried to photograph undersea life. Fernande and Simone got along well, both being bright and energetic. Both also were pregnant.

It was a happy time for Jacques and Simone. Daily swims strengthened his arm, and his naval assignment, teaching artillery techniques to enlisted men aboard the battleship *Condorcet,* allowed enough free time to experiment with filming and diving. The Cousteau home, Villa Berry, became the center of parties and all-night discussions about planned ocean adventures.

The isolated world of Sanary, at least for a time, seemed divorced from the rise of totalitarianism throughout Europe. Simone gave birth to a son, Jean-Michel, in March 1938, at the same time Hitler was marching into Austria. Several months later, while Jacques leisurely practiced free diving in the Mediterranean, Pierre traveled to the annual Nazi party congress in Nuremberg, where the Führer outlined his plan for conquering Czechoslovakia.

France, continuing to focus on its internal strife, could do little to retard Hitler's advances, and Britain's Neville Chamberlain innocently accepted the Führer's assurances and declared "peace for our time." By 1939 Hitler's troops had organized a blitzkrieg in Poland, Mussolini occupied the kingdom of Albania, and Franco captured Barcelona.

Meanwhile, as France prepared for war, Cousteau was made a gunnery officer aboard the cruiser *Dupleix,* stationed at Toulon, home port for more than sixty French warships. Because Germany and Italy opted not to wage a naval war in the Mediterranean, Cousteau's early war efforts consisted only of drills.

The "action" was concentrated in the north, where, in May 1940, German panzer divisions moved swiftly across the fertile fields of Holland and through the wooded hills of the Ardennes. It took Hitler less than a week to overrun the Netherlands and a little more than two weeks to defeat the Belgian, French, and British forces in Belgium. He cornered the remains of the Allied armies, some three hundred thousand men, in a large pocket near Dunkirk on the Channel coast.

Despite the presence of the German Army on their doorstep, the French could not unite. Marshal Henri Philippe Pétain, a symbol of the country's resistance during World War I, sought to gain some concessions by negotiating with Hitler. German troops, therefore, stormed across the border with hardly any opposition. Italy joined the act by bombing several French towns along the Mediterranean coast, including Toulon, although little damage resulted.

A French delegation surrendered to Hitler in June 1940, allowing Germany to occupy three fifths of the country, including the Channel and Atlantic coasts and most of the ironworks and coal-mining areas. Under the terms of the armistice, French officials also agreed not to aid the enemies of Germany, in particular the Free French forces which General Charles de Gaulle was organizing in Britain.

The unoccupied southern part of France chose as its capital the town of Vichy, a spa city about a hundred miles west of Lyons, and as its leaders a group of men, including Pétain, Admiral Jean François Darlan, and Pierre Laval, who wanted to avoid confrontation with Germany.

Pierre Cousteau, having been called up as a reservist to join the French Army, was one of a hundred thousand soldiers held captive by the conquering Germans and interned at a makeshift camp near Sens, about seventy-five miles southeast of Paris. Daniel sat trapped in Torquay, England, with Higgins, unable to move for fear the British would requisition the millionaire's boat. Elizabeth and Fernande struggled to survive in occupied Paris with little food and no fuel.

British Prime Minister Winston Churchill, increasingly fearful that the Germans would use the French fleet to gain control of the shipping lanes throughout the Mediterranean and Atlantic, sought to seize or destroy the warships. In fact, British ships bombed and torpedoed French vessels as they tried to escape from the Algerian harbor of Mers-el-Kébir.

Angry that British "allies" would bomb French boats, Admiral Darlan ordered ninety warships to sail into Toulon so that they could be disarmed. Artillery specialists placed explosives aboard the anchored French vessels and prepared to scuttle the fleet should the British or Germans attack. Cousteau was transferred to a gunnery encampment on the hills overlooking Toulon.

Because Hitler and Mussolini focused their expansion elsewhere, Cousteau's tasks allowed him to spend many hours with Simone, Jean-Michel, and Philippe, a new baby born in December 1939 and named after Philippe Tailliez. Life in war-torn France, even in the unoccupied sections, remained stark for most citizens, but Cousteau, Tailliez, and Dumas supplied abundant food from the sea for family and friends. They also convinced naval authorities that their undersea experiments deserved "heavy worker" ration cards, which yielded a few grams of butter and more fish. Early family photographs and home movies paint a cheerful portrait of Jacques and Simone playing lighthearted games with their children.

The German occupation eventually offered enormous opportunities for far-right journalists. After spending a year in a prisoner of war camp, Pierre-Antoine Cousteau was appointed editor in chief of *Paris-Soir,* the reformatted daily promoted by German Ambassador Otto Abetz. As a German collaborator—he liked to call himself a "realist"—Pierre wrote racist editorials against the Jews, shrill denunciations of the resistance, and apologetic stories of Nazi actions. He even published a book, *Jewish America,* that echoed Nazi propaganda about how Jews had stolen much of the wealth and commerce in the United States and Germany. Pierre later explained that his youthful persecution in New York City public schools had taught him to despise Jews.

As Pierre grew more fervent in his support of totalitarianism and Hitler, his brother slowly became associated with the French resistance. Jacques was never particularly fascinated with politics or ideologies, but French officers were expected to participate in some way. Largely because of his diving experiments in Mediterranean harbors, Cousteau was asked by Allied intelligence to provide detailed notes on Axis naval movements. He openly displayed his homemade diving and photography equipment to German and Italian patrols, which considered him a harmless eccentric. Cousteau later declared, "I did all I could to reinforce the impression."

Jacques's war record demonstrates that he was anything but innocent. In fact, he proved to be an effective spy. One night Cousteau posed as an Italian officer and slipped into the Italian headquarters at Sète. He spent four tense hours taking pictures with a miniature camera of the enemy's code book and other top secret papers. The Allies used the information to decipher Italian naval signals before the invasion of North Africa. For his underground services, Cousteau was decorated after the war with the Légion d'Honneur, the highest military award in France, as well as with the Croix de Guerre with Palm.

Family members say the political differences between Pierre and Jacques never caused a serious rift, not even a heated argument. In fact, the brothers eventually agreed to send their four children—Jean-Michel and Philippe and Françoise and Jean-Pierre—to the safety of Mégève, a small Alpine village near the Swiss border. For the war's duration Simone supervised the children's education, while Fernande stayed in Paris to participate in her husband's work.

With France out of the war, Hitler turned his attention to Britain and its empire. Beginning in July 1940, the German Luftwaffe began an all-out air offensive against London and other English cities. The Battle of Britain lasted through the rest of the year, with the Royal Air Force maintaining mastery of the skies and forcing Hitler to postpone his invasion.

In June 1941 the Führer shifted his focus eastward. German forces initially rolled across Russia, killing hundreds of thousands of soldiers and civilians. The fierce winter, however, slowed their advance, and in the fall of 1942 Hitler's army lost a fierce five-month battle at Stalingrad.

At the same time the German Army, desiring the French fleet in the Mediterranean, abrogated the terms of the treaty with the Vichy government and entered the south of France. Late in the evening of November 27 two panzer divisions launched a surprise attack on Toulon. But before Hitler's troops could gain control, French officers executed the demolition plan which they had spent several months rehearsing. The explosions rocked the naval yard and surrounding countryside.

Jacques and Simone, in a Marseilles apartment preparing to leave for Lisbon where Cousteau had been assigned to be a naval attaché, were awakened by German planes flying eastward to support the invasion. They tuned in Radio Geneva and heard the roll call of sunken ships, which included the *Dupleix,* on which he had served. "Simone and I wept by the radio," he recalled, "far from the people and ships we loved, feeling a bitter exile." The next day Cousteau, his assignment to Portugal canceled, traveled to St.-Mandrier to film the smoking warships and the occupying SS soldiers.

Despite numerous examples of continuing Axis strength, it was clear by the spring of 1943 that the tide of the war was turning. German troops were losing ground in North Africa, and they were retreating across the plains of eastern Europe. Pierre and Fernande, however, maintained their active social life among leading Nazi collaborators in occupied Paris.

While the war raged around them, Jacques, Simone, Dumas, and Tailliez fashioned underwater masks from inner tubes and snorkels from garden hoses. Their initial diving experiments focused on the effects of cold. Water, a better heat conductor than air, drains calories from swimmers, forcing divers to employ adequate protection. Some coated themselves with grease, believing it insulated their bodies. But Dumas's experiences demonstrated that grease only covered the skin with a thin film of oil that actually increased the loss of caloric heat.

Cousteau, particularly sensitive to the cold, once remarked, "I have never found sea water that was warm enough for me." Therefore, he gave great care to tailoring an array of vulcanized rubber garments, many of which made him resemble Don Quixote. Most early designs also produced serious complications. His 1938 model, for instance, allowed air to leak to his feet, thrusting him into a head-down position. Eight years passed before Cousteau's team developed a constant-volume dress that a diver could inflate with his nasal exhalations; this more effective design included air escape valves that kept the diver stable at any depth or bodily position.

The crew also developed waterproof casings for movie cameras, and Cousteau spent a great deal of time filming his colleagues under the sea, particularly Dumas spearing huge groupers. Revealing a self-promotion he would continue for several decades, Cousteau even turned a second camera on himself while he pretended to film fish and flora.

Moreover, the group examined the extraordinary techniques of sponge divers, some of whom could hold their breaths, descend more than a hundred feet, and perform chores for more than two minutes. Such feats place enormous strain on a person's body. At lower depths, pressure increases, and the lungs shrink. At one hundred feet, for instance, a person's lungs occupy only one fourth the space they do at the surface.

Cousteau, aided by several pounds of belt weights, learned to make sixty-foot dives of two-minute durations. But these brief glimpses of the sea's wonders were not enough; he yearned to go deeper and stay longer.

Cousteau described his motivation to dive as a longing to return to the mother sea, the element that produced life, but he was most inspired by the thrill of adventure and the anticipated freedom from the constraints of gravity. Only years later did he view the ocean in a more materialistic way, as a resource to be managed.

Throughout his life Cousteau related his diving efforts to a historical continuum, recalling evidence of undersea activity that can be traced to the dim beginnings of human history. The Sumerian civilization, located in the valley of the Tigris and Euphrates rivers about 5000 B.C., produced the story of Gilgamesh, a bellicose and imperious king who searched underwater for a plant that would provide eternal life; with stones tied to his feet, Gilgamesh breathed through a tube of seaweed. The people of the Aurignacian civilization deposited seashells and salmon bones in their ancient burial grounds. Assyrians produced the earliest known bas-relief representation of an underwater breathing device, showing Assurnasirbal and his army crossing a river in about 900 B.C. And ama divers of Korea and Japan have gathered shellfish and edible seaweed in the same way for almost two thousand years.

The Greeks, of course, embraced a series of sea-gods, and Aristotle wrote several times about underwater breathing gear. In fact, the philosopher described how Alexander the Great's army used *lebetas*—meaning "saucepans" and referring to diving bells that received air pumped from the surface through a tube—to destroy the enemy's ships during the siege of Tyre.

Numerous other historical figures devised undersea equipment. Leonardo da Vinci drew illustrations for diving machines, most of which would have been impractical. Edmund Halley, noted for his comet, built diving bells in the late seventeeth century. Benjamin Franklin forged fins to propel swimmers. And Robert Fulton, of steamboat fame, designed a submarine for Napoleon.

The pioneers, of course, must be put in context, because most ancient cultures feared the vast and unknown sea. For centuries sailors thought the ocean led to the end of the world, perhaps to the land of the dead. Men imagined the depths filled with dangerous monsters. In the Bible's Revelation of St. John the Divine, John envisioned a utopia in which there is earth and sky but no sea: "Then I saw a new heaven and a new earth, for the first heaven and the first earth vanished, and there was no longer any sea."

Modern undersea exploration is less than 150 years old and may be marked from Henri Milne-Edwards's bold descent in a clumsy bucket helmet in 1844. The Sorbonne professor of biology employed an air tube from a ship to witness first hand plant and animal life under the water.

In the 1860's Jules Verne imagined much of the diving equipment that engineers later developed. According to Cousteau, "Verne, like many great poets, led the way for science to follow." In *Twenty Thousands Leagues Under the Sea* (a worn and marked copy of which Cousteau keeps aboard *Calypso*), Verne's Captain Nemo employed recirculating air tanks, flexible cold-water suits, underwater lamps and weapons, and the submarine *Nautilus,* which served as both a scientific laboratory and a refuge from the rest of mankind. "The ocean," exclaims Nemo, "offered us an incessant and infinite display of its most marvelous treasures."

While Verne dreamed and wrote, Augustus Siebe devised much of the initial diving equipment. The Englishman introduced weighted shoes that enabled a diver to stand erect, a watertight rubber suit that protected him from the cold, and a communications system that allowed him to speak with surface assistants.

Half a century later two Frenchmen, the Carmagnole brothers, patented a metal diving suit with twenty-two ball-and-socket joints and a thick helmet with small windows placed in front of the diver's eyes. The rigid dress offered protection from the ocean's pressure but was too clumsy and restrictive to afford true exploration.

The development of free diving equipment—that not needing hoses to the surface—paralleled advances in the science of gas compression. As early as 1865 French naval Lieutenant Auguste Denayrouse and mining engineer Benoit Rouquayrol perfected an ingenious but simple and independent device that allowed dives to 165 feet. But because air could not yet be compressed to sufficient pressures, divers either relied on tanks that were too large or made dives that were too quick. Denayrouse and Rouquayrol eventually attached their tank to a conventional line connected to a surface pump, thus destroying much of the system's autonomy.

Progress with diving equipment in the late nineteenth century depended less on undersea exploration than on public works construction projects. The Industrial Revolution sparked a demand for bridges, quays, and lighthouses, many of which needed underwater foundations. Engineers were thus motivated to create diving bells in which laborers breathed compressed air that offset the water's pressure.

Scientists soon encountered an array of hazards associated with underwater or underground exposure. The sandhogs who worked in pressurized shafts to dig the pier excavations for the Brooklyn Bridge, for instance, came up in tortured body positions that reminded their colleagues of a contemporary fad in which fashionable women affected a drooping posture known as the Grecian bend. This painful, crippling, and sometimes fatal affliction of nitrogen gas bubbles in veins and joints, known by physiologists as caisson disease, has since been commonly called the bends.

Frenchman Paul Bert conducted the first experiments on a diver's reaction to breathing nitrogen under pressure. In 1878 he noted that the gas increased in the bloodstream because the body couldn't quickly release it as a waste product during exhalation. Bert's thousand-page treatise explained that nitrogen bubbles could block blood circulation and cause tremendous pain and damage. A diver's only recourse, he discovered, was to come up slowly, allowing the body to eliminate excess nitrogen naturally. Several years later John Haldane, a Scottish medical doctor working with Royal Navy divers, established decompression tables that specified waiting periods—depending upon the length and depth of the dive—for ascending divers.

While scientists discovered how divers could rise safely, engineers tried to devise equipment that would allow explorers to descend deeper and achieve more freedom of movement. In 1878 Henry Fleuss developed a self-contained, regenerating breathing apparatus for use in tunnels, coal mines, and other areas where the air was not safe for breathing. The English designer created a chamber of caustic soda that purified the carbon dioxide exhaled by workers.

In 1911 Sir Robert Davis advanced Fleuss's design by further increasing the oxygen's pressure while decreasing the copper cylinder's weight. Military frogmen used Davis's device—small, light, and inexpensive—because it emitted no telltale bubbles. The closed-circuit system, however, proved to be extremely dangerous at depths below twenty-six feet, where divers breathed nine times more oxygen than in air at normal pressure.

Cousteau experienced these hazards first hand with an oxygen lung he designed out of a brass box and a motorcycle inner tube. He entered the water, his bag cleansing his exhalations in soda lime to be breathed again, and felt the thrill of swimming underwater without needing to rise for air or being restricted by surface cables. For half an hour he joyously explored a cave and tried to catch a fish in his bare hands. But when Cousteau decided to chase a sunfish down to forty-five feet, his spine suddenly bent backward, and his eyelids blinked wildly. Recognizing the violent oxygen convulsion that would immobilize him in an instant, he ripped off his ten-pound belt just seconds before the convulsion hit; his unconscious body floated to the surface, where friends fished him out.

Although Cousteau suffered pains in his neck and back for three weeks, he spent the winter building an improved oxygen lung. The new design, however, proved to be just as dangerous at forty-five feet, and Cousteau's interest in oxygen ended. "In testing devices in which one's life is at stake," he noted with uncharacteristic understatement, "such accidents induce zeal for improvement."

In 1926 the French commander Yves Le Prieur developed the first high-pressure cylinder that used ordinary air. The new system did not depend on unreliable filters to purify the foul air, allowing instead for the exhalations to escape into the water under the edge of the diver's mask.

In 1937 Cousteau, Émile Gagnan, and Georges Commeinhes attached a larger diaphragm to Le Prieur's device. By using twin tanks, the team enjoyed prolonged dives, but the system proved too complicated and susceptible to breakdowns.

Cousteau, Tailliez, and Dumas made their first underwater movie without any breathing apparatus or modern photographic equipment. Shooting time was limited because both the star (Dumas) and the cameraman (Cousteau) had to hold their breaths. And since movie film was rationed during the war and the team lacked a darkroom, Jacques and Simone had to splice together rolls of still-photo film under their blankets at night. They sealed the camera, an inexpensive 9.5 mm Pathé, in a two-quart fruit jar. Despite the rudimentary equipment, the eighteen-minute film, entitled *Sixty Feet Down,* successfully conveyed the drama Dumas generated in spearing a grouper in an underground tunnel.

The difficulties with early underwater photography inspired Cousteau to spend more time devising a portable underwater breathing device. To continue experiments with Gagnan, who worked at Air Liquide's laboratory, Jacques obtained permits from his brother's influential friends and traveled to occupied Paris. Gagnan, an engineer expert at handling gases under pressure, had developed a regulator to enable wartime automobiles to run on cooking gas instead of precious gasoline. Cousteau convinced the company, whose board of directors included his father-in-law, to fund a prototype breathing unit.

Cousteau and Gagnan worked together for three weeks to redesign the car unit into a regulator that would automatically provide compressed air to a diver on his slightest intake of breath. The two men attached their new instrument to hoses, a mouthpiece, and a pair of compressed air tanks.

Cousteau brought the unit to the icy waters of the Marne River outside Paris in January 1943. Simone snapped a fuzzy picture of her skinny husband in a dark bathing suit standing knee-deep in the water, with two tanks on his back and a mask atop his head.

While Gagnan and a handful of observers stood on the bank, the experimenter disappeared into the dirty water, became a "manfish," and delivered a steady stream of bubbles from his tanks. When the bubbles stopped suddenly, the anxious engineer threw off his overcoat and started for the river. But Cousteau reappeared quickly to complain that "the darn thing runs wide open when you are standing, and it gets hard to breathe when you are upside down."

Driving back to Paris in silence, except for the mocking hiss of the regulator on Gagnan's gas tank, the two inventors evaluated their failure. Almost simultaneously the pair began shouting to each other that the first design had incorrectly placed the exhaust six inches higher than the air intake. When Cousteau turned upside down, the exhaust, now six inches below the intake, became subjected to greater water pressure, suppressing the air flow. After making a minor adjustment to the regulator in Gagnan's lab, the inventors rushed to an indoor tank, where Cousteau threw himself into crazy underwater acrobatics but still received a steady supply of air. They patented the altered device as the Aqua Lung.

Cousteau and Gagnan may have shared discovery of the first successful self-contained underwater breathing apparatus (scuba), but they displayed radically different reactions to their success. The bespectacled engineer, a quiet man with a shy smile, shunned publicity and longed to return to his laboratory. Cousteau made himself known as the father of modern diving.

That summer Cousteau tested the fifty-pound apparatus in the Mediterranean waters off the French Riviera. Dumas, one of the country's best goggle divers, stayed ashore, ready to rescue the adventurer if necessary. Simone, breathing through a snorkel, swam on the surface and watched her husband's experiment through her submerged mask. The dive went according to plan. "I experimented with all possible maneuvers—loops, somersaults, and barrel rolls," Cousteau wrote in his journal. "I stood upside down on one finger and burst out laughing, a shrill distorted laugh. Nothing I did altered the automatic rhythm of the air. Delivered from gravity and buoyancy I flew around in space."

Cousteau ended this almost spiritual diving experience on a practical note. He had followed a fish into a cave and was forced to turn on his back in the small space. Above him lay hundreds of lobsters, like flies on a ceiling. He plucked a pair of one-pound creatures from the roof and brought them up to the waiting Simone. He returned five additional times for lobsters that were served at the celebratory dinner that evening at Villa Berry.

Cousteau claimed this underwater experience ended his nightly dreams of flying with his arms extended as wings. "Now," he said, "I flew without wings." His maneuverability was most remarkable when compared with the ponderous struggle of the typical helmeted diver, whom Cousteau described as "a cripple in an alien land."

Cousteau, Dumas, and Tailliez made five hundred separate dives with the Aqua Lung that summer, gradually increasing the depths to which they plunged. It was autumn before they attained 130 feet. By October Dumas, in a carefully planned experiment, had descended to 210 feet.

Dumas's dive revealed another undersea danger, nitrogen narcosis. Upon reaching the hundred-foot knot on the anchored shot line, he had "a queer feeling of beatitude. I am drunk and carefree. My ears buzz and my mouth tastes bitter." His weighted body continued to descend, but his mind became increasingly dizzy. U.S. Navy scientists and helmet divers had explored this intoxication of the great depths for several years, suggesting that it derived from nitrogen oversaturation, but divers in occupied France knew nothing of the studies. They discovered only that the first symptom was mild anesthesia, sometimes spurring a crazed diver to offer his air pipe to passing fish. The drunken sensation, which had nothing to do with the bends, vanished when Dumas dropped his weights and bounded to the surface. Even today, after thousands of dives, Cousteau himself remains especially receptive to nitrogen narcosis. "I like it and fear it like doom," he admits. "It destroys the instinct of life."

The Gagnan-Cousteau regulator fundamentally altered diving. Its simple design and solid construction provided a reliable and low-cost unit for sport diving. Air Liquide put the equipment into commercial production, but it couldn't keep up with the demand. Competitors tried to capture the growing market by producing imitations or making slight adjustments. For instance, L. G. Arpin adapted and Healthways Company of Los Angeles distributed Divair, another popular breathing unit that featured a reserve valve within the regulator. The Scott Aviation Corporation of Lancaster, New York, devised the Scott Hydro-Pak with a mask covering the entire face for use by aviators, fire departments, and divers. And the Dacor Corporation of Evanston, Illinois, produced a double-diaphragm regulator which utilized exhaust air to help admit fresh air.

The devices revolutionized man's perception of the planet. Not unlike the Portuguese, Spanish, and Chinese explorers of the fifteenth century who doubled their knowledge of the size of the world, Cousteau and Gagnan helped open a vast portion of the globe to human exploration. They offered the opportunity for extended undersea investigation to enthusiastic scientists, engineers, and sportsmen.

The aqualung created enormous personal opportunities for Cousteau, too. The "father of modern diving" could finally seek adventure and perform productive work at greater depths than a single breath would allow. Delivered of the constraints of his own weight, he gained the freedom to witness and record the beauty and drama of undersea life. Liberated from gravity and buoyancy, the young man who dreamed of becoming a pilot had learned to fly in the sea.

CHAPTER THREE

The First Menfish

World War II dramatically altered Cousteau's career. It split his family. It divided his country and left the young naval officer without a military mission. But it also gave him the freedom to experiment with diving equipment and underwater photography.

The United States entered the war when Japanese planes bombed Pearl Harbor on December 7, 1941. Following battlefield victories in North Africa and Italy, the Allied leaders—Roosevelt, Stalin, and Churchill—met in Teheran in December 1943 to plan the liberation of France, a project they named Operation Overlord. On D-Day, June 6, 1944, General Dwight D. Eisenhower directed a massive assault that created a beachhead on the coast of Normandy.

Cousteau, on leave from the inactive French Navy to visit his mother in Paris, heard of the Allied invasion and immediately outfitted a bicycle with 110 pounds of food and wine. Despite the rush to join Simone and his sons in Mégève, five hundred miles away near the Swiss border, he found the time to have a friend take a posed photograph of the bicyclist, looking quite determined. Once started, his successful trip around German sentries and up mountain trails lasted just four days. Cousteau remained with his family for several months.

By August a second Allied amphibious force had landed on the French Mediterranean coast between Marseilles and Nice. The Germans—and Pierre and Fernande—were soon on the run.

Many years later Pierre wrote a book about his frightful experiences during the final days of European totalitarianism. Caravans of German army trucks had lined up to escort the Cousteaus and about twenty thousand other collaborators out of Paris. But chaos reigned. As delay followed delay, the Americans marched into the capital from Chartres, while De Gaulle's Free French troops machine-gunned the German rear guard. Pierre and Fernande, "sealed under a permanent avalanche of incendiary bombs and steel and the incoherence of animal panic," barely made it to Constance, on the German-Swiss border.

As British and American troops stormed across Germany's western boundary and the Russian Army entered from the east, Pierre and Fernande joined several friends on a slow and cumbersome trek across the Alps, through Austria and into Italy. While seeking shelter in Milan, they learned of Hitler's suicide, the German Army's capitulation, and Mussolini's murder. American troops eventually collected the weary Cousteaus and placed them in the prison camp at Landeck.

Pierre, having been a student in New York City, befriended the U.S. commander, who eventually agreed to release Fernande. The American also allowed Pierre to stand among the Polish prisoners when angry French troops combed the camp for Nazi sympathizers.

After V-E Day Jacques returned to Sanary with Simone, Jean-Michel, and Philippe. Cousteau's father, Daniel, visited only briefly before Higgins, freed from his entrapment within England, decided to travel again. Jacques's mother, Elizabeth, agreed to join the family and supervise Pierre and Fernande's children, eleven-year-old Françoise and seven-year-old Jean-Pierre, neither of whom could return to Paris for fear of being harassed as the children of noted collaborators.

Equipped with fake passports and transit visas that would allow his brother and sister-in-law to travel to Spain and on to South America, Cousteau drove to the Landeck prison. Pierre, however, refused to leave, repeating his promise to the American commander that he would not escape. Jacques argued strenuously, outlining the dangers he had undergone to acquire the false documents and the troubles awaiting Pierre's children if their father remained in prison. Pierre would not budge, and Jacques returned alone to Sanary.

French officials eventually identified Pierre and transferred him to Fresnes, a penitentiary outside Paris. Fernande returned to the capital to prepare her husband's defense against charges of treason. Jacques, despite warnings from his military superiors, testified at the trial in his brother's behalf, wearing his formal officer's uniform bearing several war medals. The appeals, however, proved fruitless. On November 23, 1946, the French court condemned Pierre Cousteau to death.

Jacques's display of loyalty to his collaborationist brother haunted him throughout his naval career. Admirals informally labeled him as undisciplined and suspect. Cousteau would be given responsibilities, but he remained a captain while all his academy classmates who survived the war earned further advancements.

The Cousteau children, meanwhile, enjoyed fun-filled days at Sanary, joining Tailliez and Dumas on daily dives in the Mediterranean. After several months Elizabeth took Françoise and Jean-Pierre to England, where Daniel and Higgins had resettled at the Torquay resort. She returned regularly to Paris to visit her son on death row.

Pierre was to be shot by firing squad on April 6, 1947. While the family petitioned for leniency, several French intellectuals and journalists began to demand clemency for collaborationist authors. They wrote favorable pieces about former Nazi sympathizers, suggesting that the French government could not logically do business with a resurgent Germany and execute French collaborators. Eventually the French court rescinded Pierre's sentence and transferred him to a jail in Clairvaux, 140 miles east of Paris. Fernande, stricken with what became diagnosed as a brain tumor, continued to appeal for her husband's release.

Pierre maintained a prison diary that traced his growing anger toward Jacques for concentrating on his career rather than supporting his brother. Paroled in the fall of 1953, after nearly ten years behind bars, Pierre, ill with cancer, remained bitter toward society and Jacques. According to Pierre's son, "Relations between the brothers remained incredibly tense. My father believed my uncle abandoned him in prison."

Although Cousteau realistically could have done little more to aid his brother, Pierre stewed while Jacques pursued an adventurous and creative life. He entered *Sixty Feet Down,* his eighteen-minute film completed without the benefit of aqualungs, in the new Cannes Film Festival, at which, receiving wide acclaim, it was sold to Gaumont for distribution.

With some money in his pocket, Cousteau focused his second film on a subject to which he would return several times: sunken ships. "A dead ship," he said, "is the house of tremendous fish and plant life. The mixture of life and death is mysterious, even religious. There is a sense of peace and a mood that you feel on entering a cathedral."

Locating sunken vessels for filming, however, proved difficult because most lay in filthy harbors or straits with strong currents. Few interesting specimens rested under clear water.

In 1943 Cousteau, Dumas, and Tailliez investigated the *Tozeur,* a four-thousand-ton freighter that had smashed against Frioul rock off the Mediterranean coast near Marseilles. The wreck listed to the starboard, with its mast still poking above the water and the stern sixty-five feet below the surface. The ship was, according to Cousteau, "a fine movie studio" for the team's film, *Wrecks.*

Despite its appeal, the sunken vessel harbored dangerous pitfalls. Dumas hooked his air tube on a long steel pole so tightly he could not move. He would have drowned had Cousteau not decided at the last minute to follow him down.

Cousteau recorded long sequences of Tailliez swimming gaily in and out of the *Tozeur*'s portholes, and he filmed helmet divers using oxyacetylene torches to cut up scrap metal. Under the bridge Dumas discovered the captain's bathroom and proceeded to lie in the bathtub. "It was quite lifelike," Cousteau commented in his log, "a near-naked man in a bathtub. I almost lost my mouthpiece laughing."

The wreck provoked rare religious analogies from Cousteau. The bulkheads, he noted, were arched in the fashion of cloisters. Weeds grew like lichens in a damp chapel, and light filtered down as though from clerestory windows.

The resulting black-and-white film, which conveyed the mystique of a silent tomb, enjoyed both popular and critical acclaim. Perhaps more important for Cousteau's financial prospects, it attracted the attention of Direction Générale du Cinéma Français, the government agency that promoted French film production.

Cousteau, of course, did not invent underwater photography. That distinction belongs to Louis Boutan, a brilliant zoologist who worked around the turn of the century at the Arago Marine Station at Banyuls-sur-Mer in the Mediterranean.

The major problem Boutan confronted was the way water absorbs light. Even in a clear sea, only about 40 percent of sunlight's intensity, as measured at the surface, still remains at a depth of three feet. At thirty-three feet, only 14 percent persists.

Boutan's first photographs, made in 1892 with a rudimentary camera anchored in shallow water, required exposures lasting up to a half hour in order to obtain sufficient light. Undersea currents, however, disturbed the meadow of green plants, making his early pictures extremely fuzzy.

Boutan quickly discovered the need for artificial lighting that would illuminate the subject to be photographed. He experimented with an array of alternatives, from flares to magnesium flashlights within an oxygen atmosphere. After three years of vain attempts, he enclosed combustion arc lamps in watertight housings and produced decent photographs at the incredible depth of 165 feet. But the exercise proved enormously costly, primarily because Boutan's equipment permitted only one flash per bulb. Moreover, the effort still produced blurred pictures since early cameras could obtain only one-fortieth-of-a-second exposures, whereas the movement of sea life required at least one five-hundredth of a second.

Cousteau carefully studied Boutan's *Undersea Photography,* published in 1900, which explained the initial experiments with elementary lighting and clumsy wet glass plates. He also followed the 1914 efforts of J. E. Williamson, an American who made the first underwater movies. And he scrutinized the efforts of Dr. W. H. Longlet and Charles Martin from the National Geographic Society, who, in 1926 in the Dry Tortugas, used magnesium powder and a floating reflector to produce the first underwater color photographs.

Cousteau and his colleagues began their filming efforts with simple equipment, their first camera being an obsolete Kinamo I purchased for only twenty-five dollars. Unable to obtain movie reels, team members spliced together fifty-foot rolls of Leica 35 mm film for still cameras. And before perfecting small, lightweight camera housings, they fitted steel oil drums with watertight gaskets and pressureproof glass windows.

When trying to photograph in color, the group had to overcome not only the water's absorption of light but also its significant filtering effects. Cameramen discovered that daylight quickly became so blue under the sea's surface that other colors of the spectrum virtually disappeared. They spent months photographing at various levels color charts with squares of pure red, green, blue, yellow, orange, and purple. According to Cousteau's notes from these experiments: ''At 15 feet red turned pink, and at 40 feet became virtually black. There also orange disappeared. At 120 feet yellow began to turn green, and everything was expressed in almost monochromatic colors. Ultraviolet penetrated quite deeply, while infrared rays were totally absorbed in inches of water.''

The color metamorphosis of the sea produced some startling results. Dumas once harpooned an eighty-pound liche just off the rocks of La Cassidaigne in southern France. The large fish, although well hooked, mustered a fierce struggle, dragging Dumas in circles. The diver eventually hauled in the cord, gripped the harpoon shaft, and plunged his dagger into the liche's heart. The fish's blood flowed green. "Stupefied by the sight," Cousteau noted, "I swam close and stared at the mortal stream pumping from the heart. It was the color of emeralds."

Cousteau and Dumas had begun swimming to the surface, anxious to share their discovery of green blood, when the substance began to change color. At fifty-five feet it turned dark brown, at twenty feet, pink. On the surface the liche's blood became, like everyone else's, bright red.

Artificial lighting had to be extremely powerful to correct for such undersea distortions. A flashbulb of four hundred thousand candlepower used on land at night allowed a color shot fifty feet away in one twenty-fifth of a second. Under the sea, with the murky multitude of microscopic organisms and suspended minerals, the same flash illuminated only a five-foot radius.

Photographic pioneers tested hundreds of cameras, emulsions, and lights to obtain combinations that gave true rendering. Cousteau turned to color movies in 1948, using a powerful incandescent light fed by a cable from the surface. Three years later, seeking an independent means of lighting, he developed a magnesium flare that burned underwater like an oxyacetylene torch. But because the flare's combustion time was limited and its handling proved dangerous, Cousteau eventually adopted a series of portable silver and zinc batteries.

Such batteries and powerful lights proved to be extremely sensitive, especially when subjected to undersea pressures. If used on land, without the cooling effect of the sea, Cousteau's bulbs would have melted within a few seconds. During one of the group's early dives, moreover, a crew member forgot to release the valve that admitted compressed air to his enclosed reflector. When he and the equipment reached fourfold pressure, the glass port imploded, shaking the entire camera team, increasing the reflector's weight, and dragging the diver to the seafloor. The same accident, which did not injure the diver, occurred three additional times that same day.

Cameras, too, had to be ballasted to a positive buoyancy of one pound to assure their easy handling. Cousteau attached to each housing a miniature aqualung that fed compressed air in proportion to the sea's pressure. Before descending, a diver opened a valve on the camera, providing air to the regulator. As he swam down with the camera, its regulator automatically adjusted the intake of compressed air.

Evolving cameras, when immersed in water, usually remained stable enough to produce clear pictures. But to provide divers with maximum flexibility, Cousteau devised a torpedolike mount with two pistol grips. As the Captain explained, the diver simply had to "train his camera on the subject like a charging submachine gunner." By revolving one grip, he changed the aperture; the other altered the focus.

Early underwater photography required engineering skill, an artistic inclination—and a good bit of luck. To obtain a shot, four divers typically descended. One operated the camera, two held the lights, and one acted as subject. At the signaled moment the team pressed the flash buttons and tripped the camera. The darkness, wrote Cousteau, "would flower for a long instant into blinding light, a light that had never dwelt on this particular cross-section of marine life since the seas were formed; then it would be gray and shadowy once more." The divers blinked their eyes, repeated the exercise hundreds of times, and hoped they had captured the sea's vibrant colors. Success, however, was not certain until the team returned to the surface and developed the film.

Between diving and photographic experiments, Jacques-Yves Cousteau tried to rear a family. Shortly after France's liberation in the summer of 1945, he devised miniature aqualungs for his children. Jean-Michel, then eight, was just learning to swim. Philippe, five, had only been wading. The proud father, however, was convinced his sons would take naturally to diving. He forgot that young boys like to chatter more than listen.

Cousteau began by delivering a stern speech on the basic principles of diving. The boys didn't pay attention. When they stuck their masks beneath the surface, they shouted excitedly about the bright wonders revealed, dropped their mouthpieces, and swallowed a fair amount of water.

The father "gave another lecture on the theme that the sea was a silent world and that little boys were advised to shut up when visiting it." Neither youngster remembered his first experience, but both quickly learned to dive deeper and to catch octopuses and other undersea creatures with their bare hands.

Simone, according to her husband, loved the sea and exploration, but she lacked enthusiasm for diving. He once commented on Simone's interests: "For reasons of their own, women are suspicious of diving and frown on their menfolk going down."

One of the Captain's favorite photographs is of his young family joining hands in the clear depths of the Mediterranean. It was a rare show of familial unity because shortly after the diving lesson Jacques and Simone headed for international adventures and sent their sons off to board at the École des Roches in Normandy. During holidays the boys visited their grandparents in Paris, Torquay, or Sanary. On the few occasions when the parents were nearby, they spent their vacations as a family. Many years later Cousteau admitted, "I deeply regret the lack of time I've had with my sons."

Wrecks convinced French admirals that Cousteau could help remove German mines and retrieve valuable cargo from the scuttled French fleet and torpedoed ships. After the war, they transferred the filmmaker from his assignment at a Marseilles processing center for returning sailors and gave him a commission to resume diving experiments in Toulon. Tailliez, Cousteau's superior, was promoted to commandant of the newly formed Undersea Research Group.

Military leaders also decided to invest in oceanography, believing that future control of the seas could result from knowledge of the undersea world. They began by assigning several scientists to the Undersea Research Group's oceangoing diving tender, which Cousteau renamed *Ingénieur Élie Monnier* after a naval engineer he knew who had perished in a diving accident. Ever the hustler, Cousteau noted that his new organization "neglected no opportunity to make ourselves known as a powerful bureau of the *Marine Nationale*." The team quickly acquired funds, trucks, insulated suits, underwater lights, and a new launch.

The group also developed several innovative items, including an undersea sled, on which a diver could be towed at six knots, tripling the horizontal range of search missions. Moreover, it attracted energetic divers and seamen, including Maurice Fargues, Guy Morandière, and Jean Pinard. Champion spearfisherman Dumas, an easygoing bohemian and artist, was designated a civilian specialist in charge of training the new recruits.

Élie Monnier's first drill was to clear the harbor at Sète. Four diving teams worked in half hour shifts for five weeks to remove fourteen mines, a task that would have taken conventional hard hat divers several months to complete. Using the sled, they trolled day after day, sending up yellow buoys when they located an explosive. Unfortunately, the group missed at least one katymine, which blew up a ship two years later.

Cousteau quickly became bored with minesweeping tasks and tried to focus the team's attention on diving experiments. "We were aware of the dangers and limitations of diving," he says. "We placed a reasonable premium on returning alive, but we tried all the time to flirt with the limits."

The Captain looks back on the Undersea Research Group's early dives as "insane," committed with all kinds of imprudence. "We were young, and sometimes we went beyond the limits of common sense," he acknowledges.

Tailliez, for instance, went searching for fish in December alone. When he could no longer stand the cold, he returned to the surface and discovered that he had drifted several hundred yards from the deserted shore. Tailliez struggled back, only to pass out on a rock. He would have died from exposure had it not been for his dog, Soika, a wolfhound, which covered the diver with its body and breathed hot air on his face. When Tailliez awoke, numbed and dazed, he stumbled to a shelter.

The group's incorrigible curiosity about odd effects under water led them to other dangers, including experiments with explosives. From early research by the Royal Navy, scientists assumed that shock waves from underwater blasts would blow nearby helmeted divers to pieces. One afternoon, however, Dumas tossed a grenade into the water, hoping to determine how many dead fish sank to the bottom rather than floated to the surface. After the explosive failed to detonate, Dumas waited several minutes and entered the sea to investigate. The bomb, lying fifteen feet underwater, emitted tiny bubbles. The diver approached cautiously, only to have the grenade detonate directly below him.

Racked but uninjured, Dumas staggered to the shore. The team quickly checked the British tables on underwater explosions and found that Dumas had been within the range of certain death. They hypothesized, therefore, that a naked man's shock resistance was more substantial than that of a fully suited diver.

To prove their theory, pairs ignited one-pound dynamite charges at progressively nearer distances until the bursts caused too much discomfort. While waiting for the explosion, Cousteau noted in his log, "the divers would look at each other and wince at the lunatic idea." He conceded that the experiments "boxed our ears disagreeably and dealt a sort of dry smack against the body."

For fun the group filmed submarines navigating and laying mines beneath the sea. To record the *Rubis*'s launch of a torpedo, Dumas climbed atop the vessel's hull while Cousteau took his camera thirty feet away, just off the missile's probable trajectory. On command Dumas smote the metal with his hammer, and the crew opened the tube hatch. Like a racing car, the projectile roared past Cousteau as he struggled to keep it framed in his camera lens.

The team also set out daringly to establish depth records and to examine the effects of nitrogen narcosis. From a navy ship Dumas donned an aqualung and a heavily weighted belt, descended feetfirst to progressively deeper levels, removed his weights, tied them on an anchored line, and sped to the surface. When the rope was raised, it showed the depth Dumas had attained. Cousteau and other colleagues then examined the dive's impact on Dumas's body and mind.

Divers experienced different reactions to deep descents. Tailliez, for instance, wrote an unintelligble message on the final marker board and returned to the surface with a headache that lasted two days. Dumas responded to the nitrogen with intense childlike nightmares.

Once in the mid-Atlantic Cousteau spotted a large school of dolphins and stopped the *Élie Monnier* to dive among them. He descended to 100, then 150 feet. "The intoxication was there," he later wrote, "flooding my entire being, but it seemed to me to be controllable, like the first puff of opium."

Deep dives were particularly threatening for neurasthenics like Cousteau who suffered from nervous tension and malaise. Testing his limits to nitrogen rapture, he described his first descent to 300 feet: "I was sufficiently in control to remember that in this pressure, ten times that of the surface, any untoward physical effort was extremely dangerous. I filled my lungs slowly and signed the board. I could not write what it felt like 50 fathoms down. I was the deepest independent diver. In my bisected brain the satisfaction was balanced by satirical self-contempt." Cousteau released his iron weight to ascend, quickly passing the 260-foot level, where the rapture disappeared. "I was light and sharp, one man again, enjoying the lighter air expanding in my lungs."

Cousteau's worst diving experience occurred not in the ocean but in an inland water cave. Divers had long feared, almost instinctively, such underground adventures. There was the discomfort of cold spring-water, the foreboding darkness, the potential for rock slides, and the danger of being swept away by unseen currents. Declared Dimitri Rebikoff, a diving pioneer: "Diving in fresh water tunnels corresponds to the tortures of hell."

Despite initial reluctance, the Undersea Research Group decided in 1946 to explore the mysteries of the Fontaine-de-Vaucluse, not far from Avignon. The famous spring erupted each year for about five weeks in late winter, causing the nearby Sorgue River to swell. Scientists had mapped the region and analyzed the water but failed to determine the cause of the annual flood. They couldn't explain the Vaucluse mystery by the simple overflow of an inner pool because the swelling did not entirely respond to rainfall. One hydrologist described the spring as the "most exasperating enigma of subterranean hydraulics." Cousteau and his colleagues thought they could solve the puzzle by locating a huge inner reservoir or a series of inner caverns and a system of siphons.

Vaucluse was the site of both scientific mystery and poetic romance. There in the early fourteenth century Petrarch wrote sonnets to Laura, his seventeen-year-old golden-haired love. There local poets wove tales of a smiling nymph who controlled the spring's flow by withdrawing huge diamonds from the bottom of the abyss.

The fountain lay at the bottom of a valley, near the town of Apt, surrounded by two-hundred-foot limestone cliffs. It was a quiet pool of crystal-clear water in the dry season. Beginning in March, however, it became a violent spring, rising some seventy-five feet to touch the roots of a legendary fig tree that rests precariously on the cavern's wall.

Cousteau was not the first diver to descend into the cave. In 1878, Ottonelli, a helmeted adventurer from Marseilles, followed a sloping tunnel to a depth of ninety feet. There, overcome by fear of darkness and falling rocks, he stopped, lowered a zinc weight another thirty feet, then returned to the surface to write about the siphon's depth.

Cousteau had studied the accounts, admiring Ottonelli's daring feat with the primitive equipment of his era. He pledged to locate Ottonelli's zinc weight.

In September 1938 Señor Negri from Marseilles renewed the effort to discover Vaucluse's mystery. The exhibitionist installed a microphone in his helmet to broadcast to the eager crowd onshore a running description of his adventures. Villagers recalled for Cousteau Negri's thrilled announcement that he had located Ottonelli's weight at a depth of 120 feet. Negri's written reports, however, contained little new information on the fountain's topography.

To obtain more detailed data in preparation for his dive, Cousteau tried to meet with Negri, but the salvage contractor refused to see him. What Cousteau would not know until he entered the pool was that Negri was a self-promoter who had probably descended no farther than fifty feet.

In late August 1946 the Undersea Research Group set out from Toulon with a convoy for Vaucluse. Two years old, the navy unit had accumulated an assortment of diving and photographic equipment, including a compression chamber, resuscitation apparatus, medical supplies, cameras, diving suits, and compressed-air tanks. With the help of local porters, the divers carried the heavy luggage down the steep slope to the fountain's edge.

The rainy season had not yet arrived, and the water was at its lowest level. While the divers could make out the bottom of the shallow basin through the crystal-clear water, their eyes were drawn to a large black spot near the cliff's base, the site of the siphon into which they would descend.

Cousteau and Frédéric Dumas formed the first pair, attached together by a thirty-foot cord and connected to the surface by a rope. They planned to don weights and sink to the bottom of the siphon. Cousteau would then try to climb up the siphon's other arm, uncoiling a separate rope as he proceeded, hoping to reach the surface of an interior lake.

Petty Officer Maurice Fargues, unable to descend because of a broken eardrum suffered the previous week while he dived too fast, served as the surface commander. He guided the divers by paying out or raising the rope, which served as the only means of communication between the deep men and the shore. One tug from below signaled Fargues to tighten the rope to clear snags. Three tugs called for the release of more cable. And six tugs were the emergency plea for Fargues to pull the divers up immediately.

Assistants began the expedition by moving a canoe to the middle of the pond and releasing a cable with a heavy pig-iron weight at the end. It dropped only fifty-five feet, and stuck on a stone ledge. Torpedo Petty Officer Jean Pinard dived, without protective clothing, to free the weight, and it fell to ninety-five feet. He returned lobster red from the cold.

Both Cousteau and Dumas stretched their rubber diving suits over long woolens. They waded into the pool at about 11:00 A.M., burdened by their knives, waterproof torches, supplementary air cylinders, pressure gauges, hundreds of feet of line, and mountaineering ice axes. Cousteau looked back to see a young priest standing in the crowd. He sensed that the cleric "had come no doubt to be of service in a certain eventuality."

The pair floated motionless for several moments to test their ballast and equipment before Cousteau led the way down, descending facefirst, past the triangular rock reported by Ottonelli and on to the weight dropped by Pinard. He pulled the rope three times and pushed the pig iron farther down into the sloping chasm. It landed on a sandy beach, and the two divers marked the depth at 150 feet.

The water grew dark, cold, and silent. Cousteau couldn't even see his flashlight beam because the clear liquid contained too few impurities to reflect light. The water felt icy. The divers could hear only their increasingly rapid breaths.

Slowly Cousteau began to suffer a throbbing earache. He tried to collect his thoughts, but he was drained of initiative. He lost hold of the rope.

Dumas, encumbered by his bulky equipment, struggled vainly to inflate his waterlogged frogman suit with compressed air. The mouthpiece fell from his face, and he swallowed a lot of water before replacing it. While fearing that Cousteau suffered from nitrogen narcosis, Dumas himself fell into a stupor.

Several times Cousteau swept the beach with his torch. Exhausted and disoriented, he finally grabbed the guide rope and pulled on his lifeline to the surface. It fell slack.

Fargues, on the surface, had grown worried about the lack of signals from the divers. Believing the exploration was proceeding, he payed out more and more rope. In fact, he knotted another length to the original. Unknown to him, Cousteau stood at the bottom, frantically pulling in more than four hundred feet of cable, hoping it would tighten so he could climb, dragging Dumas, to the surface.

When Cousteau felt Fargues's knot, he knew that the surface team was encouraging him to dive deeper, that it was not helping him to return. He would make it to safety only by scaling the steep and dark cliff like an alpinist. Dragged down by Dumas's weight, he struggled to find fingerholds in the rock. Out of breath and faint, he climbed only fifty feet before slipping off a crag and tumbling to the beach.

The conditions were bleak: two divers, almost unconscious, floundering in a dark maze 150 feet below the surface. Cousteau's only option was to try the rope once again. He remembered the six-pull signal for an emergency, but the line remained limp. Why couldn't Fargues understand the situation? he thought.

Fargues, increasingly concerned, could feel only a slight tremor on the rope. No regular tugs, no clear signal. He stood, hesitated, and asked aloud, "What do I risk? A bawling out?" He tightened the cable line.

Cousteau grabbed his partner and strained to hold on. Dumas's air cylinders banged against the rocky ledges during the ascent, which seemed to last for hours. Fargues, noticing that Dumas had broken the surface without his mouthpiece, threw himself into the water and dragged his colleague to shore, where Dumas vomited. Cousteau, extremely pale, managed to stumble out of the pool. Assistants pulled off the divers' rubber suits and prepared a blazing gasoline fire. The pair warmed themselves and slowly gained sufficient lucidity to explain the horrible dive, which they learned had lasted only twelve minutes. Dumas soon clambered to his feet and requested a bottle of brandy.

A nervous Simone, who had warned her husband not to enter the cave, had left the area before the descent for her own stiff drink in the village. There a young man burst into the tavern yelling that one of the divers had drowned. Simone frantically demanded to know the color of the diver's mask. It was red; her husband's was blue. Her joy collapsed, however, as she thought of Dumas. She sprinted to the fountain and found Cousteau and Dumas describing their trial with great animation. She embraced them both.

Team members could not immediately determine the cause of the unusual malaise. In deep-ocean dives the early symptoms of nitrogen narcosis were exhilaration and giddiness. But Cousteau and Dumas had grown heavy and lost their vigor.

Two other members of the group, Tailliez and Morandière, decided to try again, this time with less equipment. The results proved no more favorable.

The second pair quickly reached the same sandy beach and began to search for the other side of the siphon. But according to Tailliez, "Suddenly I felt my breath quicken. I was conscious, but I felt strangely powerless, emptied of all energy."

The divers gave the return signal to Fargues, and although the rope tightened this time, it became stuck on the wall. Tailliez, feeling increasingly numb, managed to seize his dagger and cut the entangled loop. Like Cousteau earlier, he grabbed the remaining rope and his partner.

Morandière collapsed on the surface and was dragged toward the fire. The wild-eyed Tailliez staggered to the shore. His left hand clutched the dagger by the blade, and he bled profusely but felt nothing.

After the second team had recovered, Dumas and Cousteau made another shallow dive to draw a diagram of the siphon near Ottonelli's zinc weight. Then the entire crew retired to the restaurants of Apt, where some individuals, according to Cousteau, "made a subjective comparison of cognac narcosis and rapture of the Fountain."

The group drove back that evening to Toulon, discussing the enigmatic stupor that had overtaken them in the spring's lifeless limestone water. The next morning a lab test on air in the cylinders revealed a trace of carbon monoxide, enough to kill a man at a depth of 150 feet. Cousteau then discovered that exhaust fumes from the new compressor had been sucked into the cylinders. The teams, he concluded, had suffered from carbon monoxide poisoning. (Although subsequent expeditions avoided the poisoning, they too failed to discover the fountain's secret.)

More than forty years later Dumas remembered the experience vividly. "It was extraordinary that we did not stay in that cave," he declared. Turning toward his old friend, Cousteau responded, "I was terrorized. What gave me courage was to know that your life depended upon me."

About a year after the Vaucluse expedition, in the autumn of 1947, the hazards of underwater exploration again confronted the Undersea Research Group. Fargues, trying to test diving limits in the open sea, descended more than 390 feet, tugging regularly on the line to signal the deck crew that he remained safe. Suddenly the signal stopped. Jean Pinard, the safety man, jumped immediately into the water, and the team began hauling in the line. At 150 feet Pinard reached Fargues, whose mouthpiece dangled on his chest. For twelve hours the crew tried to revive the diver, but the drunken delusions of nitrogen saturation had stolen the air tube from his mouth and drowned him.

Learning from such disasters, the group temporarily turned from deep diving experiments to undersea archaeology, trying first to locate a Roman argosy that reputedly carried priceless Greek art treasures.

The expedition proved to require as much detective skill as underwater expertise.

In June 1907 Admiral Jean Baehme, Simone's grandfather and commander of the French Tunisian naval district, spotted the Roman merchant vessel after following a tip from a Greek sponge diver who had worked in the Mediterranean waters off Tunisia's east coast. He paid particular attention to huge cylindrical objects, assumed to be cannons, at 127 feet below the surface.

Baehme sent helmeted divers to investigate and raise one of the columns. Removal of the encrusted marine life revealed no cannon but an elegant Ionic pillar attributed to Athens in the first century B.C. Art historians, realizing that the wreck's cargo consisted of an entire temple or lavish villa that Roman plunderers had taken apart in Athens for shipment to their home, sought funds for a full-scale salvage operation. James Hazen Hyde, the American millionaire and employer of Cousteau's father, contributed twenty thousand dollars to the effort.

The five-year project eventually recovered enough artifacts to fill five rooms of the Museum Alaoui in Tunis. Much more could have been obtained, but funds ran out in 1913, forcing divers to abandon their salvage operation.

Jacques Cousteau learned of the argosy in 1948. From records in Tunisia's archives he concluded that many treasures still lay below. And because his wife's grandfather had supervised the drawing of detailed site sketches, he decided to investigate.

The Tunisian landscape, however, had changed a great deal in the thirty-five years since the admiral completed his survey. Of the three alignments needed to locate the vessel, Cousteau could identify only one, a castle. The second bearing was to have been an isolated bush on the dunes, but a forest had grown throughout the area. The third was to have been a windmill, but no such building remained on the horizon. Cousteau led a shore party to locate the windmill's former site, but a withered octogenerian led him to the stone remains of three such structures.

Divers, therefore, had to spend six fruitless days searching for the famed wreck by being dragged in the sled behind the *Élie Monnier*. Cousteau commented on his frustration: "I mentally composed a report to my superiors in Toulon which would explain why it was necessary for me to work two naval vessels and thirty men for a week on a wreck that was salvaged in 1913."

On the seventh day the ship's lookout spotted Tailliez's personal signal buoy. When the diver broke the water and tore off his mouth grip, he announced the discovery of a column. The crew spent the evening celebrating in Mahdia.

Cousteau examined the wreck site the following morning and located fifty-eight remaining cylinders covered with thick blankets of corals, sponges, mollusks, and worms. He ordered the crew to begin a salvage operation, using diving schedules designed by Lieutenant Jean Alinat of the Undersea Research Group. Instead of relying on the tables for helmeted divers, which required men to spend an hour in staged decompression after forty-five minutes of work at the wreck's depth, Alinat figured that aqualunged divers could perform three fifteen-minute dives without decompressing if they rested an hour on the surface between each descent.

To maintain the rigid timetable, Cousteau fired warning signals into the water five minutes after the divers had gone down, again at ten minutes, and he discharged three rounds at fifteen minutes to signal the need to surface. Dumas usually obeyed the shooting clock religiously, but on one late-afternoon dive he made an extra plunge to investigate a shiny object. When at dinner Dumas commented on a twinge in his shoulder, Cousteau locked him immediately in the recompression chamber on deck. Dumas complained of being starved, but the Undersea Research Group had learned to take no chances on the bends.

Cousteau's superiors finally ordered him to return to more pressing tasks. After six days of excavation he had recovered only four columns, two capitals, and two bases. He noted, "We were merely scratching at history's door."

Cousteau, an energetic tinkerer, delighted in designing equipment that might improve performance or allow a diver new freedom. He demonstrated his genius time and again with the Aqua Lung, the constant-volume diving suit, camera mounts, and floodlights.

Like every creative inventor, however, Cousteau developed several failures. Unlike most, the Captain usually admitted his mistakes.

One noted disappointment was an iron cage, which Cousteau initially described as "the finest antishark defense ever devised by the mind of man and the stout blacksmiths of Toulon." The collapsible structure could be erected quickly, and it allowed divers to be lowered directly from the ship through the surface waters, where scientists assumed that sharks threatened most frequently. Once at the bottom, the frogmen could emerge from the cage's door and perform their tasks, return to the cell's safety, ring a buzzer, and be hoisted back to the ship.

Cousteau, Dumas, and Tailliez first tested this "human zoo" off Madeleine Island near Dakar. Loaded down with three-cylinder tanks and heavy cameras, they entered the cage on deck and grasped the bars as the winch swung them out over the water. The trio soon realized that the *Élie Monnier*'s gentle roll became amplified for those dangling at the end of a boom. The bumpy carnival ride, however, had just begun.

As the divers broke the surface, the water lifted them against the roof of the cell. The effect, said Cousteau, "was rather like a preposterous underwater birdcage, with three men tumbling in clumsy flight. The dipping ship's crane bounced the cage up and down, dealing us smart blows on the crown and feet, and swaying us against the bars violently."

The trio spotted no sharks, but a six-foot barracuda, equipped with razor-sharp teeth, passed by slowly. They quickly calculated that the thin fish could have swum easily through the bars and attacked the trapped divers. Cousteau called off the experiment and abandoned the equipment.

As the iron cage demonstrated, aqualung divers may have been freed from cumbersome air lines to the surface, but they had much to learn about descending safely and efficiently. Even the relatively simple mask presented problems since the glass plate refracted light in such a way that objects appeared one fourth nearer than their actual distance. Of his first dive with a mask, Cousteau observed, "I reached for objects, saw my hand fall short and was dismayed at my shrunken flipper of an arm."

Experience enabled divers to correct for distance and size, but it led to filming distortions. Because the porthole over a camera had the same refractive qualities as a mask, a photographer's compensation caused his movies to go out of focus. Cousteau experimented with an array of optics to correct for the diver's adjustment, only to find that the answer lay in psychology. He and his cameramen had to learn not to compensate for any distortion, to estimate focal length by what it *seemed* to be.

Divers also had to adjust for water's buoyancy. Undersea tools had to be ballasted so they would not sink or float away. Knife blades needed to be counterpoised with cork. Air had to be added to camera housings to make them weightless.

The diver had to be ballasted carefully, too. Cousteau noted that when fully dressed for diving, he looked "like a beast of burden staggering into the water with a 45-pound triple aqualung strapped on my back, four pounds of lead on my belt, and the weight of knife, pressurized watch, depth gauge, and compass on my wrists, and perhaps a four-foot shark billy on a wrist thong." On the surface he weighed almost 265 pounds. Under the water he was transformed to a mere pound—the deliberate overweight that allowed him to descend slowly. By the end of the dive, with air taken from his cylinders, he would have lost about 3 pounds, enough to assure an easy return to the surface.

Cousteau and his colleagues also studied the migration of cold zones within the sea. "The warm and cold layers meet with the precision of wood veneers," he concluded. "There is no transition. One can hang in the moderate zone and poke a finger into the cold and feel it as sharply as one sticks an exploratory toe in the sea on the season's first dip." During winter months, he discovered, the cold zone rose. Storms also extracted the warm layer temporarily, allowing cooler waters to ascend.

Moreover, divers had to account for the effects of increased pressure. A person on the surface bore several tons of atmospheric pressure on his body without noticing it. At thirty-three feet beneath the surface, the impact doubled. It tripled at sixty-six feet, and so on down, in multiples of thirty-three feet. Swallowing usually cleared the ears, but increased pressure caused pain and exhaustion.

Cousteau learned, ironically, that "pressure changes become progressively easier on a diver the deeper he goes. . . . Between 33 and 66 feet he experiences only half as much change as in the first layer. In the next 33 feet pressure is increased by only a third, and by a fourth in the next strata." The most dangerous area, therefore, was near the surface.

More troubling than the pressure, however, was the body's absorption of gases. Scientists had to devise schedules for stage decompression that would allow a diver to dispose of excess nitrogen absorbed by his blood and tissues from the compressed air he had been breathing. They learned, for example, that if a diver spent one hour working at 100 feet beneath the surface, he had to make three decompression stops totaling thirty-eight minutes before he could safely leave the water. For a half hour's dive at 150 feet, he had to wait thirty-five minutes for his body to readjust.

Cousteau employed much of his growing knowledge to stalk undersea animals, especially the dolphin. He had encountered his first specimen in 1934 while serving as a young naval officer in the Far East. Assigned to test the recently repaired *Primauguet,* he had maneuvered out of the harbor and accelerated the engines to full power. The mighty cruiser reached 33.5 knots. Standing on the bridge, Cousteau was enthralled by the machine's performance. He glanced to the side, however, and noticed a school of dolphins moving alongside the *Primauguet.* The mammals kept pace with the ship for some time before several of the more playful decided to ride the crest of the cruiser's bow wave. Each frolicked for two or three minutes directly before the vessel's prow. After becoming bored with the game, the school swam on, outdistancing the *Primauguet.*

A baffled Cousteau calculated that the dolphins had been swimming at a speed of almost fifty knots. He marveled that the animals were "faster, and infinitely more maneuverable, than the best machines that human ingenuity had yet been able to devise."

Fourteen years later, when the Undersea Research Group was returning to the Strait of Gibraltar after an Atlantic Ocean expedition, Cousteau spotted a large school of dolphins headed in the same direction. He moved the *Élie Monnier* so that it joined the mammals, which began to play beside the ship's bow.

Cousteau decided to test the school's sense of direction by turning the *Élie Monnier* ever so slightly. The dolphins, however, remained with the ship only for a few minutes before they resumed a true course toward Gibraltar. Despite Cousteau's repeated efforts to redirect their movement, the mammals consistently abandoned their playful games around the ship. He concluded "that here, some 50 miles from land, the dolphins knew the precise azimuth of Gibraltar and were on a direct course toward their destination."

Shortly after the *Élie Monnier* had passed through the strait, the team spotted another school of the fast and directed mammals. Cousteau decided to join these more relaxed dolphins in the water, to film their activities, and to touch their sleek skins. In 1948 this marked his first attempt at such an encounter, one he described as "marvelous and exciting for us." The dolphins, however, had other ideas. When the divers hit the water, they swam away frantically. "We learned," the Captain concluded, "that, in the water, dolphins are extremely wary of divers."

The rejection made Cousteau only more determined to befriend the mammal, which he described as "the most attractive and intriguing form of marine life." He spent decades observing the dolphin, initially confirming the obvious facts: The mammal normally swims at about ten knots per hour; it uses its numerous and conical teeth to hold rather than chew prey; it can leap as high as ten feet out of the water and soar for a distance of twelve feet; it weighs between 150 and 175 pounds; it possesses a sophisticated sound navigation system; and it communicates with its colleagues by a complex array of squeaks. Despite these observations, Cousteau often remarked on how little he and others knew of the mammal's life beneath the sea.

The dolphin's mystery, its "intelligence," and its knowing smile remained magnets for the Captain's attentions. The mammal's facial expression, which was made famous by the American television series *Flipper*, presented, according to Cousteau, "a keen look, slightly melancholy and mischievous, but less insolent and cynical than that of monkeys—[it] seems full of indulgence for the uncertainties of the human condition."

Cousteau particularly enjoyed the ancient legends about dolphins cooperating with man. He marveled at the prehistoric engraving, found in South Africa, of a swimmer playing among dolphins. He frequently recounted Homer's story of Telemachus, the young son of Odysseus who fell into the sea and was rescued by a dolphin. And he celebrated Plutarch's story of Korianos, a native of Asia Minor who convinced a group of fishermen to release a dolphin caught in their nets; a few months later a dolphin returned the favor by saving the shipwrecked Korianos.

Myths even suggested that dolphins were once men, providing an explanation for the communion that existed between the creatures. In the *Homeric Hymns,* pirates captured the child god Dionysus and began to transport him via ship to a slave market. But the child, possessed with divine powers, made leaves sprout from the mast, caused red wine to flood the decks, and transformed himself into a lion. The terrified pirates leaped into the sea, where the gods immediately changed them into dolphins, altering both their form and character. Thenceforth, according to the legend, dolphins aided mankind.

The Undersea Research Group also turned its attentions to the whale, which Cousteau described as the "monarch of the sea." In 1948, on the same trip through the Strait of Gibraltar during which the team spotted dolphins, Cousteau sighted his first large school of pilot whales. With Dumas and a sailor, he jumped into a small motorboat to catch a glimpse of the graceful giants. For almost half an hour the trio tried to foresee where the whales would resurface, only to have moved their launch to the wrong location. Finally, a pilot whale erupted right next to them, flipped its tail, and sent everything—the boat, the cameras, and the adventurers—flying into the air. While the school sped away, Cousteau and his partners remained in the water, waiting for the *Élie Monnier* to pick them up.

Not long after this encounter the team was tracking a particularly thick layer of cuttlefish with its sophisticated sonar equipment when Cousteau spotted another group of pilot whales on the surface. This school, however, seemed to be going nowhere. The whales drifted about slowly, disappearing occasionally for a lazy dive.

To analyze this odd behavior, Cousteau harpooned one of the animals and dissected it. Inside the large male he discovered the remains of several hundred cuttlefish. The observation, he later boasted, proved for the first time that pilot whales hunted for food at great depths, particularly within the deep scattering layer composed of cephalopods. It also demonstrated that cuttlefish lived in open waters, not only along the coast, as had been thought. Finally, Cousteau reasoned that these whales seemed lethargic because they were resting after having stuffed themselves on a cuttlefish feast.

More revealing than Cousteau's discoveries, however, was his willingness in 1948 to kill a whale for the sake of scientific observation. He launched the harpoon, as he later wrote, "without feeling the slightest twinge of conscience." This detachment from undersea life was to change as Cousteau matured. About twenty-five years later he remembered the harpooning incident and admitted, "We still had much to learn, not only about life in the sea but also about ourselves."

After five years of minesweeping, diving experiments, and mammal hunting, the Undersea Research Group moved into a three-story building in Toulon's navy yard. The diving center contained compression chambers, a machine shop and photo lab, stalls for captured animals, and a conference center. Rising through the building was a diving well that could simulate pressures found eight hundred feet below the surface.

Such signs of material success, however, offered little satisfaction for Cousteau. The group's early experiences only increased his obsession with the incredible realm of oceanic life waiting to be explored, and they sharpened his passion to captain his own research ship and publicize his accomplishments.

CHAPTER FOUR

Calypso

Cousteau, Tailliez, and Dumas had spent much of the war dreaming about ocean exploration, longing for a sturdy, maneuverable boat with a shallow draft that could avoid sharp coral reefs. Not just any ship would do. Although the French Navy donated the *Ingénieur Élie Monnier* to the Undersea Research Group in the late 1940's, the assignment convinced Cousteau of the need for a specially designed ship dedicated to undersea research.

The three explorers eventually convinced naval architect André Mauric to draw plans for a seventy-five-foot craft. Cousteau took the blueprints and a proposal to the Direction Générale du Cinéma Français. In charge of encouraging French film production, the agency convinced the Crédit National to provide Cousteau with some financing for a movie—but not enough to construct a ship.

Inadequate money remained a problem for many years. During the war, however, Jacques and Simone had met a wealthy British couple at a bar in Auron. The woman offered Simone half of her remaining cigarette, a generous gesture at a time when tobacco was scarce throughout war-torn Europe. They became instant friends. Jacques and the woman's husband, a former member of Parliament, talked passionately most the night about the sea, often suggesting the components of an ideal research vessel. The pair agreed to look each other up after the war.

After the setback at Crédit National, Simone convinced Jacques to arrange another meeting with Noel Guinness, this time in London. The veteran British seafarer remembered his initial conversation with Cousteau, but he argued that a custom-designed boat wasn't necessary when scores of war surplus ships were available. Guinness suggested that Cousteau travel to Malta to review the Fairmiles, mass-produced coast patrollers. More important, he said, "I'll give you a grant to buy and refit one."

Overwhelmed by the offhand generosity, Cousteau exclaimed, "I won't know how to repay you."

"Forget it," Guinness replied. And Cousteau had achieved his first major fund-raising success.

Guinness set only two conditions on his generosity: that Cousteau neither reveal the donor's name nor solicit additional money from him. The Captain accepted these grant requirements, but on several occasions, including two of his books, he identified Noel Guinness as his benefactor.

Cousteau flew to Malta in early 1950 to examine the Fairmiles, but he despaired that the small wooden ships didn't offer sufficient room for diving and research equipment. At the other end of the shipyard Cousteau spotted a boat marked J-826, a YMS (yard motor sweeper)-class minesweeper. Much larger than a Fairmile, the 360-ton vessel possessed a double hull of wood, double planking, and very narrowly spaced timbers. It was, in short, a solid ship with a shallow draft, designed for easy maneuvering around mines. Such characteristics, Cousteau reasoned, would enable it to skirt natural undersea hazards, too.

Only a few snapshots remain of the vessel's original launching on March 21, 1942, at the Ballard Marine Railway yards at the foot of Seattle's Twenty-fourth Avenue Northwest. Isobel Prentice, then a smiling schoolgirl and the daughter of the shipyard's foreman, held a bouquet of roses and smashed a ribbon-sheathed champagne bottle against the boat's bow. The vessel slipped stern first into the ship canal.

The U.S. Navy had intended the YMS vessels to operate only near their home ports or yards. The durable vessels, however, became the Jeeps of naval warfare, and the United States constructed more than 560 YMS minesweepers from 1941 to 1944. J-826 was one of 80 vessels sent to the British under the U.S. lend-lease program. Little is known of its actual activities during the war, but most of the British boats sailed initially to Malta, a key Allied naval center, and ended the war in Naples.

Records show that J-826 returned to Malta in July 1946. The British transferred its commission back to the U.S. Navy, which sold the vessel in 1949 to an entrepreneur who converted the minesweeper into a civilian ferryboat that could carry eleven cars and four hundred people between Malta and neighboring Gozo Island. The new owner christened the ship *Calypso,* after the beautiful sea maiden in Homer's *Odyssey* who reigned over the island of Ogygia. Calypso, according to the legend, loved Odysseus and promised to make him immortal if he would stay and be her husband, but the soldier begged to return to his home in Ithaca. Still, this ''sea nymph'' held Odysseus for seven of the ten years of his adventure in a bondage abounding with delights. Similarly, the ship *Calypso* has captured Cousteau's time and imagination for almost four decades.

For a ship with such a grand reputation, the *Calypso* appears surprisingly small. Four men can stretch their arms across its beam or width, and it is only 139 feet long, less than half the span of a football field.

Cousteau signed the sales papers in Nice on July 19, 1950, placing the vessel for tax purposes under his newly formed nonprofit organization, Campagnes Océanographiques Françaises. Guinness's generous grant covered the ship's war surplus price and an extensive refit as well. After transferring *Calypso* to the shipyard in Antibes, Cousteau supervised the battle gray minesweeper's further conversion into a sprightly white oceanographic research vessel. He stripped the ship to its carcass, enlarged the crew quarters, planted a crane on the port afterquarters, and installed navigational aids. After a year's effort the warrior had become an explorer.

Tailliez, Dumas, and Cousteau added several of their ideas for an ideal vessel to *Calypso*. They placed an underwater observation chamber on the forefront of the ship, eight feet below the waterline, with the steel chamber and entry tube outside the hull in order to avoid weakening the bow structure. This false nose allowed two crew members to observe and film underwater life through five circular windows.

The trio also installed a high observation platform over *Calypso*'s bridge house. The concept came from an adventure book by Henri de Montfreid that Cousteau had read as a child, in which an Arab smuggler always managed to avoid capture by being guided through coral reefs by a young observer sent up to the crow's nest. Cousteau thought a similar watchtower would enable his team to scan the horizon for whales and other intriguing creatures of the sea.

The Captain often recounted his early financial struggles to cover *Calypso*'s substantial operating and maintenance costs. ''Beyond the more obvious adventures was always the ghost of the financial adventure,'' he complained. No doubt Cousteau labored—he claimed to have mortgaged his home three times—but he enjoyed unusual access to significant financial assets. Simone, who came from a wealthy family, sold some of her expensive jewelry. Simone's father served on the board of the multinational Air Liquide Company and convinced corporations to donate major pieces of equipment for the ship. Cousteau's father, employed by an American millionaire, gained additional materials from U.S. and British manufacturers. And the Captain proved to be a premier fund raiser, charming rich individuals to make donations and lobbying the French government to hire *Calypso* as a research vessel for scientists.

Particularly generous contributions came from Roger Gary, a Marseilles industrialist; Gary's brother-in-law, the marquis Armand de Turenne; Edmond Maruic, an architect; and Pierre Malville, an Antibes restaurateur. These wealthy friends joined the Cousteaus—including sons Jean-Michel, then aged thirteen, and Philippe, eleven—on *Calypso*'s maiden voyage as a research vessel in June 1951.

During these short preliminary tests off the coast of Corsica, *Calypso* lacked its full array of equipment. Lifeboats, for instance, had not yet arrived, so Malville had to bring along his own dinghy. Moreover, official papers had not been processed to register *Calypso* as a French vessel, even though it flew the French flag.

Cousteau, having taken temporary leave from the French Navy, spent several weeks making final arrangements and hiring a full crew. He selected François Sâout, a former navy chief boatswain and a sailboat racer, as the first skipper. Frédéric Dumas supervised the diving, and Simone assumed the stewardship. The Captain also acquired the assistance of several marine biologists from the Sorbonne, the National Museum of Natural History in Paris, the Roscoff Marine Station in Brittany, the University of Nancy, and La Rochelle Laboratory.

As Cousteau energetically prepared his new ship, personal tragedy struck. His mother, aged sixty-four, died of a stroke in Paris during one of her regular journeys from Britain to visit Pierre in prison. Elizabeth's life had been filled with struggles, but she was the source of strength for the family during their early wanderings and Daniel's wartime separation. She had withstood her elder son's disgrace and assumed responsibility for raising his children.

On Jacques's seventy-fifth birthday he declared that of all the people he ever met, his mother had the greatest influence on his life. She was a sincere, hardworking woman who Cousteau said never committed a sin, never hurt another human being. She demanded performance and quality. She promoted the arts. She provided stability. And as the Captain began his most challenging and productive decade, she was gone.

Cousteau explained his approach toward undersea exploration as an "almost militant insistence on the necessity of man's presence in the water to arrive at a true understanding of that world." From *Calypso*'s very first expedition, Cousteau pushed his crew and the accompanying scientists to adopt his motto of personal observation: *Il faut aller voir* (We must go and see for ourselves).

The creed translated into a unique documentary film style in which Cousteau's cameras focused as much on *Calypso*'s crew as on undersea animals and plants. Over the years it justified the team's involvement in industrial projects, undersea habitations, and other incursions of man into nature. Moreover, it produced an anthropomorphic perspective on life within the sea.

Cousteau's explorations commenced on November 24, 1951, when *Calypso* steamed from the Toulon arsenal for the Suez Canal and the coral reefs of the Farasan Bank off the Saudi Arabian coast in the Red Sea. The ship met its first major test on the third day out as the sea began to roll violently. Cameramen humorously recorded crew members falling on the floor and lunging for airborne luncheon dishes. But the laughter stopped suddenly when the engines failed. Unable to clean the dirt quickly from the clogged fuel filters, the Captain struggled helplessly to keep *Calypso* from smashing broadside into a towering wave. One giant swell tipped the ship at a forty-five-degree angle, but the vessel shook off the water and rolled back. Several more waves attacked, and *Calypso* recovered each time. Cousteau smiled broadly and yelled, "She can take it!"

Upon reaching the island of Abu Latt, the crew established camp. Scientists aboard *Calypso* employed soundings to demonstrate that the Red Sea contained undersea basins of volcanic origin, while divers snapped thousands of underwater photographs, collected sample organisms, and identified previously unknown species of flora and fauna.

After returning from the Red Sea to Toulon in February 1952, Cousteau turned again to underwater archaeology, in part because his research vessel could advance the young science, but also because such projects could attract grants from the French government and the National Geographic Society. He wanted his first major project to be a success, so he chose to explore a sunken vessel from the first century B.C. known to be lying 140 feet underwater near Île Maître off the Mediterranean coast of France.

On the way to the well-examined site, the Captain serendipitously decided to investigate an uncharted wreck that a free-lance diver told him was filled with lobsters. Dumas found nothing of interest on his first descent. Cousteau experienced the same frustration until he was almost out of air, when he spotted a pile of dishes and pots. The Captain quickly grabbed three cups and returned to the surface.

Professor Fernand Benoît, director of Marseilles's Archaeological Museum, immediately identified the pottery as rare Campanian goblets from the third century B.C. Rather than proceed to the original destination, he and Cousteau agreed to concentrate on this site twelve miles from Marseilles, along the southern coast of Grand Congloué. From subsequent observations, Benoît reasoned that the large Roman ship, which had sunk in about 140 feet of water, measured 93 feet long and 27 feet wide. Since only four other ancient merchant vessels had been partially excavated by the early 1950's, Cousteau confidently declared that his newly identified wreck would prove to be the most ancient and that he would orchestrate the most thorough salvage operation ever undertaken.

With a temporary home base established in Marseilles, *Calypso* shuttled back and forth to Grand Congloué. The ship spent as much time as possible moored off the rocky island, allowing the men to make several dives each day.

The process proved arduous. At 140 feet a diver could work efficiently for only seventeen minutes before having to begin stage decompression. By the third dive of the day he experienced a touch of depth drunkenness.

When the team members realized they were making little progress relying only on baskets to raise the thousands of ceramic pots and dishes, they turned to an underwater vacuum cleaner, operated by a mammoth pump onshore, that sucked sand, fish, stones, and ancient relics to the surface. The powerful pipe devoured the bottom, chewing up silt and shells. If its mouth had accidentally grabbed a diver, it would have sucked his blood away, too.

When operated properly, the air lift spewed tons of materials into a metal strainer. Mud and small shells passed through and returned to the sea, leaving behind the larger objects, including relics from the wreck. The strong hose, however, often destroyed the fragile pottery. More frequently, large shards or stones clogged the pipe, forcing divers to shut down and clean the system.

The wreck's greatest treasures were graceful two-handled earthenware jars, known as amphorae, that ancient Romans used to carry wine, water, oil, olives, resin, and grain. Filled with about six and one-half gallons of wine, a single vessel weighed nearly a hundred pounds. On land, the amphora's conical bottom could be punched into the earth. On shipboard, it fitted into holes in the cargo racks. The wreck off Grand Congloué had carried an estimated ten thousand amphorae.

The expanding project required expanding financial support. The French Navy, the French Ministry of National Education, and the National Geographic Society offered initial backing, but Cousteau increasingly turned to Marseilles merchants for equipment and supplies. Demonstrating the skills of a talented publicist, he made the ship's salvaging a civic cause.

Cousteau's excavation became widely known, and it attracted many visitors and volunteers. Albert Falco, who was to become chief diver, joined the *Calypso* team in 1952. A seasoned undersea explorer from Sormiou, near Marseilles, Falco had worked as a postwar volunteer clearing mines from French harbors, a hazardous assignment that cost him three fingers on his left hand. Social security doctors refused to approve Falco's working papers until Cousteau personally appealed to a special physician, stressing *Calypso*'s needs and the diver's superior physical strength and stamina. The Captain eventually obtained a permit that confined Falco's employment to *"le navire océanographique* Calypso'' and shoreside fishing.

Falco joined a team of skilled and high-spirited divers, including leader Frédéric Dumas, Henri Goiran, Raymond Kientzy (known as Canoe because of a long, narrow boat that he cherished), André Laban, and Jean-Pierre Servanti. The work, while thrilling, was dangerous, and disaster struck in early November, when Servanti offered to retrieve the chain attached to a buoy that had been blown away during a storm. Cousteau agreed reluctantly to allow the experienced diver to descend to 230 feet alone. All seemed to be going well until Servanti's air bubbles ceased. Falco and two colleagues dived into the water instantly and soon found Servanti lying unconscious on the bottom. The trio retrieved his body and placed it in a recompression chamber aboard *Calypso,* which quickly steamed back to a hospital in Marseilles. But nothing would revive the young diver.

One of the project's bright spots was the discovery of twenty-two-hundred-year-old wine. Several of the initial amphorae to arrive aboard *Calypso* were sealed at their mouths with stoppers made of pozzolana, a volcanic substance. Each, however, had been emptied through a tiny hole drilled in the neck. Dumas joked that the ship sank because raucous sailors had sampled too many wine vessels.

Late in the fall the team found an amphora with an inner cork and a resinous-pitch lining under the pozzolana stopper that had sealed the wine inside. Cousteau, a connoisseur of life's pleasures, couldn't resist sampling the well-aged pink liquid. The sour expression on his face, however, moved one crew member to ask, "Poor vintage century?" The Captain later expressed regret for not having delivered the intact amphora to a laboratory where the ancient wine could have been analyzed professionally.

This persistent conflict between adventure and science prompted numerous pranks among the crew. When the archaeologists lamented the wreck's lack of ancient coins, divers offered a deceptive thrill by feeding modern five-franc pieces into the suction pipe. They also delivered small octopuses, alive and writhing, up the lift to the ship's deck. To torment the scientists further, they even pretended to stub their cigarettes into the ancient dishes.

As the mistrals advanced their cold northerly winds, *Calypso* could no longer remain moored safely off Grand Congloué. Cousteau, therefore, asked French army engineers to construct a yellow tin hut, dubbed Port Calypso, on the island to allow six divers to live and work at the site throughout the winter.

Calypso returned in April 1953 with some of the first underwater television equipment, donated by the British Thomson-Houston Company. Nondiving archaeologists, such as Professor Benoît, could then observe the wreck and direct the excavation while sitting comfortably in a darkened room aboard the ship.

Benoît took it upon himself to discover the meaning of the initials "S.E.S." and the images of dolphins and anchors that were engraved on the necks of the amphorae. After ransacking classical genealogies and epigraphs throughout Europe, he concluded that the marks belonged to a Greek shipowner named Markos Sestios. This merchant of a powerful clan had lived in Delos during the second half of the third century B.C. Benoît eventually identified his preserved villa by matching floor mosaics with the jar's symbols.

After two years of digging, Cousteau grew increasingly anxious, wanting *Calypso* to travel the seas and explore the depths. He had not struggled to obtain a research vessel only to have it remain stationery. While less than half the wreck had been recovered, Cousteau delicately released himself from further obligations, encouraging others to continue the work.

Undersea archaeologists toiled for a total of five years at Port Calypso and recovered more than seven thousand amphorae and an equal number of pottery pieces. The unique and extensive discoveries still grace the collection of the Borély Museum in Marseilles.

The early 1950's were years of exuberance for Cousteau and his crew as they experimented with novel equipment and encountered new wonders underwater. Each discovery seemed to spur them to further explorations.

Experiments and adventures, however, would not satisfy Cousteau, who eagerly sought public recognition. "I wanted to translate the underwater world and to share it with people," he declared.

By 1950 the Captain had produced award-winning short films and published two books in French. He broke into the huge U.S. market with a November 1950 article in *Life* magazine, entitled "Underwater Wonders: A French Diver Explores the Haunts of Sea Monsters." The seven-page color spread, according to the editors, revealed "undreamable scenes such as one of his men waltzing with an octopus or pacing the deck of a long-sunken ship."

To portray life in the murky, fish-speckled half world under the sea, Cousteau wrote, "When I first dive down the water is clear and very blue. I am reassured and not frightened. At about 90 feet I lose sight of the surface, and before I find the bottom I am alone in an inky blue surrounding in which I have trouble deciding which way is down. Then I discover the bottom and feel safe. It is relatively clear here because light is reflected off the bottom."

A separate article in the October 1952 issue of *National Geographic* described how a small group of Frenchmen had discovered an underwater cosmos. Cousteau began his magazine piece dramatically: "The best way to observe fish is to become a fish. And the best way to become a fish—or a reasonable facsimile thereof—is to don an underwater breathing device called the aqualung. The aqualung frees a man to glide, unhurried and unharmed, fathoms deep beneath the sea. It permits him to swim face down through the water, roll over, or loll on his side, propelled along by flippered feet.''

The Captain became an instant celebrity in 1953 with the publication of *The Silent World,* a fast-paced and colorful description of his early diving exploits. Millions of readers enjoyed tales of Cousteau's adventures, but they also learned of an unknown world from a poetic instructor.

His descriptions of undersea life were clear. "Fish," he informed the reader, "do not like to go up or down, but swim on a chosen level of the reef, like tenants of a certain floor of a skyscraper. The ground-floor occupants, wrasses, groupers and Spanish bream, rarely venture to upper stories of the cliff dwelling. The dentex pace back and forth just above the sandy fields."

"What do fish do all day long?" Cousteau asked rhetorically. His answer was simple: "Most of the time they swim."

Cousteau offered sensitive observations, but he didn't exaggerate his findings. "The more we experience the sea," he admitted, "the less certain we are of conclusions."

He tried to contrast his findings with popular conceptions. Several phonograph records then in vogue broadcast the sea's noises, complete with the clamor of whales singing, dolphins whining, and some fish croaking like frogs. Cousteau argued that the recordings had been amplified grossly. "It is not the reality of the sea as we have known it with naked ears," he wrote. "There are noises under water, very interesting ones that the sea transmits exceptionally well, but a diver does not hear boiler factories." The sea is, in his words, "a most silent world."

Popular culture also assumed the worst about octopuses, morays, mantas, squids, and other "monsters" of the sea. Cousteau responded, "The monsters we have met seem a thoroughly harmless lot. Some are indifferent to men; others are curious about us. Most of them are frightened when we approach closely."

Cousteau, however, remained puzzled about sharks, the powerful and ancient creatures that seemed immune to most human interference. One afternoon Dumas tried to use his super harpoon gun to kill a fifteen-foot nurse shark. When within twelve feet of the fish, he released the six-foot spear with an explosive head. It punctured the shark's skull, and two seconds later the harpoon tip exploded. The eruption shook Dumas and Cousteau violently, but the shark continued to swim away, calmly, with the spear still sticking out of its head. The divers reasoned that the harpoon had gone clear through the shark, because no internal organ could have survived such a blast. Still, a being capable of living through such an explosion only inches from its head demonstrated to Cousteau "the extraordinary vitality of sharks."

The Captain admitted that increased experience had changed his attitude toward undersea life. In his early days of diving, warned by fishermen that mantas smothered and devoured divers, he harpooned rays for pleasure and food. He later dissected several, including a pregnant manta that delivered an eight-inch calf, to examine their nutritive systems. Discovering no teeth or grinders but a stomach filled only with plankton, he came to appreciate the beauty of this gentle winged creature swimming—or "flying"—through the water. "Spearing rays has no further interest for us," he stated. "The killing is simple and unworthy."

The Silent World resulted from the Captain's daily logs. "I never planned to write it at all," he claimed. "As we went along, I did keep notes, mainly for my own records and pleasure. These were in French. Then, I thought there might be a book. With the help of an associate, James Dugan, I wrote it out in English. After that I rewrote it in French."

Dugan, while a U.S. journalist covering the war in Europe, had seen Cousteau's early films in Paris shortly after Germany ended its occupation. The undersea shots thrilled Dugan so much that he returned to the theater several times with a small camera in order to capture proof for his American friends that menfish were exploring beneath the ocean's surface. He tried for several months to meet the creative filmmaker and finally caught up with him in London, where Cousteau had come to promote his Aqua Lung to the Royal Navy. The breakfast meeting at the lively Le Petit Club Français on St. James's Place lasted through lunch and dinner as the two men fantasized about sea exploration.

Dugan, described by critics as "a writer of great wit and enormous curiosity," quickly composed an article about his encounter, entitled "The First of the Menfish," but U.S. magazines in the late 1940's rejected the topic as uninteresting. Three years passed before *Scientific Illustrated* ran his piece. An editor from Harper & Row read the story and contacted Dugan about a book project on Cousteau and his adventures.

Cousteau jumped at the opportunity, but he had little time for writing. On the rare weekend away from expeditions, he traveled to Dugan's home on Long Island, where he'd elaborate to Dugan's wife, Ruth, on the impressions noted in his and Dumas's personal journals. The sessions, filled with enthusiasm and hope for the undersea world, lasted until the early hours of the morning. James Dugan molded the notes into a manuscript, which Cousteau polished.

The Silent World became a popular and critical success. It eventually sold five million copies and was translated into twenty-two languages, from Russian to Icelandic. According to one literary critic, "Awe and beauty are two sides of wonder. Therefore, this volume is truly wonderful."

Struggling to locate funding for new adventures, the emerging celebrity had convinced the Ministry of National Education to support French scientists working aboard *Calypso,* only to see the government fall and a new minister installed. Cousteau began afresh with successive Cabinets, but they all lost office before approving his formal application.

One drizzling afternoon the Captain left his wife aboard the docked *Calypso* and trudged off for another day's fund raising. While he was gone, a gentleman in a tight Savile Row suit approached Simone and said, "I say, Madame, would Captain Cousteau be interested in conducting a submarine prospection for the British Petroleum Company?"

As Cousteau later recounted the story, Simone replied, "Please come in out of the rain," as she offered the guest a whiskey and soda. "I have heard of British Petroleum," the well-connected Mme. Cousteau continued. "My cousin, Basil Jackson, is the head of it."

"Yes, rather," responded the curious visitor. "However, Sir Basil does not know of my call. I represent D'Arcy Exploration Company, a subsidiary of BP. My chief read your husband's book and thinks he could do a good job of looking into our offshore concession at Abu Dhabi."

"Where is Abu Dhabi?" inquired the increasingly ecstatic Simone, trying to remain calm and composed.

The gentleman responded, "A sheikhdom on the Trucial Oman Coast of the Persian Gulf, formerly known as the Pirate Coast." Simone then offered a toast to pirates.

Later that afternoon the dejected Cousteau returned to find his wife laughing with the stranger. After a short explanation of the offer from D'Arcy Exploration, the Captain joined the celebration, quickly calculating that the proposed fee would cover *Calypso*'s wages and operating expenses for four months, with enough left over to purchase new equipment. The oil company, believing that divers could conduct the survey at a fraction of the cost of typical sea-exploring rigs, wanted detailed maps and samples of the seafloor throughout BP's twelve-thousand-square-mile mining concession.

Conditions off Abu Dhabi proved to be oppressive. Not only was the region one of the world's hottest, but *Calypso* arrived during the season of the khamsin, a raging southerly wind that brought sandstorms and squalls. The water, ironically, delivered a chilling cold, more frigid than the team had found during winter descents in the Mediterranean. Moreover, divers had to contend with seven-foot-long sea snakes and an array of circling sharks. Because the protective cages proved to be of little use against the slithering snakes, workers abandoned their chambers and swam amid the unpredictable sharks.

The task itself also required more hardships than Cousteau first imagined. For petroleum geologists to locate the appropriate Eocene fossils associated with oil deposits, he had hoped a drop corer—a bomb-shaped seven-hundred-pound steel drill—would collect bottom samples. The tempered-steel coring pipe, however, failed to penetrate the rock bottom. In fact, it bent into an S, unable to pierce the armor-hard ocean floor. According to the Captain, "The super-tempered cutting mouth was crumpled like a paper napkin."

Dumas, a stocky man of few words, then tried a pneumatic chisel rigged to a compressed-air pipe. But the volatile instrument bounded the diver ten feet off the bottom.

Rather than spend the time and money required for blasting, Cousteau eventually sent one diver down with a sledgehammer and another with a chisel. As if they were driving tent stakes, they swung the mallet through a medium at least eight hundred times heavier than air. The men returned exhausted, but over a four-month period they chiseled out samples at 150 sites, twice what D'Arcy expected.

Sufficiently encouraged by Cousteau's findings, British Petroleum installed a test drilling platform off Abu Dhabi. Within eight years BP's field was producing more than forty thousand barrels of oil each day.

"We located the oil," Cousteau boasted. "And now a little village of nomads has turned into a modern city with skyscrapers and big hotels—all due to our efforts.'' Then he added with a smile, ''Unfortunately, we didn't ask for any royalty.''

With the contract completed, Cousteau sailed to the Qatar Peninsula for supplies and received his own personal bonanza: word that the French Ministry of National Education finally had approved a major grant. In fact, the government agreed to underwrite about two thirds of *Calypso*'s annual operating costs if Cousteau would carry French scientists nine months a year. *Calypso,* in essence, became the official French oceanographic vessel.

In November 1954, after a few biological dredging projects in the Mediterranean, *Calypso* returned to France, where the ship underwent four months of repair. The tired crew enjoyed a vacation, while Cousteau dreamed of new projects made possible by the government grant.

He spent much time with Frédéric Dumas and cameraman Louis Malle trying to perfect photographic equipment. ''We had to make the underwater cameras ourselves because there was nothing that we could use at the time,'' recalls Malle, the renowned director of *Pretty Baby, Atlantic City,* and *Au Revoir les Enfants* who began his filmmaking career as a Cousteau assistant. ''We called the cameras SM-one (for *sous-marine* or 'underwater'), SM-two, and SM-three and made them from the mechanism of a hand-held Bell and Howell outfitted with wide-angle lenses.'' Cousteau, according to Malle, ''was always a great technician, improving constantly.''

Calypso departed from Marseilles in early March 1955 on a journey that was to bring fame and fortune to the ship and its captain. The 13,800-mile trip took Cousteau's twenty-five-man team through the Red Sea, to the Seychelle Islands in the western Indian Ocean, and down to Diégo-Suarez on the northern tip of Madagascar. They made hundreds of dives to obtain the footage that Cousteau assembled into the feature-length film—entitled the same as his best-selling book, *The Silent World*—that won the Palme d'Or grand prize at the Cannes International Film Festival and an Oscar from the American Academy of Motion Picture Arts and Sciences.

The movie's first and most memorable scene was conceived not by Cousteau but by Louis Malle, then only twenty-three years old and fresh out of film school. Malle had become fascinated by an underwater flare—developed by Frédéric Dumas, the team's resident pyromaniac—that produced a dreadful roar and a cascade of bubbles.

With a sense of visual poetry, the filmmaker arranged for aqualunged divers to glide down into the world of silence, disturbing the sea's blue stillness with their arc torches. Cousteau, as described in an early chapter, stationed himself beneath the surface to record the flight of this torch team. Complementing the dramatic images, the narrator announced: "This is a motion-picture studio sixty-five feet under the sea. These divers wearing compressed-air aqualungs are true spacemen, swimming freely as fish."

To reflect his sense of man's separation from the ocean world, Cousteau followed this supernatural scene with self-deprecating shots of the divers returning to *Calypso*'s deck, appearing as awkward, waddling ducks burdened with grotesque apparatus and heavy air tanks. Despite his jab at the human condition, the Captain had no interest in presenting nature alone; rather, he sought to record the interactions of man, the temporary ocean visitor, with the sea's permanent residents.

The film's "star" was a sixty-pound grouper nicknamed Jojo le Merou by the crew and Ulysses by the English translators. Set to a Viennese waltz, the brownish fish "danced" with Dumas as the diver circled at a slow three-step tempo. Ulysses pursued the meat in Dumas's right hand, even continuing on the beat when the diver changed direction.

Anxious for food treats, the grouper became the crew's inseparable friend. It met the divers each morning as they jumped off the *Calypso*, and it followed them to the ladder every evening. While the clever fish enlivened the crew's undersea work with acrobatic tricks, it also disturbed the filming of several scenes. Cousteau, for instance, wanted to photograph a group of yellow snappers following a diver across the reef, but Ulysses kept dispersing the smaller fish. The grouper also bumped cameras and knocked over floodlights, forcing Falco to lock it in the yellow shark cage until cameramen completed filming.

On several occasions the seemingly tame grouper demonstrated its enormous power and speed. One morning Ulysses darted for the sack of meat in a diver's hand and swallowed the canvas whole. And on the last day of diving off Assumption Island, the grouper stole a large fish that a frogman had just killed with his spear gun. In fact, Ulysses, virtually synchronized with the flight of the spear, hit the fish and instantaneously devoured all but the tail, which remained protruding from its mouth for several hours.

Cousteau recorded the violence of the undersea world most clearly after a a baby whale accidentally ran into *Calypso*'s propellers. The blades, like a meat grinder, had sliced the body of the twelve-foot calf, and it bled profusely. Dumas terminated the whale's suffering with a bullet to its head, then secured the infant to the side of the ship.

Almost immediately a crowd of thirty sharks appeared. Initially cautious, they circled, jarring and smelling the whale's body. Though this slow ritual lasted more than ten minutes, when the feeding frenzy began it was sudden and swift. The boldest shark took the first bite, extracting several pounds of blubber cleanly from the baby's hide. Cousteau described the resulting scene: "The animals would race along the length of the whale's body, taking chunk after chunk in quick succession like corn on the cob." The ocean foamed with blood.

Because the shark's jaw is located well behind its snout, marine biologists had assumed that the creature turned on its back to feed. But Cousteau observed that an attacking shark thrust its lower jawbone forward and drew back the long overhang of its upper jaw until the gaping mouth, complete with sharp and glistening teeth, moved to the front of the body.

The frenzied sharks clamped their traps into the baby whale and shook their powerful bodies like terriers to loosen the meat. The sawing action was quick, as the sharks tore off twenty-pound chunks of blubber, leaving deep and clean holes in the victim. It was, recounted Cousteau, "terrifying and nauseating to watch."

The orgy ended as suddenly as it began. However, the men on deck, as Cousteau noted, "were overcome with the hatred of sharks that lies so close under the skin of a sailor." They grabbed tuna hooks and crowbars, hauled fat sharks onto the deck, and beat the flipping beasts to death. Dumas decapitated one shark to collect its jaw; when he tossed the body overboard, the headless brute swam away.

Cousteau, already a minor celebrity because of his book, knew he had produced a captivating film. Still, he launched a public relations campaign to assure awards for the movie. He strategically docked *Calypso* off the coast of Cannes for *The Silent World*'s premiere during the film festival in April 1956, and he and his crew mingled with the judges on the Croisette. The following October the Captain spent several weeks in Los Angeles meeting with reviewers and celebrities to improve his chances for an Academy Award.

No one can say if the lobbying efforts were necessary. What is clear is that on its own, Cousteau's hour and a half film stunned early audiences. Although three other producers released feature-length underwater movies at the same time as *The Silent World,* only Cousteau edited beautiful images and good music into rhythmic, dramatic adventures. A natural artist who had been fascinated with film since the age of thirteen, he had become a master editor.

The New York Times' reviewer, Bosley Crowther, described *The Silent World* as "surely the most beautiful and fascinating documentary of its sort ever filmed." He praised the "marine adventure film" for combining "the experience of looking at marvels with a wonderful intimacy." He ranked the commentary as "manifold and extraordinary" and the colors as "superb."

Crowther initially applauded *Calypso*'s crew because "like true scientists, they eschewed trickery." But he expressed concern, which numerous other critics later amplified, about Cousteau's lack of scientific credibility. "Exactly what Captain Cousteau learned for the benefit of oceanographic science . . . is not explained," concluded the reviewer. "However, his voyaging turned up a beautiful and absorbing nature film, and that is enough for anybody whose scientific interest does not range very far outside a theater."

The award-winning movie created a series of opportunities for its producer. Perhaps the most significant, from the standpoint of Cousteau's scientific critics, was his appointment to direct the Oceanographic Institute in Monaco, the oldest and largest undersea museum and research center.

Since the Renaissance, except for a brief period after the French Revolution, the sovereign prince of the House of Grimaldi has ruled Monaco. Albert Charles Honoré Grimaldi (Albert I), a modest and timid man, had enjoyed sailing more than the pleasures of the Monte Carlo Casino, which lavishly supported the small principality. In 1899 Albert, who enjoyed collecting marine artifacts, laid the cornerstone for a museum, a stately white limestone fortress placed on the prow of a great rock overlooking the bay at Monte Carlo, with buttresses and lower floors extending seven stories down the cliffside. His "Temple of the Sea" included about fifty laboratories, an extensive library, and meeting halls. He endowed the museum with a fortune in bonds of the Third French Republic, then considered the world's safest securities, and he invited an international committee of scientists to supervise the institute's operations.

When Albert died in 1922, Prince Louis, who cared little about oceanography, allowed the museum to stagnate. Postwar inflation, moreover, destroyed the endowment's value. Scientists left the labs, and caretakers sold most of the equipment. The institution would have been closed were it not for tourists who thronged into Monte Carlo to gamble but who stayed long enough to pay for admission to the lavish museum with impressive skeletons of giant marine mammals.

When Prince Rainier came to the throne in 1949, he pledged change. Impressed with *The Silent World,* he hoped Cousteau's notoriety and his connections with funding sources would enliven the research institute.

Cousteau's arrival may have vitalized the museum staff, but it almost catalyzed a constitutional crisis for the prince. A fast-living playboy who enjoyed the sea, Rainier had decided to diversify Monaco's economy and reduce its dependence on the casino. But his projects, including a massive railway tunnel, proved to be enormously expensive, and members of the National Council sought various reforms to restrict the prince's spending.

Controversies subsided briefly in 1956, when Rainier married actress Grace Kelly of Philadelphia in a Cinderella-like ceremony. But the following year, when the monarch proposed dramatic increases in the museum's budget to cover Cousteau's large stipend and expansion plans, the National Council threatened to revolt. Rainier struck back, dissolving the legislative body and outlawing demonstrations. Although labeled by his opponents "a destroyer of liberties," he took to the airwaves to argue that his plans, especially the museum's expansion, would attract even more tourist money and allow the state to continue to levy no taxes on its citizens. Council members eventually backed down, and Cousteau received a massive office and an array of new oceanographic equipment.

Cousteau's first act as director was to throw out the seat cushion used by his bureaucratic predecessor. The Captain steadfastly resisted the sedentary life of an administrator.

A master fund raiser, the Captain convinced the French government's Délégation Générale à la Recherche Scientifique to help rebuild the institute's research facilities and staff. He outlined three main fields for scientific analysis: nuclear techniques applied to oceanography and the physiology and ecology of deep-sea animals; continuous recording of physical and chemical data on seawater; and marine geophysics.

Inspired by the prosperous Marinelands in the United States, Cousteau added more aquariums, elaborate displays of oceanographic equipment, and a small theater to show short films on undersea life. He sent *Calypso*'s crew out into the Mediterranean and the Red Sea to stock the museum's tanks with exotic and colorful species.

He ordered Falco to concentrate on capturing dolphins that could be trained, not realizing that the local species, *Delphinus delphis,* or common dolphin, was smaller, lighter, and more delicate than the *Tursiops truncatus,* or bottle-nosed dolphin, which lived off Florida, adapted well to captivity, and maintained a robust constitution. The oversight caused a series of disasters.

Falco, appearing to be an oceanic cowboy, tried to lasso one of the dolphins playing about *Calypso*'s prow, but when the rope hit the water, the creatures fled. After a week of frustrating attempts, he began to experiment with a special dolphin catcher, designed by the French Bureau of Marine Research, that acted like a giant pincer, opening on contact and then immediately closing again. He modified the pincer and his original lasso so they could be shot around a dolphin's snout by a harpoon gun. He even dipped an arrow into curare, enough supposedly to immobilize the mammal. Nothing seemed to work.

The difficulty of Falco's task quickly became apparent. It was not simple to lasso a 175-pound creature that traveled at thirty to forty knots and leaped in and out of the water—especially if one didn't want to bruise the animal. Falco caught one dolphin with the pincer only to have the device tear the high-strung animal's skin; the wounded mammal had to be released.

Six months of failures passed before Falco captured and held his first dolphin. On October 31, 1957, off the coast of Monaco, he spotted a large school and positioned his boat so that three creatures took up positions in front of the bow. According to Falco's log for that day: "Fortunately, I was already on the platform, holding the loaded harpoon gun. I fired. It was a good shot, and the pincer closed around the tail of one of the dolphins."

Within three minutes a team of divers had jumped into a zodiac launch and sped to the entrapped dolphin. Falco grabbed the animal's tail, but it delivered a blow that sent him into the air. When the dolphin became immobilized by both exhaustion and fear, Falco slipped a lasso around its tail and dragged it back to the ship, where it was placed on an inflated mattress and soaked in water. Two hours later he delivered the disoriented female creature, nicknamed Kiki, to a tank at the institute.

Kiki continued to tremble and suffer a series of convulsions

throughout the day. Falco tried various remedies, including the place-
ment of an oxygen mask next to the blowhole and the injection of
vitamins and minerals into the bloodstream. Late that first night the
dolphin collapsed and sank to the bottom of the pool; it would have
drowned had not the divers held its head abovewater.

Eventually Kiki overcame her shock and seemed to desire human
company. Falco noted: "Canoe and I left the animal alone for a few
moments to see if we could find some coffee upstairs in the Museum.
Suddenly, we heard a series of shrill sounds coming from the tank.
They weren't loud, but they were piercing, like the cries of a child
trying to call someone. We returned to the tank immediately and got
into the water with the dolphin and began talking to her. The crying
stopped at once. I feel certain that just our being there with her was
enough to restore her calm."

Cousteau hypothesized that a dolphin's reaction to man changed
dramatically when it was captured. While swimming freely, it viewed
man as a source of terror. But when removed from its environment
and left alone, the animal sought human contact.

Despite the team's support and the Captain's theory, Kiki remained
despondent and ate nothing. A veterinarian injected penicillin and
theramycin, and he even administered camphor suppositories. Falco
designed plastic balloons to support the dolphin at night. Only after a
full week did she begin to show improvement by eating fresh fish and
swimming normally.

Confident that the team had successfully captured and acclimated
a dolphin, Cousteau asked Falco to seize a male companion. He returned the next day with a 125-pound mammal, which he called Dufduf. The pair seemed to relish each other's company. They ate and
exercised regularly, but both grew thin. In fact, hollows developed
next to their flippers. After three months Cousteau found Dufduf at
the bottom of the pool, dead.

Falco left immediately to trap another. Having mastered the technique, he quickly returned with a large female. When placed in the
tank with Kiki, she bolted from Falco's arms and smashed into the
wall. Falco tried to restrain her, but she wrenched free again and darted
for the side. According to Cousteau's notes: "At one-thirty in the
afternoon, the dolphin was dead. She had killed herself by swimming
at full speed from one side of the tank to the other and crashing into
the walls. Her agony was horrifying. She lay on her side at the bottom

of the tank, her body quivering. Then she began to stiffen, and her lungs filled with water and she was dead.''

Although deeply moved by the tragic suicide, Falco captured another male the following day. This dolphin, nicknamed Beps, also smashed its skull against the wall with a terrible noise.

Shortly thereafter Kiki died. She had survived only six months in captivity.

Cousteau admitted that his attempts ended in failure, but he tried to argue that his extended mission provided ''much valuable information on the reactions of dolphins not only during and after capture but also, and paradoxically, on dolphins living at liberty in the sea.'' However, the Captain's ''scientific observations''—that capture shocks a dolphin both physically and psychologically and that a dolphin's skin is extremely delicate—had been made by several others before.

Over the years Cousteau became more sensitive to the plight of the dolphin. He complained, for instance, about fishing practices that indiscriminately slaughter the creatures to provide canned food for dogs and cats, and he argued against turning dolphins into performing animals. Yet in order to obtain film footage, the Captain continued to stalk the mammals in the open sea.

Cousteau's life-style and ideas increasingly conflicted with the expectations for a French naval officer. His had been a distinguished career for twenty-seven years. But because of his freewheeling habits and his public support for a treasonous brother, Jacques, at forty-seven, remained the lowest-ranked officer of the naval academy class of 1933.

Although detached from active duty for nearly a decade, Jacques had enjoyed access to the navy's worldwide facilities and a regular, if modest, paycheck. Simone, descended from three generations of naval officers, hesitated to abandon the service's traditions. But both longed to explore. With credibility and celebrity from *The Silent World* and with some financial security from the Oceanographic Institute, Cousteau resigned from the navy in 1957 with the rank of *capitaine des corvettes*.

While Cousteau prospered, his brother struggled. Publishers had blacklisted the Nazi collaborator and initially refused to print his prison writings.

Family relations grew more and more strained, largely because Pierre felt Jacques failed to pay enough attention to him. Pierre did not see his children for the decade he was behind bars, and they had grown into independent teenagers. His wife, Fernande, died in 1954, after suffering for years with a brain tumor. To separate himself from the Cousteau clan, Pierre remarried quickly and fathered a second daughter.

Pierre eventually found employment writing weekly political commentaries for a small magazine entitled *Rivarol*. In 1956 he finally published a series of essays, entitled *After the Deluge,* that reflected on his prison experiences and focused his acerbic wit toward contemporary politics. He remained a rancorous critic of democracy.

Three years later a small Left Bank press released two more of Pierre's books. *The Laws of Hospitality* described the frenzied flight of French collaborators during the final days of Hitler's rule. *In These Days* presented an autobiographical review of Pierre's youth and career in political journalism.

When Pierre left prison, doctors diagnosed him as having cancer. The disease tormented him until 1959, when at the age of fifty-two, he slipped into a coma. Just before Pierre died, Jacques flew from Monaco and spent a few final hours with his brother. Jean-Pierre, Pierre's son, remembers his uncle's final evaluation: "Pierre was the smart one, much more than me."

Shortly after burying his brother, the Captain sailed for New York City to address the first World Oceanographic Congress. Fireboats sprayed an elaborate welcome to *Calypso*. Journalists flocked to Cousteau's numerous press conferences. Fans asked an endless stream of questions about diving and undersea life. Jacques-Yves Cousteau had become famous.

A symbol of the Captain's growing popularity appeared in the March 28, 1960, issue of *Time* magazine. In a cover story the eulogistic editors described Cousteau as diving's "patron saint," its "pioneer, foremost promoter, prophet, and poet." Noting that skin diving had attracted more than one million U.S. adherents, they outlined the Captain's background, accomplishments, and pronouncements.

The editors quoted Cousteau's almost religious attraction to his avocation: "Diving is the most fabulous distraction you can experience. I am miserable out of water. It is as though you have been introduced to heaven, and then forced yourself back on earth."

In April 1961 Cousteau returned to the United States for more publicity, this time to receive the National Geographic Society's prized Gold Medal. At a White House ceremony President John Kennedy noted that the Captain was "one of the great explorers of an entirely new dimension, and I can imagine his satisfaction in having opened up the ocean floor to man and to science." Cousteau, expressing his appreciation for others' support, responded, "For me, this is much more than a personal award. It is recognition of a team effort led by my associates in France, together with our friends of the National Geographic Society, the Woods Hole Oceanographic Institution, and the Massachusetts Institute of Technology."

The medal pictured divers and *Calypso* surrounding the inscription: "To earthbound man he gave the key to the silent world."

CHAPTER FIVE

Conshelf

Over the ages, the sea only grudgingly revealed its mysteries. Men, despite their ingenuity, had long stood at its threshold. They had sailed its surface, but adventurers waited until the nineteenth century to discover the first evidence that within the darkness, stillness, and immense pressure of the deep ocean lay a wealth of life.

By the mid-1800's divers could don helmets and stiff suits to recover riches from sunken ships, but they remained burdened and limited by lines to the surface. The Aqua Lung, developed by Gagnan and Cousteau a hundred years later, provided additional freedom of movement, but it enabled comfortable descents to only about two hundred feet. Undersea pioneers wanted to dive farther, to witness the continental shelf and the deep abyss below it.

Nineteenth-century scientists had collected some evidence of deep-sea life. Sir John Ross, dredging the Arctic seas in 1818, brought up mud from 6,000 feet that contained worms of an unknown species. Forty-two years later the crew of the surveying ship *Bulldog* retrieved their sounding line, which at one place had been allowed to rest on the bottom at a depth of 7,560 feet, and discovered thirteen clinging starfish. The ship's thrilled naturalist declared, ''The deep has sent forth the long coveted message.''

Not until the early twentieth century, however, did humans personally witness the sweet mysteries of the black ocean. William Beebe, a respected American ichthyologist, and Otis Barton were the first to develop a practical means for true deep-sea exploration, the first to descend beyond the range of visible light. Their bathysphere, a spherical watertight cabin financed by the New York Zoological Society and the National Geographic Society, dropped to a depth of 3,028 feet in the open ocean off Bermuda in 1934. Tethered to a support ship by a steel cable containing electric and telephone lines, the bathysphere (from the Greek words *bathy* for "deep" and *sphere* for "ball") possessed a self-contained breathing system that used soda lime to absorb exhaled carbon dioxide.

While Cousteau studied aviation, Beebe was popularizing undersea exploration, in part by convincing the National Broadcasting Company (NBC) to dispatch live radio reports from his surface ship in Bermuda. The first half hour segment conveyed the tense activity on deck as sailors sealed the human cargo within the bathysphere. Radios across America heard the clanging of sledgehammers closing the hatch. After an hour Beebe, then about two thousand feet below the sea's surface, broadcast his observations of luminescent creatures within the dark environment.

Not unlike Cousteau more than twenty years later, Beebe published a series of articles and pictures in *National Geographic,* including an excerpt from his book *Half Mile Down* in the December 1934 issue. What Beebe and Barton couldn't record on film with their rudimentary photographic equipment, they described to an artist waiting by a telephone on the surface ship.

More than a decade passed before Auguste Piccard, already famous for his record-breaking eleven-mile-high balloon ascent, further advanced the science of deepwater exploration with an undersea dirigible. In 1948 the colorful Swiss professor, whom Cousteau called an "elderly scientific extremist," organized an expedition off the Cape Verde Islands that he flamboyantly declared would descend five times deeper into the sea than man had ever gone.

Although Cousteau described Simone as "a Navy wife with a self-disciplined attitude toward my activities," she objected strenuously to her husband's plans to accompany Piccard. "No one ordered you to go," she pleaded. "Don't risk yourself in that craziness." Even Cousteau's parents urged him to avoid Piccard's submarine, especially since a plaster cast surrounded the adventurer's right foot, which he had broken several days before playing tennis with his son Jean-Michel. But the Captain proceeded, intrigued by the notion of descending to such depths without lines to the surface.

The Belgian National Scientific Research Fund financed Piccard's bathyscaphe (depth-craft), and the French Navy's Undersea Research

Group supplied scientists, reconnaissance, and rescue teams, as well as the *Élie Monnier*. Piccard equipped his submarine with an advanced oxygen generator that could supply twenty-four hours of purified air, a Geiger counter to measure undersea radiation, and state-of-the-art cameras and lights to record life in the ocean abyss. A small yellow and white observation car hung beneath a large metal balloon filled with ten thousand gallons of extralight gasoline. With less density than salt water, the fluid served as a lifting medium.

Launching the submarine became extremely tedious. Five days of delays passed before the crew could attach the tons of ironshot ballast that would allow the bathyscaphe to descend vertically. To ascend at the appointed time, the weights were to be released automatically by a spring-wound alarm clock.

Professor Piccard entered the observation car early on the launch morning to perform a few last-minute adjustments. Noting that one of the clocks had stopped, the Swiss scientist wound it. He failed to notice, however, that the alarm tab was set for noon. Piccard climbed out of the submarine, watched the crews apply the last of the iron weights, and invited the entire team to lunch in the mess. At noon the alarm clock sounded with a tremendous roar as tons of metal crashed into the ship's hold. Although no one was hurt, the accident destroyed the submarine's batteries and damaged the freighter.

The elderly Piccard supervised the repair and requested that he and a randomly selected colleague be the first to pilot the vessel. The two adventurers entered the observation car at 2:00 P.M. on November 26, 1948. A winch hoisted the submarine onto the water's surface, where it sat for three hours while the crew laboriously pumped gas into the tanks. The sun set before the craft, equipped with bright lights, descended. Only sixteen minutes passed before the "depth-craft" reappeared with proof that it could maneuver underwater. It would be another five hours, however, before the crew could tow, hoist, and lower the bathyscaphe into its hanger and release Piccard. Despite the brief journey and the lengthy delays, the professor made the most of his moment by ascending from the hatch holding his sponsor's patented health drink. Cameras recorded his ceremonial toast for future advertisements.

Problems continued during the bathyscaphe's first deep descent, made off Fogo Island in the Cape Verde group without divers aboard. As the hoist swung the submarine out of the hold, three tons of ballast dropped on deck. The freighter's captain demanded that the expedition be stopped before it destroyed his vessel, but the scientists convinced him to allow one more test.

The crew began final preparations the following morning at dawn, but it was not until 2:00 P.M. that the submarine went under. Twenty-nine minutes later it reappeared in fine condition. Four hours passed, however, before the bathyscaphe could be towed back to the flotilla. The crew then worked all night, tossed about in a freshening breeze, to lower the craft into its hangar. While the mild surface swell badly damaged the vessel, tearing away the motors and propellers, the instruments showed that the submarine had reached a depth of forty-six hundred feet. Cousteau, ever confident, declared the expedition a success and predicted that future designs would be more seaworthy and take men "to the basement of the world."

While Cousteau and Piccard struggled to descend farther personally, scores of scientists were developing sophisticated technologies to explore the ocean floor while they remained on surface ships. From 1950 to 1952 the Danish Deep Sea Expedition dredged mud samples from across the western Pacific, including organisms (some presumed extinct) from a record depth of 33,017 feet in the Philippine Trench. At about the same time the Scripps Institute of Oceanography in San Diego mapped the Pacific floor with three hundred thousand soundings. The International Geophysical Year, spanning 1957 and 1958, sparked a coordinated effort by eighty research ships to compose a hydrographic survey of the Atlantic Ocean.

To catch a snapshot of life at great depths, Cousteau turned to Dr. Harold Edgerton, the ingenious professor of electrical engineering at the Massachusetts Institute of Technology who invented and perfected high-speed photography. As an engineering graduate student in 1931 Edgerton tried to examine the operations of an electric motor, but the dynamo moved too quickly for his eye or camera. He solved the problem by inventing the strobe light. The Allies asked the brilliant scientist to use his device to enhance aerial reconnaissance of the Normandy beaches the night before D day. Military leaders also had Edgerton's rapid-speed cameras capture on film the blinding flash of the first hydrogen bomb.

Cousteau visited the professor in his Cambridge, Massachusetts, laboratory in early 1953 at the suggestion of National Geographic Society President Melville Grosvenor. A small, compact man with a slight stoop, Edgerton displayed a series of now-classic photographs made possible by his electronic flash: the elegant coronet of a splashing drop of milk, the patterns of shattering glass, a hummingbird's whirring wings, and the destructive path of bullets through playing cards and balloons. He had packaged many of his shots into the film *Quicker 'n a Wink,* which won an Academy Award in 1940.

The Captain convinced Edgerton and his son, Bill, to work aboard *Calypso* for several summers. That first year the scientists brought to Corsica a submersible electronic flash lamp that illuminated objects six feet from the camera lens. With a hundred-foot spool of movie film, the camera clicked off eight hundred shots in fifteen-second intervals.

In 1954 the Edgertons fitted a sophisticated camera and battery-powered flash onto a trailer that was towed by *Calypso.* The unit began operating when it touched bottom, but because the ship-bound scientists couldn't focus their camera on specific items, Edgerton compared the effort ''to photographing birds on a foggy night from a balloon.''

The two cheerful Americans, known on board as Papa Flash and Petit Flash, obtained some puzzling pictures. At about three thousand feet the camera picked up several tiny white dots of plankton. When enlarged, the photos revealed that many of the dots were blurred and had comet tails. They, Edgerton concluded, were moving. He calculated that since his flash lasted only three one-thousandth of a second, the plankton traveled at a speed of three to ten feet per second.

In 1956 the MIT scientist came by himself with new equipment to explore the Romanche Trench almost five miles beneath the Atlantic's surface. Named after the French survey ship that accidentally located the depression, Romanche lies near the equator about three days' sail from the west African coast.

Before the photographer could attempt his experiments, *Calypso* had to be anchored. Securing a ship in such depths, however, required a novel anchor chain that could support a great length without being too heavy and unwieldy. Edgerton and diver-engineer André Laban decided to try a nylon rope that possessed great tensile strength but measured only three eighths of an inch thick. Because its specific gravity approximated that of the seawater in which it was immersed, the nylon cable proved to be essentially weightless. Yet after more than five and one-half miles of line were unleashed, the weightless anchor held.

Edgerton housed his new camera in a tempered stainless steel casing that could withstand the trench's five and one-half tons of pressure per square inch. He also developed a more powerful electronic flash and a transducer that would signal the bottom's approach, allowing the camera to focus nine feet from the seafloor. The scientist set his camera to delay for the two-hour lowering and then to snap four exposures every minute. But because the transducer failed, Edgerton had to bounce the camera up and down, hoping that some of the eight hundred exposures would occur at the right height and moment. Only two photographs were clear, but they showed the remarkable outlines of deep-sea life. The first revealed an ocean bottom of granular texture with four unknown white creatures casting small shadows. The second picture exposed a brittle starfish—at more than twenty-four thousand feet below sea level.

Calypso's crew had repaired the transducer and had begun preparing for another photographic attempt when Cousteau received an emergency radio message from Nantucket, Massachusetts. Bill Edgerton, who had remained in the United States that summer, had died in a diving accident. Although shaken, his father, ever the scientist, argued to continue the experiments. Cousteau refused and sent a message to the French naval base at Dakar: "Request special aircraft at Konakry for compassionate reasons to fly Professor Edgerton and myself to quickest connection with trunk airline to New York."

Both Edgerton and Cousteau agreed that the deep-sea pictures generated more questions than answers. Who were the "artful dodgers" dashing away from the camera? On what did the lonely starfish feed? Cousteau, declaring that "robot oceanography is getting nowhere," demanded to see these spectacles with his own eyes.

The Captain was not alone in his quest for a personal view of the ocean depths. Piccard's third vehicle, *FNRS III* (named for the sponsoring Belgian Fonds National de la Recherche Scientifique), achieved a temporary record in 1953 with a two-person descent to 12,500 feet. The submarine eventually made a total of ninety-four deepwater dives, including several with Cousteau, in the Mediterranean, the Atlantic, and off the coast of Japan. The U.S. Navy purchased a later Piccard model in 1958, and after reinforcing the spherical steel gondola, Lieutenant Don Walse and Piccard's son Jacques took this craft, named *Trieste,* to the bottom of the Marianas Trench near the island of Guam. The 35,800-foot descent lasted four hours and forty-eight minutes.

Complaining that military submarines and deep-diving bathyscaphes were too big and clumsy for intimate reef exploration, Cous-

teau argued for "a radically new submarine, something small, agile."
With financial support from the National Geographic Society, the Air
Liquide Company, and the EDO Foundation, he, along with engineers
Jean Mollard and André Laban, spent six years designing and constructing "Hull No. 1." The small turtle-shaped submarine stood only
5 feet high, with two windows, a top hatch, external lights, and viewing
ports. The flattened sphere was built to descend to a depth of 1,150
feet, stay underwater for at least three hours, and be nearly as maneuverable as an independent diver.

Cousteau equipped his yellow depth machine with a hydraulic claw
to capture undersea samples and with sophisticated cameras to acquire
undersea pictures. All he lacked was the necessary patience to wait
for appropriate weather conditions.

Even as the sea near Grand Congloué became more choppy on an
overcast day in March 1958, Cousteau's crew winched the unmanned
submarine toward the water and successfully lowered it some two
thousand feet into the sea. But while the crew attempted to bring the
sub back aboard *Calypso,* a swell lifted the ship's stern and dropped
it back into a steep trough. The cable snapped when *Calypso* rose
again, sending the precious exploration unit to the bottom, thirty-three
hundred feet below. No one was seriously hurt, although Raymond
Coll suffered a superficial cut on his cheek from the cable's whiplike
action. The submarine, however, was lost. The crew, picking up the
machine's distant echo with the sonar, took their only solace from
knowing that the hull had withstood the great depth.

Cousteau turned again to the French Department of Underwater
Research (Office Française de Recherches Sous-Marines, or OFRS),
the undersea research and development laboratory he founded in Marseilles. Technicians worked for eighteen months to complete "Hull
No. 2," which looked, according to the crew, like a comic-book
version of a flying saucer. Thus Cousteau named it *la soucoupe plon-
geante,* the Diving Saucer, or DS-2."

On October 9, 1959, the Captain located a relatively calm, shallow
spot off the west end of Puerto Rico for his new trials. If problems
arose, divers could retrieve the vessel. While the initial experiment
proved successful, several days later pilot Albert Falco and engineer
Jean Mollard felt an explosion outside the craft while ascending from
a 230-foot dive. When they reached the surface and opened the hatch,
they were engulfed in smoke and flames. They quickly closed the door,

while *Calypso*'s crew frantically lowered the saucer back into the water to douse the fire. Discovering later that the copper battery compartments had short circuited, engineers substituted power packs made of lead.

After the Puerto Rican experiments, but before heading to the great abyss, Cousteau and Falco tested DS-2 along the continental shelf, the submerged part of the landmass before it drops off to the abyssal plains and the great depths. However, even the new batteries failed, causing the vessel to scrape the slope, lose power, and sink. Only by pulling an emergency lever that released a 450-pound weight were the deep men able to return to the surface. The disappointed divers silently drank wine and ate chicken sandwiches on their slow ascent.

Perhaps the saucer's closest brush with disaster came off the Cape Verde Islands. When the unit neared the bottom, water leaked inside the interior batteries, and they imploded, sparking a fire within the tiny capsule. Cousteau quickly threw himself against a heavy iron plate to dislodge the burning material, and smother the flames.

In February 1960 Cousteau took the saucer to 1,000 feet in the Bay of Ajaccio, near Corsica. This time the winch, the batteries, and the other equipment performed perfectly. The Captain's findings dazzled scientists, the general public, and even himself. "We have no idea what the gray blobs are," he wrote from inside the submarine. "We are probably the first creatures to see such a thing alive." Cousteau and Falco opened another bottle of wine during the ascent, this time to toast their success.

The saucer's top speed registered only a knot and a half, yet it turned, as the Captain noted, "as whimsically as the fish." Rather than employ bulky propellers, rudders, or tail planes, the sub depended on a series of jet nozzles that the pilot could swivel to change direction and regulate speed. Cousteau described the depth machine, which allowed six hours of undersea study, as "a scrutinizer, a loiterer, a deliberator, a taster of little scenes as well as big."

To transport the saucer around the planet yet free *Calypso* for other expeditions, Cousteau and his team designed the world's largest inflatable ship. Measuring sixty-five feet long and twenty-nine feet wide, *Amphitrite* could be flown to any port and launched by means of air rollers. Drawing only fourteen inches of water, the ship traveled at thirty knots.

Financed in part by the National Geographic Society and dedicated by Princess Grace of Monaco in December 1960, *Amphitrite* had a pressurized vinyl cabin that could sleep five. Its powerful winch pulled the saucer in and out of the water.

Falco subsequently transported geologists and biologists aboard the saucer, while Cousteau continued to search for new ways to explore undersea life more fully. Over the past three decades the saucer has made more than 1,070 dives around the world; Falco himself piloted the unit more than eight hundred times.

The late 1950's and the decade of the 1960's were years of adventure. With World War II a memory, industrialized economies flourished, and new worlds beckoned to be explored. President John Kennedy launched the United States on a race to the moon. Scientists searched for the secrets within the atom.

The motivation to dive underwater complemented the desire to explore outer space or to climb the highest mountains. The experience of adventure, Cousteau said, provided spiritual rewards, and he dreamed of diving deeper and staying longer. The curious explorer described *The Silent World,* complete with the descending torch men, Ulysses, and the shark horde, as "our farewell to the upper layers of the sea. We wanted to leave a souvenir of the beauty and adventure our team experienced in twenty years of free diving. That period is over for us. We must move on deeper. We are going to the continental shelf next, and after that, who knows?"

The Captain, however, argued that undersea exploration could not be an end in itself: "To enter this great unknown medium must produce greater knowledge of the oceans and lead to assessment and exploitation of their natural resources."

In his new stage Cousteau described plans to help develop "amphibious man." At the 1963 World Congress on Underwater Activities in London he predicted the "conscious evolution of 'homo aquaticus,' spurred by human intelligence rather than the slow blind natural adaptation of species." He hypothesized that within fifty years surgical operations would enable volunteers to inhale water instead of air, just as fish do. These menfish would be able to swim to a depth of about a mile, far deeper than the two-hundred-foot limit for free divers. They'd reside in dry, gas-filled houses on the bottom of the ocean. While these menfish would live pretty much like their landed colleagues, their workdays would be spent in the water, farming undersea crops or mining minerals.

Skeptics mocked the Captain's notion of water people being born at the bottom of the sea. Several delegates to the congress dismissed the forecast as "science fiction."

Cousteau, not used to such criticism, responded angrily. "What's wrong with science fiction as a presentiment of reality?" he snapped. "Ever since Jules Verne, and lots of people before him, the informed human imagination has projected what is to come." The Captain also charged that his "conservative" vision of man's undersea future paled in comparison with some delegates' wild suggestions for milking whales in underwater dairies.

Ever struggling to balance his romanticism with his pragmatism, Cousteau began to play down the grand notion that human colonies would emigrate to the seafloor forever. "There would be no serious reason," he observed after the congress, "to abandon all those things we love: sunshine, fresh air, country, and landscapes." Still, he remained convinced that extended settlements on the seafloor would perform important tasks for science and industry.

The main barrier to undersea colonization had been a diver's inability to spend a long time under the water before nitrogen saturated his tissues, leading to the dreaded bends. At the turn of the century John Scott Haldane and the British Admiralty Deepwater Diving Committee had published detailed stage decompression tables explaining how divers could ascend slowly and allow nature to eliminate the excess nitrogen.

Almost fifty years later George Bond, a U.S. Navy diving physiologist, reasoned that once a diver's body had become saturated with nitrogen or helium the time needed for stage decompression no longer increased. The diver, Bond suggested, could stay underwater for several hours or a month and not absorb any additional inert gases. He then argued that divers could work below and live in an undersea colony for long periods without wasting tremendous amounts of time undergoing stage decompression after each descent.

To devise the equipment needed for extended undersea visits, Bond studied the 1918 plans by Simon Lake, a U.S. engineer, to construct a series of supply depots that divers could reach through an open hatch at the bottom of their submarine. In the late 1920's Sir Robert Davis drafted a portable manned seafloor chamber. And in 1957 Bond began to build such a colony, which, eight years later, became Sealab One.

The 1960's witnessed a virtual race to the ocean floor, as well as to the moon. On September 6, 1962, Robert Stenuit stayed underwater for twenty-four hours, using as his base a small, aluminum recompression chamber two hundred feet beneath the Bay of Villefranche. Eight days later, at Pomègues in the Mediterranean, Cousteau initiated Continental Shelf Station Number One (Conshelf I), in which Albert Falco and Claude Wesly spent a week.

Planning for the tightly organized Conshelf I lasted more than a year, with filming sequences arranged and diving experiments set. Falco actually complained that the entire operation became "too mechanized."

Cousteau's cameras seemed omnipresent throughout the project. They witnessed Wesly's farewell embrace with his wife and young daughter, and they eyed Falco, a bachelor, kissing his mother and sister. They recorded the oceanauts' descent down the diving ladder in the early afternoon of September 14, 1962. Just under the surface they traced the passage of the divers to their undersea home.

The complex arrangements required copious finances. Cousteau could not yet launch major projects on movie contracts alone, despite a history of award-winning films. So, as he had several times before, the Captain turned to the major oil companies interested in undersea technologies that might enhance their drilling operations.

Cousteau designed his project both to produce his own film and to foster extensive media coverage, and he did not spare hyperbole in describing his adventure's significance. Falco and Wesly, he declared at frequent press conferences, were to be the "first men to occupy the continental shelf without surfacing for a significant amount of time." They were the "pioneers into a new world."

The undersea pioneers, however, faced few hardships. They enjoyed hot freshwater showers piped through a plastic tube from the surface ship. They ate gourmet meals, sent down in pressure cookers. Scores of men attended to their every need.

The true tests of the experiment became more psychological than scientific. How would the divers respond to living under thirty-five feet of water for a week? Would they become claustrophobic within a cylindrical dwelling only seventeen feet long and eight feet high? Would they remain motivated to dive several hours each day at depths to eighty-five feet?

Albert Falco almost failed these challenges. This man, whom Cousteau described as having "as much courage as anyone I have known," suffered terrible nightmares in his undersea prison. He felt suffocated and imagined a hand strangling his neck. He longed to return immediately to the surface, but his nitrogen-saturated body lay trapped. "I feel completely alone and isolated," Falco wrote in his diary. "We are sentenced to remain underwater for a week."

The normally serene Falco grew increasingly irritated, snapping at an attendant who brought a breakfast of broken biscuits. He complained that frequent telephone calls from the surface disrupted his experiments. He berated the "surface people" for diving around his home, stirring up the silt and creating a murky haze.

Cousteau wisely altered the team's routine to give Falco and Wesly more peace. He restricted telephone calls and ordered the surface divers to avoid disturbing the undersea men in their home.

The changes enlivened Falco. "The water is beginning to come into our grasp," he noted at the end of his stay. "I feel happy when I am alone with Claude . . . because it is the first time in 20 years of diving that I really have time to see."

The undersea dwellers became philosophical about their mission. Wesly began to sense that he was part of the water environment. "Under the sea," Falco pronounced, "everything is moral."

While Conshelf I's few scientific experiments had limited value, the exercise did demonstrate that men could live underwater for an extended period—if fully supported by an elaborate surface crew. The mission also provided good copy for journalists, especially when Cousteau orchestrated the arrival of his undersea dwellers into a press extravaganza. After again declaring the project's importance, the Captain, microphone in hand, asked Falco what he would most like to do. The thirty-five-year-old diver, returning to his land-based pragmatism, responded simply, "To walk."

As astronauts soared around the earth, Cousteau dreamed of descending farther within the planet's depths. He outlined an ambitious six-stage plan that eventually was to create an underwater home 660 feet below the surface. While the final segments remained an unfulfilled vision, the Captain dramatically advanced the techniques of undersea habitation, and his films introduced millions to the ocean's wonders.

Compared with the well-equipped Conshelf I, Conshelf II was a luxury operation, at least for the five divers who spent a month at Starfish House, thirty-five feet below the surface of the Red Sea. The aquanauts ate fresh fruit and cheese, drank fine wine and cognac, and enjoyed a high-fidelity tape player.

The undersea research station consisted of four main buildings and

eight ancillary structures. Starfish House, the air-conditioned headquarters, contained sleeping quarters for eight, a kitchen, dining space,
biological laboratory, and photography room. The Deep Cabin, anchored at eighty-five feet and large enough for only two explorers,
resembled a diving bell with an open bottom. A domed hangar housed
the diving saucer, and a wet or underwater garage serviced the expedition's tools and submarine scooters.

On the surface, *Rosaldo* served as powerhouse, supply depot, and
billet for the fifty-two scientists, technicians, cameramen, and divers
supporting the oceanauts. The ship anchored five miles from shore in
a protected lagoon within a coral outcropping known as Shab Rumi,
Arabic for "Roman Reef." *Calypso* shuttled back and forth for supplies
to Port Sudan, twenty-five miles away.

While the oceanauts relaxed, life topside proved to be torturous.
Temperatures hovered in the nineties, and humidity seemed to remain
at 100 percent. To anchor the undersea station, workmen had to carry
some four thousand lead ballast bars, which the fierce sunlight had
baked. Cousteau, already lean, lost twenty pounds during the expedition. One member of his team, after a particularly fatiguing day,
appealed to the Captain: "What on earth put this idea in your head?"

Life in the Deep Cabin also lacked comfort. Cousteau failed to
provide air conditioning because he planned the expedition to begin
in March 1963, when the Red Sea would have been cool at ninety
feet. But fund raising and administrative hassles postponed the operation until July, when the vessel sweltered at eighty-six degrees and
constant high humidity. Raymond Kientzy and André Portelatine complained that they "perspired like fountains."

Cousteau selected oceanauts less for their diving skill or prowess
than for their ability to participate in an undersea society. He desired
"to see what would happen to a group of average men during a month-
long sojourn." One member of the unathletic team, forty-three-year-
old cook Pierre Guilbert, even suffered from mild arteriosclerosis.

Cousteau supported this elaborate expedition with a $1.2 million
grant from the Bureau de Recherches des Pétroles, the French national
petroleum office. The persuasive fund raiser again convinced the oil-
men that drilling stations on the seafloor would be safer and less
expensive than traditional surface platforms. He argued that the continental shelf contained untold riches in sea life and minerals and that
the Conshelf experiments would prove that seabed stations could provide vast industrial and scientific benefits.

Conshelf II, despite careful planning, did not begin smoothly. Just before the oceanauts descended to Starfish House, an advance team of divers discovered a heavy fog in the headquarters that obfuscated their outstretched hands. Technicians eventually found that the compressor aboard *Rosaldo,* burdened by the hot, humid air, delivered tiny beads of water coated with an oily film. Because organizers had failed to pack an assortment of filters, an engineer had to take a three-hour ride aboard *Calypso* to Port Sudan, where he waited half a day for an airplane and then to fly for twenty hours to France. Only after five days of travel did he return to the Roman Reef with a filter that blocked the aerosols and allowed the expedition to continue.

Anchoring the Deep Cabin also presented a series of frustrations. Before Kientzy and Portelatine arrived, electricians entered the chamber, supposedly secured at ninety feet, to install electric, telephone, and television equipment. But as they exited, the tall steel cylinder shook, tore loose from its moorings, and rolled down the reef.

Divers eventually attached cables to the wayward cabin, and a strong winch on *Calypso* brought it back into place. Electricians returned to reinstall the power and communication lines. But as two men made a final routine examination inside the chamber, the tower again began to vibrate and slide back down the hill. Raymond Coll quickly tried to escape through the open bottom hatch, only to have the falling vessel catch his foot flipper and air tanks. His partner sat trapped in a pocket of air at the top of the cylinder.

Coll, demonstrating his typical Catalan calm, described his predicament: "There were cables everywhere—a real spider's web—and one of the electric cables caught on my tank. Well, the house was going down, so were the cables, and so was I. When I saw that I couldn't disentangle myself, I got rid of the tank at about 40 meters (131 feet)—but the falling tank removed one of my flippers. So I had to surface with no air and one flipper. When these little accidents happen, you have to figure out pretty quickly how to cope with the situation."

The Deep Cabin landed on a sandy ledge and lodged against the reef. Engineers had to install another set of cables before the fallen chamber could be recovered and the trapped electrician released from his prison. After round-the-clock efforts they finally secured the wandering cylinder.

The shark-infested waters offered other dangers. One afternoon Cousteau and Falco entered the diving saucer to film the efforts of four divers among the sharks. For almost half an hour they photo-graphed a circling band of killers. After one of the larger sharks had darted for the diving team, Pierre Goupil rang the alarm to raise the antishark cage. Since the steel bars would protect only three divers, Goupil made a quick decision, shoving his least experienced colleague into the cage and placing the remaining three men atop the structure. They sat back to back, ready to ward off an attack from any direction. The assault came, and the divers struck back frantically with cameras, lights, and shark billies. When the cage broke water, the frustrated sharks thrashed on the surface.

Cousteau and Falco remained in the diving saucer to film Goupil's return amid the sharks' frenzy. This time only one partner accompanied the diver in the shark cage. But as the sharks circled frantically, the pair suddenly abandoned their protective structure, wildly slapping their ankles. They rushed to the surface and were scooped onto the deck, where their legs dripped blood. Meanwhile, the saucer moved closer to investigate the submerged and abandoned shark cage, shining its lights on thousands of swirling white dots, or sea mosquitoes, known for their vicious bites.

Conshelf II, however, delivered more than setbacks and dangers. The five oceanauts came to enjoy the comfortable and calm surround-ings of Starfish House. Able to look out their windows on schools of colorful reef fish, they played leisurely games of chess.

The pleasant headquarters even lured Simone Cousteau. Weary and half ill from the punishing tropical climate, she announced her intention late one afternoon to take a break at Starfish House. Before her husband could dissuade her or summon a diver to accompany her, she dressed and descended. She arrived in time for dinner, thoroughly enjoyed herself in the air-conditioned atmosphere, and called the *Calypso* by phone to request that her belongings be brought down in the next shipment. Thus Mme. Cousteau became the first female oceanaut.

Jacques and Simone celebrated their twenty-sixth wedding anni-versary in Starfish House with a gala party. The chef aboard *Calypso* baked a large cake and brought it dry to headquarters in a special pot. Only the champagne lost its fizz because of the increased pressure thirty-five feet underwater.

As on most Cousteau adventures, the team tried to befriend crea-tures of the sea. The Starfish House cook, for instance, conditioned a triggerfish to respond to his taps on the window by sticking its mouth into the chamber's open entry hatch to receive the crew's table scraps. Several divers adopted a sinister barracuda and named him Jules. And Claude Wesly encouraged a parakeet within Starfish House to commune with a parrot fish outside the window; both creatures, however, seemed uninterested in otherworldly dialogue.

The project's most useful scientific data focused on the physiological impacts of extended life underwater. A doctor dived from *Calypso* each morning to test the divers' vital signs and reflexes. He observed only minor surprises; for example, the increased atmospheric pressure at thirty-five feet inhibited the growth of beards, and the doubled-oxygen environment of Starfish House healed cuts and abrasions with tremendous speed.

The oceanic physician also evaluated the ability of the deep men to withstand a week in an environment of air and helium. Cousteau had projected that the mixture would allow Kientzy and Portelatine to perform useful work down to 165 feet and to make short dives to 330 feet without the risk of nitrogen narcosis. In fact, they safely reached 363 feet.

Cousteau and Falco piloted the diving saucer much deeper. At minus four hundred feet, they passed the thermocline layer, the paper-thin boundary between the warm surface water and the denser cold liquid of the depths. At minus six hundred feet, they encountered the deep scattering layer, a massive collection of tiny plankton which had mystified sonar specialists. They also spent time below a thousand feet, exploring the bizarre life that existed in absolute darkness and under tremendous pressure.

Of particular interest to Cousteau, the expedition proved that the diving saucer could operate entirely from a submerged base. DS-2 returned from its voyages to an undersea garage, safe from surface winds and waves. It was hoisted by an electric winch into the dry and pressurized hangar, where it discharged its crew and received maintenance.

To return to the surface, Starfish House residents experimented with a short decompression program that required them to breathe for two hours a mixture of 80 percent oxygen and 20 percent nitrogen, the inverse of the atmosphere's blend. They ascended, by pure coincidence, on the fourteenth of July, Bastille Day, to extol both their country's freedom and their expedition's success. The Captain toasted the ''ever-enchanting realization that we are living inside the sea.''

* * *

Cousteau edited thousands of feet of film about Conshelf II and the diving saucer into the movie *World Without Sun,* which premiered in the United States in December 1964. Critics applauded the ninety-three-minute film. The Motion Picture Academy, for instance, awarded an Oscar, Cousteau's second. *The New Yorker* declared that "the Captain is persuasive, largely thanks to the fact that his cameras make everything we behold so ravishing." Veteran *New York Times* critic Bosley Crowther found the film to be "a beautiful and awesome excursion into an underwater realm."

Crowther went on to say, however, that *World Without Sun* "combines superb actuality experience and a touch of science fiction fantasy." He suggested that the filmmaker resorted to "obvious faking" to heighten the drama of his pictures. The Captain became incensed at this challenge to his credibility.

The flap focused on the film's final scene, during which Falco explored a deep-sea tunnel, slowly edging the saucer within the tight walls and following an incline up to an open grotto. Viewers witnessed him break the surface, open the top hatch, and stick his head out to shine lights on the steep walls. Cameramen obviously had been placed along the path and within the undersea cavern to record Falco's every movement.

Crowther complained that the film inplausibly suggested that the saucer operated at a thousand feet. Leading oceanographers he had consulted declared that an underwater cavern at that depth couldn't contain a pocket of air, that any bubble at such depth would consist of noxious methane or marsh gas, and that the pressure would be too great for an unprotected man to bear. The reviewer also questioned whether the filmmaker had resorted to filming such difficult scenes in a studio.

Cousteau, responding to the charge of fakery, wrote a terse letter to the *Times:* "May I strongly state that we don't need tanks or studios. Not one shot from my film was made in an aquarium or in a studio, and those takes that had to be rephotographed for editing purposes were reenacted inside the very structures (Headquarters or Deep Cabin) that were used for the experiment."

The Captain also argued that his film clearly suggested the cavern was close to the surface. "The visual and verbal description of an upward voyage to the lake," he noted, "covers two minutes of playing time and mentions a period of ten minutes logged by the saucer during the ascent.''

Crowther remained skeptical. The critic viewed the film again, as Cousteau had requested, and concluded that the final scene is ''so trickily staged and so vaguely explained that it tends to confuse the viewer and leave the scientifically-minded wondering whether he isn't being hoaxed.''

Over the years Cousteau frequently referred to this critical exchange with anger. He devoted several pages of two books to descriptions of his filming techniques for *World Without Sun*. The filmmaker, however, was to face many more allegations that he adjusts natural scenes for dramatic effect.

Despite Cousteau's successes and renown, he couldn't win the growing competition with astronauts for funding and public attention. Again and again he preached that his undersea habitations would ''lead mankind to greater rewards than the space race.'' Yet the Captain could only watch enviously as the space program received millions of dollars while he struggled for movie and industrial contracts.

Maintaining funds from the French government required *Calypso* to complete numerous tasks with oceanographers. In early 1964 Cousteau's crew helped tow and anchor a new laboratory-buoy, nicknamed the Mysterious Island; the two-hundred-foot-long tube floated vertically in the Mediterranean, halfway between Nice and Corsica, allowing scientists to work within the sea despite adverse weather and sea conditions. In midyear they tested new air guns, boomers, and other seismic-refraction equipment. Later they participated in a detailed geophysical and geological study of the Strait of Messina to determine the feasibility of building a high bridge between Sicily and mainland Italy. Early in 1965 they mapped the zone covered by the RANA radio navigation system—from Italy to Toulon, including most of Corsica.

Cousteau's empire had grown to 190 scientists, engineers, electronic experts, technicians, divers, and sailors. In addition to admission fees from the museum, he needed to raise two million dollars each year to support his teams at the Oceanographic Institute in Monaco, at the Underwater Research Center in Marseilles, and on the exploring vessel *Calypso*. The National Geographic Society gave him a yearly appropriation. The French government provided research grants. Numerous businesses contracted for specific oceanographic services. And the Captain rounded off his personal financial needs with money for being chairman of U.S. Divers, the world's largest diving equipment company.

Added to the growing competition for money was the quickening race to the continental shelf. Twelve weeks after Conshelf II, Captain George Bond, the first to propose the principle of saturation diving, organized a U.S. Navy project 193 feet below the surface, off the coast of Bermuda in the Atlantic Ocean. The tubular Sealab I habitat looked like a 40-foot-long cigar. Four aquanauts stayed for only eleven days, their experiment cut short by the threat of a hurricane.

Cousteau, struggling to take his own underwater-living experiments a step farther, proposed that Conshelf III would have six divers working for twenty-one days in the chilling darkness of 325 feet below the surface of the Mediterranean near Île du Levant. Although he consistently sought to reduce his reliance on the surface, the expedition required the extraordinary support of 150 technicians and a dozen ships.

The six-member crew, including Cousteau's twenty-four-year-old son, Philippe, entered their sphere from the docks of Monte Carlo at noon on September 17, 1965. *Calypso* towed the 140-ton structure to the prepared site, but an unexpected storm broke the power and communication cables that ran from the Cap Ferrat lighthouse, forcing the vessels back to Monaco for two days.

Noting the persistent dangers, a reporter at the second launching cornered the reluctant Simone and asked, "Madame Cousteau, are you not concerned about your son in there?" The Shepherdess replied, "Monsieur, I have six sons in there, and I am thinking of all of them."

The oceanauts worked in almost total darkness because sunlight barely penetrated to 325 feet. They also operated in isolation because compressed-air divers from the surface could not safely visit a site so deep. Their spherical chamber, eighteen feet in diameter, contained two stories, the lower for sleeping, sanitation, and diving, the upper for dining and communications. The oceanauts commuted to work through an open hatch at the chamber's bottom; since pressure inside the house equaled pressure outside, the water could not enter the sphere.

Cousteau and his team again filmed almost every aspect of the adventure. The Captain descended daily in the saucer for five or six hours in order to record the oceanauts' actions. Philippe, who had recently graduated from l'École Technique de Photographie in Paris, the French government's school of motion pictures, shot other footage from within the submerged habitat.

Because the nitrogen content of air would be lethal at eleven atmospheres, the oceanauts had to breathe a mixture of 98 percent helium and only 2 percent oxygen. While this heliox disrupted some of the machinery within the chamber, the lighter medium had little impact on the divers' bodies, other than to cause their vocal cords to vibrate rapidly, creating high-pitched squeaks that made them sound like Donald Duck. Living in high-pressure heliox also seemed to dull their senses. Divers, for instance, complained that their skin consistently felt wet with perspiration, even when they were dry. They also protested that they couldn't taste their food or smell odors. Albert Falco remarked, "On air, we find everything so beautiful, but with heliox, the reality is there, gray and sad."

Cousteau again orchestrated a sophisticated public relations campaign to advance his image and his film. But the divers' distorted voices combined with language barriers to disrupt the Captain's grand plan for his oceanauts to talk through an elaborate satellite phone connection with U.S. astronaut Scott Carpenter in Sealab II, 205 feet below sea level off the coast of Southern California. Philippe and Carpenter exchanged animated greetings for several minutes while the cameras rolled, but both admitted later that they couldn't understand a word their counterpart said.

More successful was Cousteau's arrangement for Eurovision to broadcast to seventeen countries a live report of the oceanauts' return from the deep. The Captain held a microphone before the television cameras and proudly greeted his crew as they emerged onto Monte Carlo's dock.

Conshelf III, despite its successful mission, dramatically altered Cousteau's orientation away from scientific experiments and full-length movies. Like previous efforts, the undersea colony proved that divers could perform practical work at substantial depths. In fact, his accomplishment sparked a proliferation of submerged stations, most of them more simplified, in Japan, Great Britain, Italy, the United States, the Soviet Union, West Germany, Canada, the Bahamas, the Netherlands, and Cuba. The Captain soon realized that his initiatives had lost their uniqueness.

Cousteau also discovered that funds for such projects were evaporating. The French petroleum office had supported the Conshelf experiments, hoping to demonstrate that oceanauts could efficiently operate equipment below the two-hundred-foot limit imposed on surface divers. Oil executives watched *Calypso*'s closed-circuit television approvingly as the undersea crew, trained for five months as petroleum technicians, performed sophisticated wellhead repairs. They were particularly impressed that the divers—whose tools and equipment became lighter in water—replaced a four-hundred-pound valve in only forty-five minutes, about twice as fast as the operation could be done on land.

Yet despite these accomplishments and Cousteau's dream of ongoing undersea contracts, executives calculated that neither surface drilling rigs nor underwater stations provided a practical and economical means for recovering natural resources from beneath the ocean floor. Industrialists didn't abandon either method, but they turned more and more to less expensive robots and small submarines that could perform a myriad of functions at great depths.

Cousteau concluded that his future belonged elsewhere, and he found it in television. Because theaters had rejected his feature documentary of the experiment, *Experience Precontinent III*, the Captain hustled his dramatic and colorful footage to the National Geographic Society, which had begun producing a series of television specials on nature.

The society's Melvin Payne agreed to promote Cousteau's program, but only if David Wolper, a respected Hollywood television producer, supervised the editing. Cousteau, who took an immediate liking to Wolper and who had few other options, accepted the deal. CBS broadcast *The World of Jacques Cousteau,* narrated by Orson Welles, in April 1966 as a National Geographic-Wolper Production. The hourlong show introduced the Captain to a huge American audience. Cousteau's life was never the same.

CHAPTER SIX

Television

Cousteau, although a keen adventurer and a clever inventor, is at heart an artist. Since his youth he has demonstrated skill as a pianist, painter, and poet, but cinema has remained his favorite form of expression. "The only field in which I know I'm gifted is cinema," the Captain declares. "In fact, I made my first film at the age of 13. It's a built-in sickness. I feel miserable if I don't make a film."

Cousteau has demonstrated a rare ability to deliver drama and poetry on the screen. Cinema, he explains, "encompasses many other art forms. You have to have a good script or a good text. You have to have good images, beautiful images. You have to have good music. You have to have the sense of rhythm. You have to pack all these things into a neat, interesting and beautiful piece, which is a piece of art."

Louis Malle, the celebrated French director who coproduced *The Silent World,* maintains that the Captain is one of the world's few "brilliant" cinematographers. "For someone wanting to become a filmmaker," says Malle, "the *Calypso* was a fantastic education. The Captain really invented underwater photography."

Throughout the early 1960's Cousteau dreamed of producing his own television films on undersea life, but the idea, according to Philippe, "ran up against the ingrained habits of Madison Avenue." Credit for realizing Cousteau's vision must go to David Wolper, the eventual producer of *Roots,* the 1984 Los Angeles Olympics extravaganza, and the Statue of Liberty bicentennial celebration. As Wolper watched the rushes of the National Geographic Society special on Conshelf III, he realized that a television set resembled a fishbowl. Viewers, he concluded, would enjoy regularly spending an evening at home watching undersea adventures. In 1966 Wolper flew to Monaco to encourage the Captain to prepare a proposal for an American television series that would feature his travels aboard *Calypso* across the seven seas.

Cousteau didn't need much convincing. "I love films," the Captain responded to Wolper, "but television is for me the greatest reward there is. With television, you know that on one evening 35 to 40 million people are going to see dolphins." Cousteau willingly sacrificed some of film's clarity, believing that television's widespread exposure compensated for any minor technical imperfections.

Television diverted Cousteau from further efforts to research the ocean environment, to improve diving technology, or to expand undersea habitation. But the Captain made the conscious choice, as he liked to put it, to awaken millions to the wonders of the oceans and the dangers they faced.

Cousteau's decision favoring television over science was made easier when the French government transferred its grants to a new oceanographic ship, the *Jean Charcot*. Concerned about Cousteau's increased subjectivity and his association with "Yankee producers," French ministers cut off funds for research they had been supporting aboard *Calypso*. "The government was very tough on us, very unfair, taking away work that we used to do and making it very difficult for us to compete for new research projects," complained Jean-Michel. "It really shocked us, really hurt. It made my father's life very difficult."

But the frustrations did not last long. After weeks of late-evening negotiations in New York, Cousteau and Wolper signed a $4.2 million contract with the American Broadcasting Corporation (ABC) to produce twelve hourlong television specials. Cousteau's filmmaking company, Les Reguins Associés (Sharks Associated), would shoot the film, and David Wolper Productions (working through Metromedia Producers Corporation) would complete all the editing and postproduction in Los Angeles. In addition to receiving up-front funds from ABC, Cousteau could market the series throughout Europe, Asia, and Africa.

Wolper ushered Cousteau into the television age and changed his image. "Lookit, this is showbiz," the producer argued. "You can't use the same old stuff, that one tank hanging down the back. You need futuristic stuff, a lot of jazzy underwater inventions." Cousteau, said Wolper, caught on quickly and acquired hydrodynamic air tanks, bright yellow helmets with built-in lights and radiotelephones, electric scooters, and a Hovercraft. "You have to be attractive," Cousteau agreed.

Calypso also received a face-lift. The deckhouse was entirely remodeled. A new stateroom was added on the upper deck for the Captain and Simone. Research laboratories became photographic darkrooms. Winches used for scientific research were abandoned to make room for two new minisubs, called sea fleas. The old false nose was replaced by a larger observation chamber, whose eight portholes provided better visibility. A media room was outfitted, and closed-circuit television monitors were installed. Even the engines, generators, mufflers, and rudders were overhauled.

Beginning in 1968, Cousteau delivered four television shows a year for presentation on ABC-TV's *The Undersea World of Jacques Cousteau*. With his distinctive red woolen cap, hooked nose, and boyish smile, the Captain created and starred in the most popular documentary series in broadcasting history. The dramas were eventually shown in more than a hundred nations, from the Soviet Union to Brazil and Japan.

The ABC series, extended several times, ran for almost nine years. Cousteau analyzed his success by stating, "We are not documentary. We are adventure films. The kids identify with Falco on the diving saucer. The entire environmental content of my films is wrapped into adventure, with the same heroes."

Cousteau initiated his maiden filming expedition for ABC in mid-February 1967 at a press conference aboard *Calypso*. He discussed the growing destruction of the world's oceans as a result of pollution and overfishing, and he declared his intention to record on color film for future generations the marvels vanishing from pristine waters.

"The great expedition," Cousteau explained, would be unlike his previous efforts, offering more spontaneity and adventure. The Captain would still develop detailed operational plans, but he would also allow himself the freedom to explore whatever secrets of the sea he might encounter.

Concerned with charges about his lack of scientific credentials, Cousteau went out of his way to highlight the participation of researchers from the Oceanographic Institute. He also promised to carry a noted scientist aboard *Calypso* for each program to verify the accuracy of his team's work and observations.

Despite his enthusiasm at the press conference, the Captain appeared pained, having fractured two vertebrae in an automobile accident several weeks before. Simone argued for postponing the expedition, but he decided that bathing in the Red Sea would be the best possible treatment. Nonetheless, movement for him proved to be pure agony. "I am like a child," Cousteau admitted, "who does not quite know what he is strong enough to do and what he is too weak to attempt."

Prince Rainier and Princess Grace of Monaco attended a farewell reception and presented to Simone a rare St. Hubert dog, which she christened Zoom. As the dog and crew left the port, crowds on the wharf showered the ship with flowers and confetti.

Cousteau and his son Philippe decided that the series' first segment should focus on the shark, a legendary fish that could attract a large viewing audience. The Captain felt the shark symbolized the contrasts characteristic of the undersea environment. On the one hand, he believed the sleek cartilaginous fish "ranks among the most perfect, the most beautiful creatures ever developed in nature." Yet he described a pack of sharks in a feeding frenzy as "demons incarnate."

Jacques and Simone had first encountered sharks in 1939 on a dive near Djerba Island off Tunisia. Cousteau claimed to have been "uneasy with fear," and Simone was outright scared; but the sleek creatures passed the divers by haughtily.

Several years later, while filming triggerfish, Cousteau and Dumas spotted a twenty-five-foot-long *Carcharodon carcharias*, more commonly known as the great white shark, a confirmed man-eater. They watched in terror for several moments as the monster lazily swam closer. Cousteau, imagining that the brute would at least get a bellyache from eating his metal air tanks, was totally unprepared for the shark's response when it spotted the divers: The feared man-eater stopped abruptly, released a cloud of excrement, and sped away. Cousteau and Dumas burst into nervous laughter.

These initial experiences engendered a foolish self-confidence and negligence for safety. Because "the camera demanded lively sharks," for instance, Dumas and Tailliez regularly pulled on the tails of sharks to encourage them to perform their bit parts.

The streak of good fortune ended in 1948 off the Atlantic coast of Africa. Dumas had harpooned a small bottle-nosed whale, which turned the water around the *Élie Monnier* blood red. Cousteau dived with a camera to record Dumas slipping a noose over the whale's tail, only to encounter an eight-foot shark of a species he had not seen before. Believing the sleek gray creature would retreat like the others, the two divers boldly chased it, coming to within ten feet. Cousteau welcomed the opportunity to film the beast, and he directed Dumas to swim in front of the shark and to pull on its tail—all in the spirit of acquiring good photographs.

The gray displayed no apprehension and led the divers down to sixty feet, where two more sharks, these being fifteen-foot blues, appeared. The trio slowly closed their circle around the divers.

Cousteau, admitting that "a sense of danger came to our hearts," began to experiment with an array of popular shark repellents. He released cupric acetate tablets, but the brutes swam through the copper-stained water without hesitation. He tried flailing his arms and releasing a flood of bubbles, but the sharks continued to close their circle. Dumas turned his back toward Cousteau, hoping to maintain an effective watch, and drew his knife.

The gray broke away for a moment and then glided rapidly toward Cousteau, whose only weapon was the camera, which he slammed into the shark's muzzle. The Captain didn't realize at the time that his finger remained on the camera trigger and that he was filming the oncoming monster. He felt only the smashing impact of its snout.

Cousteau and Dumas decided the time clearly had come to call for help, but they knew that a diver floating on the surface offered the perfect target for hungry sharks. While one diver faced the beasts, therefore, the other rose to the surface and waved his hands wildly to attract the attention of colleagues on the *Élie Monnier*, which had drifted three hundred yards away. They received no reply.

The two divers, nearing exhaustion, continued to repel the trio of sharks for what seemed like an eternity. The men became cold and worried about their diminishing air supply. Dumas, heeding a yelled warning from Cousteau, turned at the last moment to push back one of the blues at his feet. The shark returned to the circle.

With only five minutes of air left, Cousteau and Dumas reached for the emergency valves on their oxygen tanks. Suddenly a shadow fell over them. The sharks grew agitated, turned down, and disappeared. The weary pair looked up to see the hull of a launch from the

Élie Monnier. The crew had seen the distress signals after all and located the bubbles. Cousteau and Dumas, weak and shaken, flopped into the boat.

Fascinated with shark behavior, Cousteau and his crew killed scores of dolphins for bait in order to witness the voracious eating habits of different species. They also created a dummy, nicknamed Arthur, to test the shark's reaction to a fully dressed diver; Arthur was torn to bits. And they attached identification tags to the creatures' dorsal fins in order to track their movements. Cousteau religiously kept a diary of such shark experiences for twelve years, stopping in 1951 during his first trip to the Red Sea when he came upon too many creatures to examine.

An unusual encounter occurred on that first Red Sea voyage as the Captain and three scientists explored the Shab Jenab reefs. A moderate-size *Carcharhinus* and Cousteau spotted each other simultaneously at a distance of about seventy-five feet. The shark paused for a moment and then rushed directly toward the divers. Lacking a weapon to defend himself or the time needed to retreat to the reefs, Cousteau froze. When the speeding shark, traveling at a velocity of at least ten knots, came within an arm's length of Cousteau's body, it executed an about-face. The Captain felt only the rush of the creature's wake as it returned to the open sea.

Cousteau met one of the largest sharks, a three-thousand-pound cow shark, almost nine hundred feet below the ocean's surface. From within the diving saucer he spotted the enormous form that seemed to be blinded by the vehicle's lights. At first he could not identify the species. The giant swept gracefully around the saucer, which was only half its bulk, before swatting the submarine with its powerful tail. Although the crew faced no real danger inside the steel cocoon, the impact, according to Cousteau, "shook us up considerably."

From these experiences Cousteau described the shark, which physiologically had changed little since the Devonian period some 350 million years ago, as the "epitome of muscle power and streamlined design." He said the creature was no more a "killer" in the criminal sense than "the housewife who served bacon at the family's breakfast table." Noting that only 27 of the world's 344 species were known to present a danger to human beings, he criticized journalists and other moviemakers for portraying the fish as a bloodthirsty butcher.

Cousteau found sharks to be an integral, if disquieting, part of the undersea environment. He often repeated the conclusions he first expressed in the early 1950's: "The better acquainted we become with sharks, the less we know them, and one can never tell what a shark is going to do."

The first segment of *The Undersea World of Jacques Cousteau,* promoted by ABC as a "beautiful, terrifying study of the most ferocious creature in the ocean," won very favorable reviews. *Time* marveled that "one crewman rode the back of a 60-ton whale shark. . . . Cousteau's red-capped divers fearlessly ran off experiments right in their menacing midst." *Saturday Review* awarded the show a citation, describing it as "unusual adventure-entertainment . . . [that] successfully combined the derring-do of divers amid dangers underwater with some meaningful marine experiment laboratory work." *Variety* labeled Cousteau "a master of the entertaining message—his style and content stand in sharp contrast to hoked up efforts." The show also won the Ohio State Award for being "a milestone of foresight and value . . . a rare combination of instruction and entertainment."

The show's few critics focused on the Captain's preference for purple lyricism over scientific purity. Eugenie Clark, the professor who worked aboard *Calypso* on the segment, complained that the rushed production schedule forced inaccuracies. "Cousteau's films are misleading in a way, because they portray him as a scientist," said Clark. "I can't think of any particular scientific contributions he's made, because he just doesn't have time. He's trapped. He needs to keep up that big image, to make it look like he's moving forward. When you get up there, when you have all that power, sometimes you lose track of what you started out to do."

Responding to such criticism, Cousteau said, "Our films have only one ambition—to show the truth about nature and give people the wish to know more. I do not stand as a scientist giving dry explanations. I'm an honest observer."

The Captain's broadcasts, however, rarely explained the true behind-the-scenes maneuvers used to obtain dramatic photographs of undersea life. For example, the second television segment, entitled "The Savage World of the Coral Jungle," tried to demonstrate that groupers aggressively protect their territories. Rather than wait for an intruding grouper, Cousteau planned to trick the fish into attacking its own image in an underwater mirror. On the first attempt a medium-size grouper charged the mirror but couldn't break it. A thinner mirror broke when divers lightly bumped against a coral projection. The next, noted Cousteau in his log, "was smashed into a million fragments by a ridiculously tiny grouper who had no business there in any case, and who, moreover, would not look good on film."

Finally, the team surrounded a brave grouper with four appropriately sized mirrors, which the fish systematically charged and destroyed. But because the cameras jammed, the crew, after four hours in the water, had to try again. Once more the grouper conquered its four images. Riled up, the unpredictable fish began eating the mirror fragments, and by the next morning it had died. Cousteau's resulting film only portrayed a valiant grouper defending his territory from multiple "intruders."

In early June 1967, four months into the "great expedition," Cousteau learned from radio reports of growing tensions between Israel and Egypt. Although still needing to film for several more weeks in the Red Sea, he decided to escape possible trouble and ordered *Calypso* to return to France via the Suez Canal. The Captain himself caught the next flight from Port Sudan to Paris. His crew was not so lucky.

On June 5 the Six-Day War began, and Sudan entered the conflict on the Egyptian side. Two of *Calypso's* men were trapped for several hours in Port Sudan, where violent street demonstrators sought out and stoned Westerners, including sailors.

When the bruised pair returned to the ship, *Calypso* sailed quickly for Suez. Egypt, however, closed the waterway and forced all vessels to anchor. Cousteau's crew, ordered to remain on board, sat helplessly amid the crossfire, a sitting duck in an international shooting gallery. Bombs exploded all around.

After much negotiation, the Egyptians allowed *Calypso's* team to unload cameras, film, and underwater scooters for air transport to France. But once on the docks, the precious equipment was strafed by machine-gun fire from Israeli planes. Everything was destroyed.

Cousteau returned to his ship on July 15, the day after Israelis had bombed the oil refinery at Suez, and tried using his substantial charm and military connections to gain passage through the canal. He even convinced the French ambassador to beg for help. Nothing seemed to work.

Hostilities finally ended on July 21, allowing Cousteau to deliver new equipment and to replace his entrapped crew with a fresh team. To make up for the valuable time lost to the war, the Captain quickly devised an alternate filming program in the Indian Ocean.

* * *

While Cousteau traveled around the world, his father, alone since Elizabeth's death in 1951, settled in France. A vivacious seventy-five-year-old who had spent much of his life being a sports companion to American millionaires, Daniel decided to tackle diving and underwater photography. He also agreed to handle many of his son's administrative tasks. Trained as a lawyer and conversant in several languages, Daniel negotiated contracts and arranged diplomatic permits for cameramen and scientists. He proved to be a master bureaucrat, known affectionately as Daddy to the Cousteau team.

Daniel worked periodically on the expeditions for nearly fifteen years. His health failing, he returned to his apartment in Paris on the Avenue de la Motte-Picquet, where Pierre's children, Françoise and Jean-Pierre, cared for him. He died a few months short of his ninety-fourth birthday in March 1969.

Jean-Michel also helped with the thankless and behind-the-scenes tasks of finding and contracting for *Calypso*'s supplies. In contrast, Philippe starred in, directed, or photographed several of the early television segments. Cousteau's younger son, appointed vice-president of the family's film production company, appeared to be the Captain's confidant and alter ego. In reality, father and son sparred frequently.

Philippe constantly demanded more responsibility, bristling at being labeled a *fils à papa*, a derogatory French term for the unproductive offspring of a talented father. The Captain, however, refused to retire or abandon control over his empire.

The family rift cracked open when Philippe decided to marry Janice Sullivan, a green-eyed fashion model he had met in 1966 at an after-theater party in New York City. The pair spent several romantic weeks enjoying the Big Apple and Paris. Not long after Philippe returned to Morocco to film a project for his father, he called the model on the telephone and asked her to marry him. "I said yes before he could change his mind," Jan recalls.

Los Angeles-born Jan had taken up modeling in her early teens. She advanced rapidly from lunchtime assignments in local restaurants to a swimsuit manufacturer's showroom and on to a New York modeling agency. "I lived in a world of fashion shows, parties, and nightclubs," she says. The biggest influence on the tawny-haired, long-limbed beauty had been her ambitious mother. "She married too young and had to work to help support the family," Jan remembers. "She pounded into me a sense of her own mistakes. She told me not to get trapped in an early marriage but to live life and gather experience, build a career and only eventually to marry. I became aggressive and self-motivated, sort of fulfilling her fantasies.''

Jacques and Simone were furious with the relationship, in part because they believed a model was not good enough for their son and in part because Jan was not French. The parents, in dramatic scenes, demanded that Philippe call off the marriage. But the young man wouldn't back down.

In January 1967 the handsome young couple organized a wedding ceremony in Paris. Jacques and Simone refused to attend. The parents' pointed gift consisted only of French-language lessons for their daughter-in-law.

Father and son, despite the tension, had to work together. The ABC contract demanded their constant attention. In addition to overseeing the filming, they needed to unearth fresh stories, identify captivating locations, and develop new technologies.

The Captain slowly provided more freedom to Philippe, allowing him, for example, to add a hot-air balloon to *Calypso*'s arsenal of equipment. Cousteau sent his son to a South Dakota school for pilot instruction, and the certified Philippe returned in late September 1967 for tests off Djibouti, where on his first venture he plummeted the photogenic airship precipitously into the sea. A few days later Philippe succeeded in launching the brightly colored balloon from *Calypso*'s rear deck, only to have it collapse suddenly and engulf the ship's crew in a sea of nylon. Later attempts, however, demonstrated the value of the equipment, which Philippe called ''the poor man's helicopter,'' in both filming from the air and guiding *Calypso* through dangerous coral outcroppings.

In 1968 the Captain also allowed his son, then living with Jan in Marina del Rey, California, to lease his own ship and help produce a film segment on the gray whale. Philippe assumed the assignment with enthusiasm.

The young Cousteau, according to his father, had ''this belief that animals are focusing on him.'' When Philippe came close enough underwater to observe a whale's blowhole, for instance, he interpreted the modulated stream of bubbles as communication. ''Perhaps it was even talking to me,'' he said, ''a dialogue of the deaf.''

Philippe aggressively sought ways to witness whale activity. He rented a Cherokee 300 to conduct airborne photography in Baja California, but the noisy plane scared the sensitive giants away. He experimented with a vertical or ascensional parachute, but the traction cable snapped, causing the buckle to strike Philippe in the face; crew members had to rescue the unconscious adventurer from the lagoon. Philippe and Jan then tried the hot-air balloon and captured some splendid shots of the migrating grays. When the couple drifted out to sea, they dropped a line to a Zodiac and were towed back to the ship.

Philippe, despite his talents and energy, seemed to lack direction. His career goals fluctuated constantly among cinematography, engineering, and flying. His mother described him as "the biggest playboy in town."

Philippe had obtained his baccalaureate in 1961 from the Lycée de Monaco and studied at the College of Normandie and the Massachusetts Institute of Technology. To maintain his French citizenship, he spent two years as a draftee in the French Navy, stationed in Algeria. He planned to gain an advanced degree in engineering but changed his mind at the last minute to enroll in the French school for filmmakers. Cinematography, however, would not satisfy him. Even during his productive years with the ABC series, Philippe frequently announced his desire to abandon filmmaking and pursue a commercial pilot's license. Frustrated and confused by his father's efforts simultaneously to retard his ambition and to encourage his independence, Philippe struck out on his own in 1969 and established a production company, Thalassa Films, named after the Greek word for Mediterranean.

The filming formula developed by the Cousteaus combined adventure and education, providing more action than the average wildlife special and more drama than the conventional documentary. The Captain made stars of himself and the *Calypso* crew, encouraging a generation of television viewers to worry each quarter whether Albert Falco would be able to pilot the diving saucer through yet another narrow cave or whether Dominique Sumian could avoid the madness of feeding sharks. The personable team became an integral part of each show, not as tourists merely observing nature but as adventurers partaking in the wonder of discovery.

Bosley Crowther, *The New York Times* movie reviewer, remarked on the formula: "The intimacy with the explorers, intelligently and humorously set up, is largely responsible for the vivid sense of participation one gets from the films. . . . At the end, you and Captain Cousteau, his crew and their dachshund are friends."

Cousteau devoted particular care to the story line, engrossing viewers in the plot by making them wonder what would happen next. According to Christopher Palmer, executive producer of the Audubon Society's television series, "The Captain was the key pioneer in nature filmmaking not just because he was among the first but because he recognized that productions had to be entertaining if they were to maintain the audience's attention and loyalty."

The Captain also added unique touches of humor to his nature dramas. In Africa, for instance, two *Calypso* adventurers donned a life-size plastic hippopotamus disguise in order to film the giant and fearsome creatures from the water. In the subsequent film the serious close-up footage of hippos was played off against shots of the ridiculously disguised and awkward men, looking like a vaudeville team, hobbling back onto the shore and into the savanna.

Critics of Cousteau's formula complained that he spent more time photographing himself than exploring the undersea environment. Each television segment included lengthy shots of the crew planning and preparing the expeditions: Team members examined unidentifiable maps, stared contemplatively toward the sea, and laboriously loaded air tanks and cameras into the Zodiacs.

Just as unpopular was the Captain's willingness to invent drama to invigorate his films. One reviewer criticized the *Calypso* team for poking and provoking creatures until they performed as the ferocious beasts the script called for. To demonstrate the hippo's violent ways, for instance, the Cousteaus dragged their camera barge across a small pond to corner a theretofore passive herd at the shallow end. A few of the frightened creatures lunged past the camera for freedom. One accidentally smashed into the barge, giving the Captain the dramatic element he was seeking.

Even the most ardent of critics, however, agreed that Cousteau's early work consistently contained beautiful photography. The camera work and editing brilliantly captured fascinating details of the undersea world.

Producing the series demanded unusual patience. Cousteau explained:

What is not apparent on the screen is the almost insurmountable difficulty of such an enterprise: the years of technical preparation, of research and documentation; the financial obstacles involving substantial personal sacrifices for a crew of 150 men; the thousands of dives in conventional diving suits, the hundreds of dives in the saucer; the hours passed shivering in the cold water or in the decompression chamber; the nights spent repairing a piece of essential equipment or a flooded camera; the tempests of sand; the tropical cyclones; the accidents that occur in a ship in the middle of an ocean; the agonies we experience when we lose track of a diver or a saucer.

To produce four broadcasts a year, Cousteau usually kept two teams in the field at all times. Ideas for the films came from many sources, and a research team spent several months examining the literature and exploring possible filming sites. Writers developed a story line well before *Calypso* arrived on the scene, although cameramen often amended the plan to respond to natural events on location. When Captain Cousteau could break away from his busy schedule of administering a growing empire he'd check in for a few days to be filmed with the animals. Cameramen sent as much as 140,000 feet of film recorded over several months to Marshall Flaum Productions in Los Angeles, where editors cut all but 2,000 feet. Although not directly involved in the editing process, Cousteau gave final approval to each finished program and made his presence felt through his French-accented narration.

The hurried schedule, of course, demanded compromises. Even during the early years of filming, Cousteau's log included repeated complaints about the lack of time to explore a subject thoroughly. In 1969, for instance, as he prepared both to establish an archaeological dig in the Caribbean and to dive in Lake Titicaca in the Andes, he wrote, "Unfortunately, we will now have to cut short our study of the furred sea lions. We are all—*Calypso* and her teams, as well as myself—burdened with an overambitious schedule."

When it came to filming creatures in the open ocean, Cousteau was torn between his childlike affection for animals and his professional desire for dramatic footage. Unwilling to devote the time needed to obtain natural shots, he often imprisoned animals in cages or aquariums to record their movements. With regular expressions of remorse, he labeled his actions "experiments to befriend animals."

Off the coast of Seattle, for instance, Cousteau seized a giant octopus and placed it in an aquarium aboard *Calypso* in order "to examine a specimen at our leisure." He admitted that the prisoner was initially "red with emotion," but he hoped that after being fed well the octopus would "accept his situation and become accustomed to us." The octopus had other ideas and removed the aquarium cover which Cousteau had secured with several twenty-pound weights. The Captain and his crew watched the creature slither across *Calypso*'s rear deck and fall into the sea. No one tried to block its retreat because, as Cousteau later admitted, "We were already feeling guilty about having deprived an animal of its liberty—a splendid animal made for freedom."

Guilt, however, did not hinder Cousteau's efforts to "befriend" an array of marine mammals, a process he felt would bridge the chasm between man and animal. He foresaw a new phase of human evolution when "we will be in need of friends in the sea with whom we may begin to communicate." But to communicate with sea lions in Alaska, his crew trapped a large male in an isolated inlet and stretched a net over his only exit. Cousteau failed to see the irony in his describing the prison as "semi-freedom."

The Captain even tried to harness a three-ton elephant seal, proposing to tame it. *Calypso* divers scrambled over the rocks of Guadalupe for several hours, trying to corner the giant. Only when the elephant seal virtually collapsed from exhaustion did Cousteau call off the chase. And even then, he expressed less concern for the animal's comfort than for dramatic adequacy of the film footage of his bikini-clad "hunters" stalking their powerful prey.

Falco often used the Zodiac to torment and disorient dolphins and whales. With the outboard motor running wide open, he circled around the creatures continuously until they were enclosed in a ring of noise and bubbles from the Zodiac's wake. The annoyed animals sometimes sent Falco flying, but more often they became confused and quiet. Dependent upon sound for communication and guidance, they fell into a stupor. The Captain could then acquire his prized photographs.

Cousteau's desire to befriend or humanize the sea's creatures also led him, as he later stated, to become "addicted to naming animals that we meet in and on the water; and, above all, animals that we take on board, feed, and train." He christened a whale calf Jonah, a barracuda Jules, and the now-famous grouper Ulysses. The preoccupation, he noted, "reflects an effort to make these animals members of our group. This is especially true in the case of animals with whom contact is difficult, and training even more difficult, and to whom our men must accord a certain amount of patient affection. The very act of giving a name to an animal is a sign that contact has begun and that the animal is regarded as a member of the group rather than an outsider.''

Cousteau rarely considered how new group members felt about their "contact" with *Calypso*'s crew. The fifth show of the *Undersea World* series, entitled "The Unexpected Voyage of Pepito and Christobald," reported on the Captain's experiences with a pair of sea lions captured off the Cape of Good Hope, and it exposed his contradictory attitudes toward his animal subjects.

Having spent too much time at the southern tip of Africa in early 1968, Cousteau needed to rush to several filming engagements in the Caribbean. Since he had not obtained enough footage of the furred sea lions for a film, he decided to capture two of the animals and record their actions aboard *Calypso* as they sailed across the Atlantic.

While the Captain argued against the "idea of removing animals from their natural environment, especially marine mammals like these, who are so obviously attached to their freedom and so active in the water," he ordered a landing party to net two sea lions and tow them, in antishark cages, back to *Calypso*. Although he admitted that "it is useless to pretend that captivity in any form is less than cruel," he gave detailed instructions to the divers on how to seize the creatures and to the cameramen on how to film the capture. Moreover, Cousteau may have rejected "the idea of training and conditioning animals and teaching them 'tricks,' as people do in zoos and circuses," but he rewarded the sea lions with fish when they climbed stairs or stood on stools. In fact, he diligently tried to train the two sea lions, nicknamed Pepito and Christobald, to accompany *Calypso*'s divers underwater.

Cousteau described the seizure and training as an exciting experiment. Would the sea lions, he asked, "follow our divers in the depths of the sea, the way that dogs follow their masters for a walk through the woods?'' Would he be able to mount a camera on the creature's back and direct it to enter areas too small or dangerous for his divers? Could he establish friendships with wild animals?

Pepito and Christobald did not initially "appreciate" Cousteau's "sentimental adventure" or their small plastic pool on *Calypso*'s rear deck. The two sea lions frequently bit their captors, who learned to wear thick gloves, boots, and chaps when feeding or petting the animals.

Caring for the trapped pair became both a danger and an enormous chore for the crew. The sea lions required some twenty pounds of fresh fish daily, and they constantly fouled their pool, creating an overwhelming stench.

The animals eventually came to depend upon their masters, and Cousteau ordered cameramen to film the playful and photogenic pair taking fish from the divers' hands or napping alongside their trainers. Yet the Captain acknowledged that "their longing for freedom will very likely be stronger than any attachment they may feel for us." He therefore constructed harnesses that buckled around the sea lions' bodies when they dived in the open water.

The animals' longing for freedom became quite apparent when *Calypso* docked at Natal, on the coast of Brazil. As the crew tied up, Pepito escaped from his cage and lunged toward the ocean. When Christian Bonnici grabbed his hind legs, Pepito turned and bit down, hard, into Bonnici's stomach. After a full minute of struggle Pepito opened his jaws, and Bonnici quickly threw the animal back into his cage and locked him in.

Rather than risk an escape during a harness-free dive in the ocean, Cousteau tried to locate a large swimming pool in Puerto Rico in which to practice. A wealthy woman in San Juan volunteered her facility, so Cousteau rented a car to transport his team and the two sea lions across Puerto Rico. For almost a week, according to the Captain, "Pepito and Christobald were subjected to a course of progressive training which gave us every hope that they would not escape once we transferred them to the open seas."

The drive back to *Calypso* demonstrated the comic and ludicrous nature of Cousteau's "experiment." Not used to traveling by automobile, Christobald tried to climb out the window. Falco slammed on the brake, and Dominique Sumian snatched the animal just before it fell onto the pavement. The pair tried to keep the sea lion motionless, but Christobald fell into a rage, not unlike a child's tantrum, and proceeded to cover the crew and the automobile with excrement. From that time on, Cousteau remarked sheepishly, "It has been impossible for anyone from *Calypso* to rent an auto in Puerto Rico."

When the day of Cousteau's orchestrated experiment finally arrived the two sea lions, without harnesses, faithfully followed the divers to the ocean floor and returned with them to the ship. For Cousteau, who often resorted to dramatic exaggeration, the scene denoted "the perfect understanding between man and animal." He went on to say, "We had proved that men and marine mammals are able to live together—

as loyal and sincere friends—if only man is willing.'' He failed to mention that the animals also must first be imprisoned and trained.

Cousteau's euphoria did not last long. On one of the next dives Christobald deliberately swam away from the divers. The Captain ordered a launch to recapture him, but Christobald avoided the crew's nets. After more than an hour in choppy seas Cousteau called off the search and tried to rationalize the escape. Sounding a bit like an animal psychiatrist, he concluded that Christobald's ''need for freedom was something that he shared with us, something that we could understand.''

When *Calypso* returned to San Juan, the disappointed crew was greeted with a photograph of Christobald in the local newspaper. It seemed that the sea lion had traveled more than a hundred nautical miles, and, having been unable to find food, accepted fish from a local fisherman, who proceeded to slip a rope around his neck.

The fisherman sold the sea lion to another wealthy Puerto Rican woman. Cousteau arranged to meet ''Mme. W'' and to have the newspaper's photographer accompany him to her home. According to the Captain, ''I had been forewarned that I would have to use 'all my charm,' and I was prepared to do so.'' After cordial greetings, Cousteau autographed copies of his books for the woman's two sons. He described filming techniques and suggested that Mme. W would be perfect for a role in one of his productions. After sharing whiskey, the woman agreed that Christobald would be returned to the *Calypso*.

The sea lion proceeded to destroy another San Juan automobile before arriving for the great feast Cousteau had arranged in honor of the prisoner's return. Christobald, in no mood to celebrate, became very ill and within a few days died.

Almost without emotion, the pragmatic Cousteau concluded that ''it would be useless to continue our experiment. We have already proved what we set out to prove: that marine mammals are almost as capable of attachment to humans as land animals.'' Perhaps of equal importance, he realized he was late for his next filming engagement. He eventually released the lonely Pepito, an ocean away from his home, to join some Peruvian sea lions.

Despite the fact that the creatures rejected Cousteau's advances, his film asserted that ''two marine mammals were our willing companions in the sea.'' In subsequent publications he often recalled his adventures with Pepito and Christobald, suggesting that the sea lions ''had been free to come and go as they wished'' and that the seven-month spectacle had been "an extraordinary experience in communal living." Cousteau couldn't acknowledge that in his quest for dramatic film footage he had imprisoned a marine mammal, taught it tricks, and watched helplessly as it died in captivity.

Several other Cousteau expeditions also produced unexpected results. Later in 1968, for instance, the Captain searched for gold among sunken ships in the Caribbean, believing he had located the site of the famous seventeenth-century Spanish galleon *Nuestra Señora de la Concepción,* wrecked while transporting enormous riches from the New World.

The area, located to the northeast of the Dominican Republic, had been the focus of several previous excavations because historians assumed it contained more sunken ships than any other spot on earth. Some researchers estimated that at least six hundred million dollars in gold, silver, precious stones, and pieces of art lay buried in limestone and encrusted with coral.

Simone opposed the project from the beginning. Since she lived aboard *Calypso* and considered herself responsible for the crew's well-being, she feared that the treasure hunt would sacrifice solidarity. Jacques overruled her objections, but he did have the men pledge that any riches would be distributed equally among them.

The Captain expressed more concern about the tons of coral that his sledgehammers would destroy. "I am conscience-stricken at the thought of what Project Sunken Treasure will do to the lovely coral," he recorded in his log the day before the excavation began. However, his dream of treasures—either gold or captivating photographs—overwhelmed his concern for the environment. "It is too late to turn back," he continued. "Tomorrow, we must begin work, and the first step will be to turn our picks against the living coral."

Excavating the ship proved to be enormously difficult, largely because the treasure lay within a treacherous sea-level coral reef. Even reaching the site without scraping *Calypso* required Cousteau to use the hot-air balloon and the ship's sophisticated navigational aids.

In unremitting heat, crew members suctioned mounds of mud and debris up a temperamental air lift and raised rusted cannonballs and pieces of ancient crockery. To compensate for the arduous work, they dreamed about the gold. Bernard Delemotte outlined in his log the plans of a true sailor: "I think I'll buy some land; a lot of land, with trees and hills and flatlands. And a river through it. Perhaps there will be an old house alongside the river.''

After almost two months of toil and romantic dreams, however, the crew discovered that the wreck was not the *Nuestra Señora de la Concepción*. In fact, it was a simple eighteenth-century merchant vessel with no treasure in its hold.

Cousteau tried to put the best light on his setback. ''We carried out, for the first time, a systematic dig in a coral bank,'' he declared. More objectively, he continued, ''We have learned something very important: that we must not expect too much from archaeological research in tropical seas. Coral grows too rapidly, and buries too deeply the vestiges of man and human artifacts.''

Little time existed for self-pity because the Captain needed to join his advance team at Lake Titicaca, located some thirteen thousand feet above sea level, high in the Andes between Peru and Bolivia. Cousteau planned both to explore the physiological implications of diving at high altitude and to expose the geological origins of the lake and the archaeological ruins of the Tiahuanacan civilization. To convey some suspense to an otherwise straightforward expedition, he expressed hope that the team would discover the ''golden chain'' which, according to local legend, bound together, at the bottom of the lake, the Island of the Sun and the Island of the Moon.

Cousteau, however, located no golden chain, no archaeological artifacts, and no undersea creatures—other than unique frogs that lived completely underwater and breathed through their skin. With little of substance to report, the Captain and his team became the focus of their film. They recorded long sequences of themselves loading the small submarines known as sea fleas from the *Calypso* to a flatcar of a Peruvian train, which labored up the winding mountain rails to Lake Titicaca. They also filmed themselves and their equipment being transported slowly across the lake on a barge provided by the Bolivian Navy.

Adjacent to the highest navigable body of water in the world, the Titicaca region provided only half the amount of oxygen the crew received at sea level. The Captain suffered a great deal from the altitude, and *Calypso*'s divers panted as they walked with their heavy equipment. Beneath the water, however, team members were surrounded by water at familiar pressures, and their tanks provided normal amounts of oxygen.

Cousteau devoted considerable time to interacting with natives, providing patronizing commentary on their habits. He even organized an elaborate ceremony for the local priest to bless the minisubs, decorated with appropriate political sensitivity in the flags of both France and Bolivia. The Captain imagined that the arrival of divers offered needed stimulation for the poor villagers: "For these people, trapped in a bleak and barren land, deprived of all entertainment other than what they can create for themselves, the unexpected festival was a gift from heaven."

Cousteau paid particular attention to the Urus, a primitive people who lived in huts built on floating islands made of woven rushes. But rather than explore the Urus' culture, which is the most ancient in this Andean region, he contrasted their habits and poverty with the outer space-like paraphernalia of his helmeted divers. In several subsequent books he printed a picture of Jean-Claire Riant standing among an Uru family, who proceeded with their chores and appeared bored by the fully suited diver stalking awkwardly about their huts.

After almost two months the crew reboarded the train, and Cousteau shipped the disappointing footage to Hollywood for editing. Back on *Calypso* at the end of November 1968, the busy filmmaker declared that he was "ready for a new adventure."

After leaving Lake Titicaca, Cousteau's crew headed northwest to Guadalupe Island, 134 miles west of Baja California. *Calypso* deposited on the barren rock a team of cameramen and scientists, water jars, and live chickens, which would supply eggs and fresh meat. Beginning in early January 1969, the men endured Spartan conditions for three months while they recorded the elephant seal's mating habits and birth. Though ungainly and aggressive on land, underwater the massive creature displayed an elegance of motion.

The Captain and *Calypso*, meanwhile, sailed to Scammon Lagoon in the Baja Peninsula to join Philippe in tracking the migration and courtship of gray whales. The resulting segment, entitled "The Desert Whales" and broadcast at the end of 1969, garnered the team its first Emmy award.

The whale had long been a favorite subject of the Cousteaus. The enormous warm-blooded beings, according to the Captain, "bear such a strong resemblance to man, with their lungs, their intelligence, and the talent for communication."

The numerous species of whales are indeed remarkable creatures. The voice of the finback, for instance, carries almost fifty miles underwater. Sperm whales travel at a rapid twenty knots, while the orca or killer whale is capable of thirty knots. The California gray whales exhibit a sophisticated social structure.

Almost eradicated by greedy traders, the graceful whale was becoming a symbol of environmental consciousness, a new image that the Captain claims to have personally developed and promoted. "We were the first," he boasts, "to seek them out in a spirit of friendship and curiosity in the depths of the sea."

Regardless of the exaggerations, Cousteau's television shows did help change the popular perception of whales. While eighteenth century painters depicted the mammals' ferocity and malevolence, the Captain showed his divers riding peacefully on their backs. Nineteenth-century hunters may have viewed the animal from a strictly utilitarian perspective, but Cousteau's pictures painted a world of grace and familial affection.

The image Cousteau presented of whales, however, contained a predominantly human perspective. He wrote of the mammal's natural habitat, but his photographs portrayed divers trying to touch the giant. Man, according to the Captain, needed to integrate into the whale's environment if he was to learn practical diving techniques and appreciate the poetic beauty of the sea.

Philippe developed a special, almost spiritual, affection for the whale. During his first encounter with a gray, he jumped into a Zodiac, roared off in front of the whale, and dived into the water. By the time he cleared his mask, Philippe had only a fuzzy view of the whale's mouth—"a mouth unlike any that I had ever seen before." Within seconds, the fast-moving giant swept past the diver, but not before Philippe concluded that "the whale and I had reached a perfect understanding."

Cousteau's son, despite his hyperbole, did experience several remarkable encounters with whales. A unique bit of film footage taken in Bermuda, for instance, showed Philippe jumping into the water between a mother whale and her calf. The whales passed on each side of him, and the mother pulled back on the tip of her flipper so as to avoid hitting the diver. "I think that those were the most beautiful hours that I have ever spent in the water in my whole life," declared Philippe.

(The Captain, several years later, suggested that the giant creature avoided divers not because of benevolence toward man but because it feared bruising its delicate skin.)

The reverence toward the whale exhibited by the Cousteaus in their books and films was not always complemented by techniques they used in the sea. *Calypso*'s cameramen have remained, at heart, practical filmmakers, committed to producing popular television shows.

In his March 1969 log, Cousteau outlined an underwater photographer's many frustrations. On the first day the Captain spotted grays, he couldn't take quality pictures because the water was too murky. The sea cleared on the second day, but the whales refused to cooperate, diving vertically whenever the ship approached. Whale watching remained impossible the following day because a slight storm created whitecaps that were indistinguishable from a whale's spout.

Filming, even on those few calm days with clear water and relaxed whales, demanded special, often aggressive tactics. The lead Zodiac would try to move in front of the whale to slow it down, while the second dropped cameramen into the water. Five seconds usually passed before a diver could clear his mask and begin taking pictures. Often by that time the whale had disappeared. Sometimes a flick of its tail overturned the boats and sent the occupants and equipment tumbling into the ocean.

The Zodiacs quickly returned to pick up the men and repeat the exercise. If lucky, the divers obtained enough good shots for the editors in Hollywood to piece together later. At the end of the day the crew stumbled into the wardroom, their legs and arms limp from exhaustion.

To ensure that a surfacing whale was the same one that dived, Cousteau and his team used harpoons to mark the individual giants. Sensitive to charges that his actions harked back to those of Captain Ahab and other nineteenth-century whalers, Cousteau declared that he inflicted "a very superficial kind of wound, one that does not harm the animal in the slightest."

Cousteau tried repeatedly to witness the birth of a whale. He even raided the lagoons of Baja California at all hours of the day and night, but the shy mothers delivered neither a baby nor a show.

The Cousteau team adopted several whales to produce touching, personal scenes and stories for their movies and books. In Baja California, for instance, divers tried to rescue a beached baby whale, which Cousteau nicknamed Jonah. They tied the creature gently alongside *Calypso,* and accompanying scientists hand fed mixtures of clams and squid to it. After one meal the whale refused to release the scientist's hand. Believing that the mammal understood his goodwill, the professor became emotional and cried out, "He understands! He loves me!"

Cousteau, who filmed most action aboard *Calypso,* took the rare step of ordering the cameras to be shut off. "It seems somehow wrong," the Captain reasoned, "to record the great emotion of this lover of animals." The sentiment, however, did not stop Cousteau from writing about the episode in one of his books.

Recognizing that he had other commitments to keep and adventures to record, Cousteau radioed the Marine Zoo in San Diego, where scientists expressed a willingness to treat the mammal. But on the following morning Jonah died. "We have seen great animals of the sea die before," stated the Captain, "but nothing has moved us as we have been moved by the slow agony of the baby whale who did not want to die and to whom we had wished to give life. And yet, our reaction is that of creatures of land. In the sea, there is no room for pity or for sorrow."

Even today Cousteau remains emotional about the whale, expressing pride in having come face-to-face with the creature in the open sea. He still searches for the mammal, attracted to its intelligence and anxious to create a spirit of friendship. Despite periodic claims to have established a bond with the mammal, he admits that the whale remains a mystery. "A sperm could be in a frenzy of rage for an hour before he decides to put an end to us with a flick of that incredible tail, and we would have no way of knowing it," Cousteau states. "There is no experience on dry land that can compare with it."

The Captain's filming expedition off Baja lasted just two months. After a major overhaul in San Diego, *Calypso* proceeded north. Throughout April 1969 the group circled California's Catalina Island to photograph dolphins, groupers, and orcas, the black-and-white "killer whales" feared for their high intelligence, massive teeth, and ravenous appetites.

Though Cousteau mandated a strict filming schedule, he periodically abandoned it if a unique opportunity arose, as it did off Catalina with the appearance of a mass of squid in a sexual frenzy. "We had all learned before to bend to the whims of the sea," he noted. "When the sea wishes to share its secrets, it does so, and we must plan our own affairs accordingly."

The gelatinous squid announced their arrival by blocking the intake screens of *Calypso*'s water pumps, causing the motor to overheat and the circuit breakers to snap. The crew stumbled to the deck and witnessed the sea seething with activity. Divers quickly suited up and found themselves surrounded by squid, some four inches long and others almost a foot in length, some golden and others red.

Calypso's cameramen spent sixteen hours recording the frantic activities of love-crazed cephalopods. They emptied thirty-six bottles of compressed air and exposed a mile of film, edited into an hour segment entitled "The Night of the Squid."

The squid, for their part, delivered millions of babies, most of which were devoured by predators. Sharks, in particular, relished the unique feast; they cruised blindly through the mass, within inches of the divers, collecting thousands of prey with their open mouths.

As the Captain recorded violence within the sea, Philippe pleaded with his father to make a statement against the war in Vietnam. Cousteau, however, feared that political controversies would threaten his relations with ABC and damage his image with millions of "Middle Americans." The pair finally agreed that Philippe would rent a boat and produce an allegorical film about the thirty Japanese destroyers sunk during World War II off Truk Island, at the eastern tip of the Caroline chain.

Philippe didn't mention Vietnam. In fact, most of the show, "Lagoon of the Lost Ships," laboriously retraced the events of February 1944 and explored the dark wrecks. At the film's end the Captain intoned against the waste of human lives and nature inherent in any war, but he refused to protest against contemporary actions. In fact, the former naval officer concluded, "Today individual men are concerned with the choices that lead to war and peace, and with this new realization comes hope."

While Philippe worked in the South Pacific, Cousteau rushed *Calypso* north to reach Alaska during the summer solstice. The lengthy daylight provided stunning scenery and brilliant conditions, and enthusiastic cameramen took photographs for twenty-two hours straight, forsaking sleep and throwing the routine into disarray. The warmish weather also brought out swarms of mosquitoes that settled on the crew's skin, as Cousteau put it, "like a layer of coarse dust."

The Captain and his colleagues filmed "The Tragedy of the Red

Salmon'' on Alaska's Kodiak Island during the last week of June 1969. They stationed themselves within freezing waterfalls to record the fish's "majestical procession upstream" to the place of its birth. Sometimes crew members caught exhausted salmon and placed them above waterfalls so the fish could continue their journeys. At the high lakes, the filmmakers employed remote-controlled cameras to photograph males battling for mates. Finally, the Captain creatively revealed the tragic cycle of life, showing the slow death of those salmon that successfully reached the spawning grounds and laid their eggs.

Cousteau's stunning television show received Emmy awards for both music composition and cinematography. *Daily Variety* found it to be "emotionally gripping and poignant . . . a work of art. At the end, one is actually emotionally involved with the salmon.''

Calypso left its anchorage off Kodiak Island on July 4 and proceeded to the tiny Cherni Islands in the Aleutians to locate sea otters, which hunters had slaughtered nearly to extinction in search of their beautiful coats. For three days cameramen filmed these endearing shoreside mammals perform clever antics. One sequence of the award-winning show portrayed an otter floating on its back and using its small front flippers to munch in humanlike fashion on a crab's leg. Another revealed otters tearing the fins off captured sunfish, which remained alive but unable to swim away.

On Round Island, near the Alaskan mainland in the Bering Sea, the crew tried to photograph the thousands of walruses that covered the beaches. The massive mammals, however, proved to be unwilling actors, having developed an understandable fear of humans interested in their tusks. The hulking beasts, complete with flabby bodies and bloodshot eyes, flopped heavily into the sea when cameramen approached. Cousteau nonetheless tried to ''commune'' with the wrinkled walruses, which he concluded were capable of affection and intelligence.

To convey the size and temperament of a walrus, Cousteau crawled carefully to within ten feet of a three-thousand-pound creature, while Philippe filmed his every action. When the walrus expressed little reaction to the stranger, the Captain moved another step closer and rose to a kneeling position. The walrus, no longer pleased, reared its massive head, growled, and lunged forward clumsily, baring its fearsome tusks.

Cousteau interpreted the show of hostility as a mere tactic of intimidation, intended to frighten the red-capped intruder away. Becoming as much the subject as the walrus, he chose his own form of intimidation by rising to his feet and glaring down on the giant beast. The walrus halted its demonstration immediately. But when Cousteau lay flat on his stomach, the animal reared again. The two players repeated their awkward game for several minutes. Finally, the Captain jumped to his feet, flailed his arms, and shouted wildly. The walrus, probably deciding that the exchange had gone on long enough, dived into the sea. The Cousteaus thoroughly enjoyed the antics and claimed to have developed an "understanding" with the giant walrus.

Cameramen also focused on a baby walrus, abandoned after hunters they were filming had killed its parents. Believing the infant would die if left on its own, they scooped it up, nicknamed it Burke, and placed it inside the umiak, or Eskimo boat. The baby, according to Cousteau, "not only accepted man but became instantly and wildly attached to him." It snuggled up for warmth to divers in wet suits, which evidently resembled the skin of a female walrus. The Captain shot heartwarming pictures of his divers gently stroking the cuddly pet. The warm relationship didn't last, however, for having a film schedule to keep, Cousteau sent Burke to Marineland of the Pacific in California.

Less successful was the Captain's attempt to photograph the migration of thousands of starfish along the seafloor. "When they move," explained cameraman Michel Deloire after his initial dive, "they're like some incredible lawn mower. Everything in their path is devoured." During the next descent, however, a strong current kicked up enough mud to cloud the water. The crew decided to remain at anchor overnight and try again, but a thirty-six-hour storm arrested the diving efforts. When the water finally cleared, the starfish had vanished.

Cousteau tried to learn a lesson from the episode. "Despite all our technological gadgetry," he noted, "we are as much at the mercy of the elements when we are at sea as the most primitive tribesman in the Pacific. Eventually, one resigns oneself to Neptune's whims, but sometimes I cannot help wondering how many extraordinary films we have missed because of such bad luck."

The Captain's fortune was sufficiently positive, however, that for a remarkable five quarters in a row, every Cousteau television program won an Emmy award. In fact, he accepted a total of eight Emmys from 1969 to 1972.

* * *

After two months in Alaska Cousteau returned to Seattle and set out to change the octopus's bad public image. Creto-Mycenaean artists, of the third millennium before Christ, might have portrayed the creature delicately, but the modern view of the "octopus monster" began with the medieval legend of Kraken, a mile-and-a-half-long mass with shiny horns that dragged ships under the sea.

Victor Hugo heightened the fear in *Toilers of the Sea:* "The Octopus, O horror! inhales a man. It draws him to itself, and into itself; and, bound, immobile, he feels himself slowly ingested by that incredible being which is the monster. The terrible tentacles are supple as leather, solid as steel, and cold as night."

Jules Verne's famous *Twenty Thousand Leagues Under the Sea* also depicted the octopus as a sinister giant. One illustration showed the titan using one of its eight arms to seize an unfortunate sailor from the *Nautilus*.

Cousteau, admitting that "the myths on which we were born die hard," sought to portray the octopus as a gentle creature of intelligence. His task was not easy, for as *Calypso* arrived in the Pacific Northwest in September 1969, Seattle newspapers reported the dramatic story of the long and bloody battle between a pair of local divers and an octopus weighing more than two hundred pounds. Even specialists from the Seattle aquarium warned the Captain about the creature's poisonous and deadly bite.

The giant octopuses living off the coast of Seattle measured up to twenty feet in diameter, yet they stretched themselves, like rubber, into numerous configurations. They swam backward by inflating their mantles with water and then expelling the liquid through short jetlike funnels. Because they lacked any protective armor against eels, groupers, and other mortal enemies, they had to find shelter in discarded shells or jars. To distract predators in the open sea, they emitted clouds of black ink while darting away, and they adopted various colors for camouflage.

The clasp of the octopus's arm, according to Cousteau, "is a strange thing, rather like that of a noose. The more one pulls on the arm, the tighter the grip becomes. And there is little hope of being able to neutralize the octopus by turning over its mantle as one can sometimes do with smaller specimens. It is one of the parts of its body that the animal defends most diligently, for it is a weak point that plays a large role in combat between octopuses."

The television episode entitled "Octopus, Octopus" revealed as much about the misrepresented sea creature as it did about Cousteau's little-understood filming techniques and his attitude toward women. The Captain, for instance, displayed as much interest in an expert's photogenic qualities as in his or her credentials. Jean-Marie Bassot, a noted French authority on nautiluses, joined the team briefly to offer guidance, but Cousteau cautioned, "For television, what we needed was not merely an expert, but an English-speaking expert." His staff spent several weeks trying to find a replacement who could take time off to be photographed giving advice to *Calypso*'s crew.

The Captain located Joanne Duffy, an attractive twenty-one-year-old Seattle-based diver who held a master's degree in marine biology. Duffy's official duties were to teach *Calypso*'s divers about the octopus's habits and to make the creatures cooperate with the filmmakers. Cousteau, however, paid attention to more than Duffy's scientific explanations. "Joanne is very feminine," he wrote in his log, "well rounded, quite striking in a bathing suit. . . . Apart from her professional qualifications, she is an intriguing woman, with just enough reserve about herself and her private life to create a faint air of mystery. Altogether, a James Bond heroine." The eventual film featured lengthy shots of the wet-suited diver-scientist brushing back her long black hair.

Behind-the-scene action also demonstrated the Captain's manipulative approach to filmmaking. For instance, while viewers were led to believe that *Calypso*'s divers waited patiently to witness a dramatic battle between large octopuses, in reality Cousteau provoked the fight by pushing two males together in front of a single amphora shelter.

After lengthy wrestling, one octopus wrapped its arms around the other and immobilized its mantle. The defeated animal began to smother and turn gray, and on the point of death by asphyxiation it became virtually white. The victor, in contrast, turned a bright red, having penetrated its foe so deeply that the tip of its arm emerged from its enemy's funnel. Just before the blanched octopus died the divers—portrayed as sympathetic naturalists even though they had, after all, started the fight—separated the combatants. They filmed the winner entering its prized amphora, as well as the defeated octopus slinking away and settling into a rusted pail that Cousteau had recently added to his undersea set.

The Captain also wanted the film to convey his image of the animal's intelligence. In writing, he could explain that "by looking at the octopus's eyes, the diver has the sensation of lucidity, of a look much more expressive than that of any fish, or even any marine animal." But for the film he had to develop a visual experiment, in this case by placing a clear jar that held a live lobster at center stage of his underwater theater, which was fully equipped with carefully arranged floodlights and cameras. From stage left he introduced a mature and hungry octopus. The eight-armed creature, after hesitating several moments with stage fright, tried to engulf its meal, only to discover the protective glass. After almost an hour the confused and frustrated octopus seemed to discover that the cork top held the key to dinner. But suddenly the cameraman yelled, "Cut!" This supposedly natural and unrehearsed scene was not appropriately lit, so the crew took the bottle away from the octopus and began the take all over again.

On the third attempt *Calypso*'s divers allowed the staged experiment to continue. The octopus—whether by luck, practice, or reasoning—succeeded in removing the cork top and grabbing the helpless lobster. From this action Cousteau concluded that "the most remarkable thing about the octopus is its ability to grasp a problem that is presented and to find a solution to it by making proper use of its physiological and psychological equipment."

The Captain also announced his supposedly patient evaluation of the complaint by fishermen that octopuses were robbing their nets. But rather than take the time to follow an actual fisherman and record any undersea activities, Cousteau arranged his own net next to "Octopus City," baited it with enticing fish, and installed lights and cameras nearby. Not surprisingly, an octopus eventually ventured a few feet from its shelter to harvest the free and easy meal. In the film the Captain claimed to have discovered new information about the creature's habits, but he failed to mention that he had choreographed the entire "experiment."

After a month in Seattle the crew sailed back down the Pacific coast, stopping in Monterey Bay, just south of San Francisco, for additional footage of sea otters. The team arrived in Southern California in early November 1969 to film and record the sounds of dolphins around Catalina Island.

Proceeding on to the Galápagos Islands, *Calypso* crossed the equator, an event calling for the traditional initiation of sailing novices. Seeing the occasion as an opportunity to frolic and be frivolous, the crew dressed in wild costumes, Bernard Delemotte as the white-bearded Neptune and Yves de Pimodan as the stunning nymph Amphitrite. King Neptune initially read a comic list of sins committed by the equatorial first timers. Other veteran "dignitaries" then pronounced sentences against the guilty, most of whom were forced to devour éclairs stuffed with cotton and covered with mustard. Repenting his cruelty, King Neptune eventually made "amends" by cleansing the novices inside and out with an enema and a soak in the plastic swimming pool on deck. Cousteau boasted that his men "are rather expert at the conduct of these rituals."

The initiated sailors arrived in the Galápagos on February 1, ready to spend two months traversing the group of fourteen islands, approximately six hundred miles west of Ecuador, that contained seven thousand human residents and the world's most acclaimed biological breeding ground, made famous by Charles Darwin. Just as *Beagle* before it, *Calypso* sought to examine and report on the archipelago's rare species.

Cousteau focused on the iguana, the only land animal to derive its sustenance exclusively from the sea, predicting his investigation would yield clues to how human physiology could be modified to allow deeper and longer dives. Dragonlike and with a dorsal chest, the iguana appears to be left over from the Age of Reptiles. Darwin described the creatures as "being of hideous aspect, having a dirty black color, stupid, and sluggish in their movements."

To sink rapidly, an iguana empties its lungs. Although it lacks gills to extract oxygen from the water, its tissues store enough for most dives. A sailor aboard Charles Darwin's *Beagle* submerged an iguana for an entire hour, and the reptile still lived. *Calypso* cameramen pushed a male iguana down to ninety feet, where its chest became concave from the pressure.

In his subsequent film and book on the Galápagos, Cousteau suggested that he and his divers allowed UCLA scientist Dr. George Bartholomew to further his studies in the iguana's natural environment. In fact, it was Bartholomew who demonstrated his previously obtained knowledge to the Captain and his cameramen. The scientist wired a male iguana to various monitors to show that the creature, when submerged, could moderate its heart rate from fifty to only eight beats per minute. Bartholomew explained that the reptile's heart could slow to four beats per minute and even stop entirely for a short period.

The television show may not have advanced the study of iguanas, but it did reveal Cousteau's fascination with fancy equipment. Most of the broadcast's first section featured the team's new "wet submarine," an undersea scooter with two small propellers and a Plexiglas cone in which the diver placed his head. The yellow sub could travel at five knots and withstand the strong currents around the islands. The film's first shot of the featured iguana, in fact, came several minutes into the show and pictured the creature clinging to an undersea rock as the wet sub zoomed just over its head.

This film also contained some of Cousteau's most entertaining animal photography. Cameras underwater and on a small boat traced the trials of a single iguana trying to escape the playful antics of a team of acrobatic sea lions. As cats might taunt a mouse, the sea lions grabbed the iguana's tail and neck. They swam circles around the awkward reptile, trying to push it away from the rocky shore so that their game could continue. The iguana trudged on determinedly, making slow advances. When it finally reached the shore and crawled up a rock, the narrator declared that "the iguana is free at last from its tormentors." With the skilled hand of a practiced comic, Cousteau paused the film for a moment. As the narrator added, "Or is he really free?" the camera slowly panned from the exhausted iguana to a sleepy sea lion resting its head on the rock above.

While Cousteau cruised aboard *Calypso* throughout the ten-thousand-square-mile archipelago, Bernard Delemotte directed a land team. Delemotte's diary recounted the strict filming schedule and his constant efforts to withstand the equatorial islands' 120 degree temperatures. It also described the team's typical after-dinner relaxation: Jacques Renoir filmed background shots; Michel Deloire and Henri Alliet repaired an underwater camera; Jacques Delcoutère wrote a letter; François Dorado plucked his guitar; and the cook cleaned up the kitchen.

Not all evenings, however, provided such peace. To obtain footage of iguanas mating, the team had placed cameras and floodlights in the midst of some five thousand reptiles resting on the lava. Switching on the lights after dusk created such a panic that the iguanas stopped all sex, crawled feverishly over each other, and seriously clawed the legs of overrun crew members.

As *Calypso* was leaving the Galápagos, an uncharted underwater boulder imposed its own bruise. The collision overturned tables and sent several men tumbling to the floor; but damage was limited to the ship's false nose, and no leaks occurred. The crushed observation chamber prompted Cousteau to sail the ship quickly through the Panama Canal and on to dry dock in New Orleans, where the false nose was rebuilt, the keel repaired, and the exterior repainted.

The refitted *Calypso* left for Belize, on the Gulf of Mexico in northern Central America, in early May 1970 to search for blue holes, deep circular caverns surrounded by flat-topped coral reefs. The Captain had first encountered the geological phenomenon in popular American magazines. Learning of legends that these sunken caves were bottomless and housed monsters, Cousteau decided to explore the mysteries of the hole at Lighthouse Reef.

The depression's diameter measured approximately a thousand feet, and the circle was broken by just two narrow passages. Cousteau had to rent a helicopter to guide *Calypso* through the widest of these coral-lined and winding channels.

Visiting geologists informed the Captain that the ocean had flooded the cave at the end of the Glacial Epoch, causing the ceiling to collapse and a hole to form. Divers quickly located the underwater stalactites which confirmed that the blue hole had once been a true cave above the surface of the water. They retrieved one "icicle" that weighed a ton and measured about twenty feet in length.

Using minisubs, the new wet submarine, and underwater scooters to explore the indigo lake, the team also discovered steep walls beneath the rim and, at about 50 feet down, an immense stone forest, lined with massive limestone pillars and columns. At a depth of 250 feet, the water became motionless, despite the tides, and fish disappeared, suggesting that no water was exchanged between the bottom of the blue hole and the ocean. Further exploration in the minisubs revealed that this sunken cave descended 400 feet.

Cousteau claimed that he "did everything possible to insure that our investigations would prove valuable from a scientific standpoint. At the same time, however, we had a television film to shoot." So with insufficent natural wonders or colorful fish to fill an hourlong segment, the Captain ordered his divers to mount their new scooters and to play tag amid the stalactites. He described the activity, duly recorded by cameramen, as a "bizarre underwater ballet, with the two scooters crossing paths and then pulling away from one another in a stream of silvery bubbles."

While *Calypso* remained off the coast of Central America, Cousteau decided to examine another blue hole—near Andros in the Bahamas —in which independent divers had located a large cavern. He entrusted what he described as "the most difficult exploration of my career" to his son.

Philippe rented a boat and spent three weeks and thirty dives preparing for the adventure. The Captain arrived, courtesy of a U.S. Navy helicopter, for only three days to be filmed descending to 180 feet and then proceeding along an 800-foot tunnel that emptied into a cave filled with stalactites. Philippe and other cameramen hurried ahead of Cousteau to record his arrival at each major checkpoint. In print and on film, the Captain later fretted that tidal currents might have swept through the corridor and trapped the divers, but no hazards appeared.

Back on the surface, the boastful Cousteau wrote in his log: "We are the possessors of a secret shared by only a few divers. We had lived through one of the most exciting adventures. We had dived to the outer limits of reasonable risk, and we had survived because our team was expert, ready, and confident of its own abilities. And also because Philippe had foreseen all the risks and taken them into account."

Calypso headed back to France on August 22, 1970, having spent almost four years at sea, journeying over a half million miles and generating enough film footage for almost twenty hourlong television segments. The dramatic and well-photographed films catapulted *The Undersea World of Jacques Cousteau* into the most acclaimed documentary series in television history, and they transformed the Captain into one of the world's most renowned celebrities. Dick Cavett, a popular American television host, gushed that "most people would rather meet Jacques Cousteau than anybody."

Despite Cousteau's public success, his log periodically revealed deep depression. In a 1968 entry, for instance, he wrote: "I have renounced my ambitions in all other areas, even though, at times, I have been sorely tempted by the attractions of a different kind of life." He lamented that he was neither physically nor mentally prepared for the adventurous life he led. He resented the required sacrifice of money, time, family ties, "and almost everything else that people generally regard as precious in life."

The Captain's sense of wonder at the sea, he continued, had "been interlaced with pain and disappointment. For every pleasure that I have derived, I have had to scale a mountain of aversion. I was the only one who knew this; and even I refused to admit it completely to myself.''

In public Cousteau frequently claimed to possess an insatiable curiosity about the sea. Privately he admitted a need ''to possess the sea, to dominate it, to conquer it.'' On several occasions he described his frustrating struggle in sexual terms. After making a small discovery, he noted, his ''satisfaction is that of a man who succeeds, at least momentarily, in having his way with the woman he loves.'' But the sea, as a lover, also bore ''temptation, disappointments, betrayals, misunderstandings, quarrels, and rages.'' Beneath the adventure and exploration, Cousteau concluded, ''there has always been a sense of being trapped.''

The Captain took setbacks harshly. After failing to discover sunken treasure in the Caribbean, for instance, he recorded his ''resentment, and almost hate, toward the unceasingly evasive and artful love of my life.'' He spent several days sulking about the sea's betrayal, talking with no one, refusing to dive. His only outlet was to write angrily: ''I will remain alone on this little ship, bitter, with accusations of infidelity running through my mind.''

A particularly troubling blow occurred in 1971, when the French government canceled Cousteau's contract to build a mobile undersea settlement. Without warning, the minister of industrial and scientific development halted the grand effort to engage oceanauts in long-term oil drilling, undersea farming, and other productive ocean activities.

The Captain had decided against pursuing Conshelf IV and V, but he continued to dream of cutting the energy, communication, and air lines that chained undersea stations to the surface. ''It became obvious to me,'' he said, ''that all the support complex had to migrate from the surface down to the immediate vicinity of the diver's habitat. The support systems had to leave the remote, unstable, stormy surface and go to the peaceful quiet of the ocean's deep.''

Cousteau had signed a $1.5 million development contract with the French government in 1968 to build ''the ultimate in deep-diving equipment, a submarine bearing the name of our water spider, the *Argyronete*.'' The three-hundred-ton vessel was to carry four ocean-auts, who would work up to eight days, for several hours a day, at two thousand feet beneath the sea. With sufficient air, electricity, and food supplies, *Argyronete* would eliminate the need for a tender ship.

The submarine was more than half built when the government halted construction. Cousteau, claiming to be caught in the crossfire of a political struggle, sued for $1.5 million in indemnities, plus a symbolic franc to cover the harm to his reputation. France's highest administrative court eventually ruled against him.

Years later Cousteau admitted that the ministry had suspended the project less because of politics than because oil companies had decided to use remote-controlled tools rather than divers to perform their deep-sea tasks. Still, he continued to glorify the submarine: "The concept remains above criticism, and the *Argyronete* family of steel water spiders will multiply in the future."

The Captain never completed the vehicle. The frustrating experience only further encouraged him to concentrate on television instead of engineering.

That Cousteau waited until his twentieth television episode to showcase dolphins suggested the difficulties inherent in filming the free-spirited mammals. As the Captain had learned in 1948, when he first slipped into the water to touch them, dolphins feared divers and scattered when approached. The filmmaker, therefore, faced a conflict. He was riding the crest of the environmental movement, portraying himself as a protector and friend of the sea's creatures; but he had a filming schedule to complete, and dolphins promised to provide a popular broadcast—if difficult to produce.

As the Captain began a renewed contract with ABC, he declared his intention not to film dolphins in aquariums and marinelands because "they seemed to me to be deformed and perverted by their captivity and their contact with man." Trained animals, he said, would not give "a true representation of the way that marine mammals lived in freedom in the sea." More important, Cousteau knew that performing dolphins had been filmed extensively; he needed a fresh angle.

The Captain, busy with other projects, entrusted most of the dolphin project to Jacques Renoir, great-grandson of the famous painter and grandson of the acclaimed movie director. The young Renoir began by constructing a camera boom that extended over *Calypso*'s prow in order to capture rare frontal views of dolphins swimming in the open sea. The team tested the device in early January 1971, off Málaga in southern Spain, but no dolphins approached the ship, even though the Captain tried to maneuver into their midst.

With typical ingenuity, Cousteau concluded that the bright yellow paint on the arm's bracing and camera housing disturbed the mammals. He ordered the *Calypso* to return to Málaga, where his crew painted the instrument a dark red, the same color as the ship's hull. When the team set to sea again, dolphins surrounded the *Calypso* and began playing about her bow.

Renoir and Cousteau also devised a floating pen into which captured dolphins were placed for observation and tests. The pool measured twenty feet in length, and about forty feet of net hung from a string of air bags, giving the unit buoyancy. The filmmakers arranged three hydrophones at different angles in the tank and positioned two underwater television cameras in the enclosure to relate the mammal's sounds to its movements.

Cousteau rationalized that the pool offered the most humane means of imprisoning wild animals. The netting, he claimed, permitted the captives to see and communicate with other dolphins. Although the mammals regularly roamed over vast distances, the Captain argued that his twenty-foot tank was "sufficiently large for a dolphin to feel practically free." He also promised to release the prisoners after no more than two or three days, thereby not allowing the dolphins to have "the opportunity to adapt to captivity, or to be deformed by it."

Initial experiments in the pool, however, proved tragic. The first seized dolphin remained dazed and motionless for hours; Falco had to affix small bolsters under the animal's snout to keep its blowhole above the water's surface. That night a storm twisted the floating tank, and the dolphin became entangled in the netting and drowned.

The following day Falco placed another specimen into the pool, but this dolphin refused to move, too. The team tried to prod it, but it would not swim. The frustrated filmmakers finally released the animal, which became alert immediately and darted away.

The third captive ate and swam about but refused to speak. According to Cousteau's log: "We've spent the day waiting for our dolphin to 'talk.' We are beginning to feel slightly ridiculous." Frustrated, the Captain decided to abandon Operation Dolphin for two months while the *Calypso* crew completed some lucrative and more productive industrial assignments.

In April Cousteau returned to his ship, off the coast of Gibraltar, and finally succeeded in placing two lively and talkative mammals in the floating pool. He proceeded to conduct a series of experiments in echolocation.

Scientists had long recognized the dolphin's range of sounds, its communication, and its sonic navigation. In fact, Aristotle wrote extensively about the mammal's abilities twenty-three centuries ago. Dolphins, it was understood, emitted clicks to conduct a sonic exploration of their surroundings. From the echoes of these sounds the mammals were able to deduce the shape of objects in the area. The clicks varied in both frequency and amplification, being more active —say, twelve hundred per second—when the dolphin explored an unfamiliar environment. Sometimes the clicks sounded more like claps, squeaks, or grinding; some reached such high frequencies that they were inaudible to man. Dolphins also exchanged whistling noises that seemed to be used for communication rather than echolocation.

Despite this knowledge, numerous mysteries about the dolphin's behavior remained. Scientists obviously didn't know if the mammal possessed a language, and they couldn't comprehend what it was saying. They didn't even fully understand how the animal produced its various sounds.

Cousteau provided no answers. His "studies" conveyed drama rather than advanced science. Replicating Marineland demonstrations that the dolphin could maneuver without use of its eyes, Cousteau installed blindfolds on his captive subjects. As expected, the mammals swam around the pool without the slightest hesitation. The Captain then spaced iron bars throughout the tank, and the blindfolded creatures maneuvered around them, too. He repeated the experiment several times until Renoir had obtained sufficient footage.

Since divers couldn't take underwater shots of the group life of dolphins by approaching the sensitive mammals directly, Cousteau decided to place a camera atop an individual animal, to return it to its school, to activate the remote-controlled camera, and then to recapture the dolphin and retrieve the pictures. In mid-April Cousteau installed a camera on the back of a large 275-pound male. The dolphin could swim; but the bulky unit retarded his speed, and the school swam right past. The team tried the experiment several times, but no burdened animal could travel at its normal rate. The Captain finally admitted, "The film that was taken by our dolphin cameramen was totally without interest."

Frustrated by the elusive ocean mammal, Renoir completed the film by adjusting his focus toward human subjects. To convey other unique forms of communication, he filmed Canary Islanders using a whistled language to communicate from distances up to six miles over a precipitous terrain. In the film "A Sound of Dolphins" Cousteau intoned that the dolphin may be taught a similar language that would enable it to express abstract thoughts to mankind.

Seeking to convey a communion between dolphin and man, Renoir also filmed members of the Imragen tribe catching thousands of mullets with the help of dolphins. The Imragens were poor fishermen of Mauritania, along the Atlantic coast of northern Africa, who moved their huts up and down the coast in search of food. Cousteau described their homes as "windowless, and even smaller and more ill-smelling than one would think possible."

In this arid region where desert meets the sea, the Imragens had been catching mullets in a similar fashion for thousands of years. Tribesmen were convinced that when they called the dolphins by slapping their sticks on the water, the mammals purposefully herded the fish into their nets. Renoir's cameras captured the chaotic scene of thousands of mullets leaping into the air to escape the dolphins, swarming dolphins brushing against the fishermen and divers, and women on the shore screaming their delight.

"One dare not say that man and dolphin eventually became accustomed to one another's presence," Cousteau observed. He suggested, however, that the Imragens could be a modern example of the ancient legends that dolphins helped and protected men in the sea. With increased human contact, the Captain hypothesized that the dolphin would become man's partner. He concluded, "What promise the future holds for us—and what responsibility!"

Cousteau's television show on dolphins won an Emmy award for outstanding documentary program achievement.

Cousteau's photography may have been appreciated, but he increasingly revealed a disturbing elitism. Even beyond the Captain's preference for presenting more shots of himself and his crew than of undersea creatures was his condescending approach to native peoples.

Cousteau discussed the Eskimo in Alaska as would a patronizing tourist. In a chapter of a subsequent book entitled *The Happy Eskimo,* he informed readers that Eskimos "are not a saving people, and they love to spend. . . . They are trigger happy and shoot at anything merely for the joy of it." Moreover, he wrote, "Eskimos do not seem to have a knack for tinkering, and they are unable to repair their engines or even to maintain them properly."

Wanting good postcard shots of the "typical Eskimo," the Captain tried to convince the natives to build an igloo. Failing to appreciate that only Eskimos of the Canadian Arctic made use of this form of shelter, he proceeded to construct his own. While Eskimos chuckled at the Frenchmen cutting blocks of ice with a handsaw, Cousteau expressed "astonishment" and "disappointment" that "there was not a single resident of the village who knew how to go about constructing an igloo."

Though willing to torment wild creatures and patronize native peoples, Cousteau condemned tourists for doing the same. The explorer believed that only he should be allowed to enter a pristine wilderness or walk along a primeval beach. Others, he asserted, should be content to experience nature vicariously through his photographs and movies.

While in the Galápagos Islands, the *Calypso* crew returned one morning from filming undersea creatures to encounter forty tourists photographing the wild landscape, iguanas, and sea lions. Members of the group passed Cousteau's divers, smiled, and said hello. But the leader of *Calypso*'s team noted in his diary: "None of us could say a word. Like robots, we walked toward our camp looking straight ahead. We were all so upset that we didn't trust ourselves to say anything, or even to look at one another."

Oblivious of their own standard red caps and yellow-lined wet suits, Cousteau's crew criticized the usual tourist costume: straw hats and flowered shirts. The resulting film, "The Dragons of Galápagos," portrayed the visitors as fat and awkward buffoons, particularly in contrast with *Calypso*'s muscular bikini-clad divers. Background circus music mocked their less than graceful ways.

Cousteau did credit the travelers with an enthusiasm for nature, but he described their zeal as "naïve." "Seeing tourists on the islands of the Galápagos," he noted in his log, "I could not help believing that man has degenerated alarmingly." Unmindful of the physical comforts he and his crew enjoyed aboard *Calypso* and of the scientists provided to him by the local government, Cousteau declared, "If these men and women had not been led by guides and accompanied by a troop of servants capable of providing them with food and finding them a place to sleep, of entertaining them and caring for their well-being, they would never have survived. Our species, I am sorry to say, is physically decadent."

Cousteau's elitism was particularly apparent in his coverage of the Kawashkar Indians living on one of the Tierra del Fuego inlets at the southern tip of Chile. The tribe, battered by conquering armies and poverty, had declined from a population of four thousand a century before to only five family units. In his television segment, "Life at the End of the World," the Captain expressed the appropriate concern for an endangered species of humans: "It is a shame that we cannot extend to threatened human populations the same protection and encouragement that we have begun to extend to other living creatures." But John O'Connor, *The New York Times* reviewer, observed, "The protection and encouragement offered by Mr. Cousteau and his crew seemed to extend no farther than an eagerness to get the material recorded for a TV special."

Once again, Cousteau condemned tourists—this time British military men—who visited the isolated inlet. He filmed the poor Indians trying to sell souvenirs to the sailors, while the narrator remarked: "Rosa had labored long stitching her bark canoe. Nobody will buy her boat. Her picture is taken."

"But what of the *Calypso* crew that was taking a far more elaborate picture of the situation?" asked O'Connor. Rather than offer a compassionate response to the Indians' poverty, Cousteau employed his helicopter to film the village, and he brought expensive recording equipment into the tribe's huts. O'Connor concluded: "After getting all those nice shots of sad faces, the luxurious *Calypso* sailed off into the sunset. One nagging question: Did Mr. Cousteau bother to buy Rosa's boat?"

Despite his patronizing ways, the Captain produced many brilliant television adventures. Some of his best featured the ice-studded seas of Antarctica. His 1972–73 expedition generated four hourlong shows, for which Cousteau received two Emmys. More than fifteen years later he still considers Antarctica to be the most wonderous spot he has ever been. "It's the most beautiful place in the world," he declares. "Everything is pristine—not crystal clear, but much clearer than crystal. It's something you remember all your life."

Although *Calypso* had spent several months in Alaska a few years before, the small boat had never journeyed to the polar region, nor had it withstood floating ice fields. In preparation for the Antarctica adventure, therefore, the Captain reinforced his ship's planking and ordered thorough repairs. He also installed ultramodern satellite communications equipment in order to conduct a collaborative mapping project with the U.S. National Aeronautics and Space Administration (NASA).

Calypso departed from Monaco on September 29, 1972, following an elaborate reception hosted by Prince Rainier and his son, Prince Albert. Two months later the vessel arrived at Ushuaia, the southernmost settlement on the planet. Here Cousteau transferred some of his equipment, including the diving saucer, to an Argentine vessel that served as the expedition's supply ship.

A violent storm flared up as *Calypso* crossed the Drake Passage between Cape Horn and the continent of Antartica. Fierce winds and drifting ice battered the ship for four days, but the refitted vessel performed well.

About 250 miles north of the Antarctic Circle, *Calypso* stopped at King George Island, which had served as a butchering ground for whalers during the late nineteenth and early twentieth centuries, before huge factory ships began to process the mammals at sea. Cousteau's team tried to sort through the remnants of thousands of whales to reconstruct the skeleton of a ninety-foot-long blue.

Calypso then sailed farther south to Deception Island, a circular bit of land dotted with several active volcanoes. The unlikely juxtaposition of fire and ice allowed cameramen to obtain remarkable photographs of steaming glaciers.

Deception Island also hosted huge colonies of "tuxedoed" penguins, which cruised underwater at about ten miles an hour and accelerated to speeds exceeding thirty miles an hour. The Captain employed special slow-motion cameras to show the birds clearly using their wings to "fly" through the sea, their feet serving as rudders.

The crew also witnessed the penguin's elaborate mating ritual, in which couples build a nest of stones on land before exchanging a "marriage" pebble. They traced young chicks struggling to survive the harsh weather and attacking skua birds. And they learned that juveniles, abandoned by their parents, eventually enter the sea and adopt an ice floe, on which they are pushed by winds and currents for four years before they, too, return to land to breed.

Cousteau, touched by the environmental activism growing in the United States and Europe in the late 1960's and early 1970's, increasingly integrated ecological themes into his films. He converted the penguin, for instance, into a symbol of the interconnectedness of the planet's resources. "Today the penguins are protected from slaughter," he commented during the second of the Antarctic segments. "But their lives are already infected by toxic chemicals—as deep-sea currents carry wastes from heavily populated continents to these remote Antarctic seas. As the world's waters mix, there is but one ocean. Not until we understand this unity can we safeguard the pathways of future penguins in flight.''

A more immediate tragedy struck *Calypso*'s crew three days after Christmas. Michel Laval, the first mate, had climbed one of the glaciers to examine the properties of ice at higher elevations. When he went to meet the helicopter on its regular trip between the ship and the island, he slipped on the ice and struck the helicopter's tail. He died instantly. Cousteau ordered *Calypso* to return to Ushuaia, where he made arrangements to transport Laval's body aboard a plane to Paris.

Calypso quickly headed back to Deception Island, picked up the camera crew left there, and headed south. Temperatures dropped and ice floes increased. Drifting glacial masses often forced the boat to change course suddenly. On several occasions the crew had to send the helicopter ahead to aid navigation.

Calypso crossed the Antarctic Circle on January 19, 1973, and soon encountered a monumental iceberg rising 240 feet above the water. Divers donned their bright red insulated dry suits and entered the frigid sea to discover that the iceberg's underwater portion was shaped like a giant golf ball, symmetrical and pebbled.

The weather turned crystal clear the following day, allowing the cameramen to capture spectacular footage of stark white angular landscapes against the rich blue sky. Philippe launched his multicolored hot-air balloon while other crew members ascended in the helicopter. They photographed each other, with *Calypso* and icebergs in the background.

Through the poetry of his pictures and narration, Cousteau revealed to millions of television viewers the exotic elegance of the sculptural ice formations that dotted the lonely southern seas. "Surrounded by a majestic beauty that still haunts me today," he commented, "I know that here the sea is only a couple of degrees from freezing solid, that life teems at the edge of death."

Cousteau created an assortment of adventures to dramatize his images. Divers, for instance, followed seals through enlarged holes in the iceberg that had been formed by the salt water's corrosive action. Two crew members used the diving saucer to examine walls of ice at a polar depth record of twelve hundred feet; there they obtained the first photographs of the elusive icefish, a semitransparent creature with a kind of antifreeze in its blood. And Philippe led a diving party through the labyrinth of a disintegrating crystal grotto as the environment reverberated with the crackling of ice.

The most dramatic adventure, however, was unexpected, caused in part by Cousteau's failure to heed warnings and return north before the waters became an impassable ice pack. After a morning's filming of blue-eyed cormorants and fur seals, Cousteau and his crew were suddenly engulfed in a raging storm. Although at anchor, *Calypso* had to run its engines to hold position against the fierce winds.

More treacherous than the gale were the fields of drift ice, created by the crumbling face of glaciers that had weakened during the short summer's thaw. The Captain tried for hours to avoid the sharp ice rocks, pushed about by erratic currents, but a large block smashed into *Calypso*'s bow, ripping away numerous planks. Another bounced against the stern, breaking the shaft of the port propeller. A third bent the starboard propeller.

The blizzard, with gale winds reaching a hundred miles per hour, lasted for three days and three nights. *Calypso,* loaded with some thirty tons of ice and snow, limped about the small bay on one damaged propeller in zero visibility. Dependent upon radar, the vessel struggled to avoid other ice blocks. The heavy shell of ice endangered *Calypso*'s stability, making it top-heavy and vulnerable to capsizing. According to the Captain, "Without exaggeration we were in grave danger of losing the ship and the crew. There was no certainty at all that we could make it."

The wind died down on February 11, allowing sailors to clear the ship of its load of ice, repair the damaged planks, and secure the broken propeller shaft so it would not jam the rudder. Alerted to Cousteau's troubles through the NASA communications system, the Argentine Navy sent a vessel that offered to tow *Calypso* to safety across the rough Drake Passage. On film the Captain boldly declared that his trusted ship would make it under its own steam; in reality, the damaged *Calypso* followed a path cleared by the Argentine icebreaker.

Cousteau converted his pictures of the vast white realm into four award-winning television shows and a feature-length movie. The *Los Angeles Herald Examiner* called the series "a remarkable amalgam of poetry and science." *Variety* declared that "Cousteau and his men brought that remote part of this earth to the living room in all its natural beauties, its splendor, its sheer magnificence." The *Oakland Tribune* said, "The Cousteau scripts rank with the finest writing in television." Concluded the *Philadelphia Inquirer:* "Through the petty schools of intellectual sardines and cultural piranhas who infest television, Jacques Cousteau sails like a slim and stately marlin, majestic and serene. . . . He gives television what it usually lacks: class."

Such success, however, would not last forever.

Jacques-Yves Cousteau.

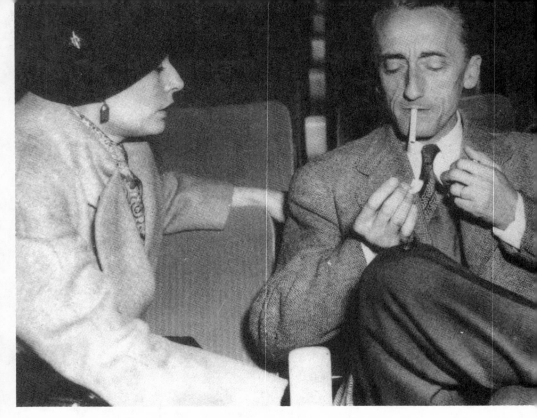

Above, Cousteau relaxes with his wife, Simone, at Royal Festival Hall, London, before a 1954 showing of his films. The Captain made his first underwater movie without any breathing apparatus or modern photographic equipment. Shooting time was limited because both the star (Frédéric Dumas) and the cameraman (Cousteau) had to hold their breaths. *(Wide World Photos)*

Left, Cousteau, aged forty-seven in 1957, speaks at a scientific conference shortly after he was selected to direct the Oceanographic Institute in Monaco. Cousteau's first act as director was to throw out the seat cushion used by his bureaucratic predecessor. The Captain steadfastly resisted the sedentary life of an administrator. *(Wide World Photos)*

Prince Rainier and Princess Grace of Monaco observe the Galeazzi diving suit, on display at the Oceanographic Institute. The Prince, impressed with *The Silent World,* hoped Cousteau's growing notoriety and his connections with funding sources would enliven the research center and museum.   (*Wide World Photos*)

Cousteau appears in the film *World Without Sun,* his ninety-three-minute movie recounting the Conshelf II expedition. Five oceanauts spent a month thirty-five feet below the surface of the Red Sea in the 1963 project financed by the French national petroleum office.   (*Wide World Photos*)

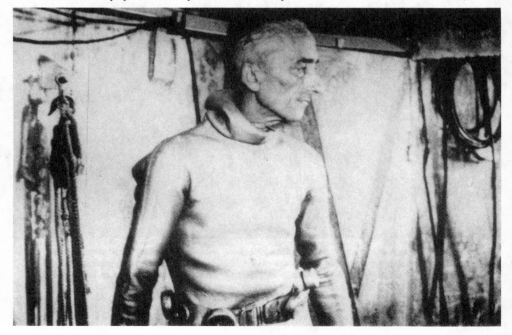

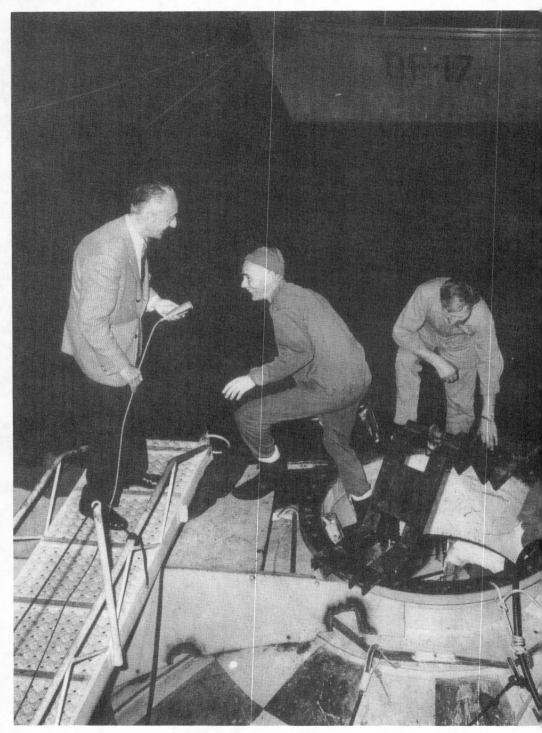

The Captain, microphone in hand, welcomes André Laban, one of six Conshelf III adventurers, as he returns from working twenty-one days in the chilling darkness 325 feet below the surface of the Mediterranean. Ever the promoter, Cousteau arranged for Eurovision to broadcast to seventeen countries a live report of the oceanauts' return from the deep. (*Wide World Photos*)

Jacques, Simone, and their pet dachshund pose aboard *Calypso*. The Captain had arrived in New York City to participate in an international oceanographic conference. (*Wide World Photos*)

Thomas Moore, left, president of ABC Television Network, is joined by Cousteau and producer David Wolper in announcing *The Undersea World of Jacques Cousteau,* a series of ABC-TV specials begun in the fall of 1967. Television diverted Cousteau from further efforts to research the ocean environment, to improve diving technology, or to expand undersea habitation. But the Captain made the conscious choice, as he liked to put it, to awaken millions to the wonders of the oceans and the dangers they faced.   (*Wide World Photos*)

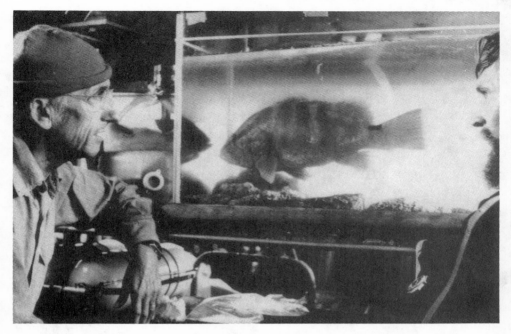

The Captain and diver Bernard Delemotte examine a small grouper. In one segment of the *Undersea World* series, Cousteau tried to demonstrate that groupers aggressively protect their territories. But rather than wait for an intruding grouper, Cousteau tricked the fish into attacking its own image in an underwater mirror. The behind-the-scenes maneuver ended in tragedy when the conquering grouper ate mirror fragments and died.   (*Wide World Photos*)

Calypso and Cousteau weather a blizzard within the Antarctic Circle. Gale winds reaching a hundred miles per hour battered the ship for three days and three nights. *Calypso,* loaded with some thirty tons of ice and snow, limped about Hope Bay on one damaged propeller in zero visibility. ''Without exaggeration,'' said Cousteau in 1963, ''we were in grave danger of losing the ship and the crew.'' The Captain received two Emmys for the four hour-long shows on Antarctica.   (*Wide World Photos*)

Philippe Cousteau, the Captain's younger son, starred in, directed, or photographed several of the early television specials. Appointed vice-president of the family's film production company, he appeared to be Jacques Cousteau's confidant and alter ego. In reality, father and son sparred frequently.   (*Wide World Photos*)

Philippe and Jacques Cousteau appear at an Involvement Day, a carnival-like conference on the ocean environment that promoted the Captain's celebrity and highlighted his ideas. The regional U.S. gatherings were organized by the Cousteau Society, a membership-supported organization founded in January 1974 and dedicated "to the protection and improvement of the quality of life."   (*Wide World Photos*)

On June 28, 1979, Philippe banked his seaplane and prepared to land on the Tagus River, not far from the Portuguese capital of Lisbon. Suddenly and without warning, the plane flipped over and tore apart, violently throwing the crew forward. One of the plane's two engines slammed into the cockpit, crushing Philippe's body. The French Embassy arranged a funeral service in Lisbon's St. Louis-des-Français church. Jacques and Simone, left, flank the coffin, while Philippe's widow, Janice Cousteau, stands at the right. *(Wide World Photos)*

After a short ceremony, officers placed the coffin aboard a Portuguese warship. Eighteen miles from shore, mariners saluted while friends slid Philippe's coffin into the Atlantic Ocean. ''Cousteau lost his future when Philippe died,'' commented Philippe's widow. *(Wide World Photos)*

Left, after ABC-TV canceled *The Undersea World of Jacques Cousteau*, citing critical reviews and continued rating declines, the Captain developed a series for the Public Broadcasting Service that tended to focus on human tragedy, environmental disasters, and lost cultures. Here, Bernard Falco and the Captain examine two bronze statuettes recovered during Cousteau's search for the legendary city of Atlantis.   (*Wide World Photos*)

Below, Detroit Mayor Coleman Young presents Cousteau with the keys to the Motor City in September 1980. The Captain was filming two television segments on the Greater St. Lawrence Seaway for the National Office of Canadian Film. According to a Canadian working with the *Calypso* team, ''It seems Cousteau was content with simply using his famous name to get the film board's million dollars.'' (*Wide World Photos*)

Jean-Michel Cousteau, the Captain's older son, shows a model of *Calypso* to Norfolk, Virginia, mayor Vincent Thomas in 1980. Using his administrative skills, Jean-Michel consolidated many of his father's operations in Norfolk, where he proposed to develop a major museum and entertainment center. But after the Cousteau Society refused to contribute its $5 million toward the center's construction, Norfolk's city council withdrew its support.   (*Wide World Photos*)

Jean-Michel and Jacques Cousteau cuddle with a rare giant river otter during their trip through the Amazon basin. The Captain billed the two-year adventure, begun in February 1982, as "the greatest and most difficult expedition I have ever undertaken," as well as "the most ambitious land-sea-air expedition in history."   (*Wide World Photos*)

Alcyone, Cousteau's windship, set sail from La Rochelle, France, in May 1985. The vessel features two Turbosails, which lower fuel costs by up to 40 percent. In summer 1985, Cousteau's two ships began a five-year around-the-planet adventure, entitled *Rediscovery of the World,* that is the focus of twenty hour-long television specials financed by Ted Turner's cable network.   *(Wide World Photos)*

Calypso, a converted World War II minesweeper, is named after the beautiful sea maiden in Homer's *Odyssey,* who reigned over the island of Ogygia. Calypso, according to the legend, loved Odysseus and held him for seven years in a bondage abounding with delights. Similarly, the ship *Calypso* has captured Cousteau's time and imagination for almost four decades.   *(Wide World Photos)*

CHAPTER SEVEN

Setbacks

Despite favorable reviews of his four-part Antarctic series, Cousteau was losing his television audience, and executives at the American Broadcasting Company became openly concerned about the show's popularity. The distraught Captain also had to wait over a year for *Calypso,* damaged by ice storms, to be repaired. He finally left for Isla Mujeres, off the northeastern tip of Mexico's Yucatán Peninsula, on October 17, 1974, but his heart was not in the expedition.

The resulting film, "The Sleeping Sharks of Yucatán," exposed the unique behavior of cave-dwelling bull and lemon sharks, which unlike other species, didn't need to swim constantly in order to obtain enough oxygen to survive. Yet Cousteau couldn't develop an hourlong program around sleeping sharks alone, primarily because the only drama occurred when his divers, in a cave about eighty feet beneath the surface, provoked a large bull shark to lunge at them. He had to turn to other subjects, including a massive manta ray, with a wing span of nearly twenty-six feet, that eclipsed the sun as it "flew" above the cameramen. Most of the show, however, consisted of unrelated "filler" needed to complete ABC's time requirements. With film footage of Chichén Itzá and other fabled Mayan ruins taken from a converted World War II seaplane, the show degenerated into little more than a disjointed travelogue.

Critics said the disappointing film lacked Cousteau's personal attention. The Captain, in fact, had abandoned his filming schedule several times to assume lucrative mapping contracts with NASA. On one occasion he helped test the accuracy of LANSAT 1 and LANSAT 2, which photographed well-defined areas of the Bahamian reef from the sky, while Cousteau and a small crew measured the transparency and reflective properties of the water and marine sediments. Cousteau Society scientist Richard Murphy defended the diversion by declaring that satellite mapping was "totally consistent with the Cousteau spirit of ocean exploration—to use the latest technology to develop simple equipment which will give more people greater access to the environment."

With the Captain distracted, his cameramen spent an additional month off Isla Mujeres trying to photograph the annual migration of tropical spiny lobsters. Day after day they located only a few scattered creatures huddled inside their dens. The closest to marching crustaceans—before the cameras and bright lights disturbed them— were three lobsters moving a few yards in perfect synchronization, with one's antennule touching the posterior walking legs of the lobster ahead.

The crew abandoned the area for a few hours in early January 1975, when strong winds forced *Calypso* into shore for shelter. After the storm had subsided, they returned to their waiting spot, only to pass scores of fishing boats filled with an estimated seven hundred thousand spiny lobsters. Finding no crustaceans on the seafloor, Cousteau tried to salvage the show by presenting shoals of colorful reef fish, but reviewers complained that the film lacked both marching lobsters and drama.

In response to such criticism and continued rating declines, ABC canceled *The Undersea World of Jacques Cousteau* in early 1975. The network agreed to broadcast three already edited shows in 1976, but the Captain lost funding for new expeditions.

Long the laggard in network competition, ABC had finally struggled to achieve success with popular prime-time programs such as *Laverne and Shirley, Happy Days,* and *Starsky and Hutch.* A new breed of executives, stressing financial returns, measured only how the number of viewers translated into advertising dollars. They initially justified the cancellation by expressing the need to join CBS and NBC in barring outside documentaries, but a network spokesman admitted that the Cousteau specials had "slipped below the surface bit by bit and were not successful." He added that reviewers found the latest segments to be uneven.

Cousteau offered a different perspective. He argued that ABC executives had "systematically torpedoed his shows by airing them at odd hours." It was true that stations broadcast one of the final shows at 10:00 P.M., too late for the large audience of children who normally watched the adventure films. But Cousteau specials shown during earlier hours also had dropped in the rating charts over the previous year and a half. In fact, the last segment, aired in May 1976, averaged only an 11 rating, considered "very poor" by television officials; it ranked sixty-eighth of sixty-eight shows on the Nielsen list.

Of the networks, the Captain declared, "I think they underestimate the public. It is thirsty for knowledge. Not for the junk that is offered." He even accused television executives of "trying to murder nonfiction films." The cancellation, he maintained, was "a political reaction against the family hour," the government declaration that evening television shows aired before 9:00 P.M. had to be family-oriented.

From a strictly financial standpoint, the loss of revenue came not long after Cousteau had purchased an expensive seaplane. More damaging, he lost access to millions of viewers and admirers.

In addition to the enormous strain associated with ABC's cancellation, Cousteau struggled to reduce tensions within his own family. Philippe had broken away in 1969 to establish a production company in Los Angeles, and he remained bitter toward his parents for rejecting his wife. At the same time Jan heightened the divisions between Philippe and Jean-Michel by arguing that her husband should be the heir apparent.

Around 1974 Jacques and Philippe began to reconcile. Missing his son's ideas and enthusiasm, the Captain recognized his need for a like-minded companion to stimulate his work. For his part, Philippe realized that at least professionally, he'd be better off with his creative father. Already Philippe's cinematographic work on his father's shows had won him two Emmys and six other nominations.

Philippe, however, would not regain his mother's favor until the birth of Alexandra in 1976. When the new grandparents finally accepted Philippe's marriage, they opened the door for him to become director of his father's film production company and vice-president of the Cousteau Society, the U.S.-based environmental organization his father had founded in 1974.

Jean-Michel, relegated to administrative tasks on his father's expeditions, felt unwanted and sought independence as an architect. The Captain, however, encouraged his elder son to skip the traditional internship with a large architectural firm and concentrate on marine design. He periodically arranged jobs for Jean-Michel, including the design for a marine exhibit on the *Queen Mary,* docked permanently in Long Beach, California.

Jean-Michel's marriage never presented a problem for his parents. He had met Anne-Marie, a native of Rodez, in central France, while attending architecture school. They had two children, Fabien in 1968 and Céline in 1972. Anne-Marie took up photography, and the family moved into a rented house in Los Angeles, where Jean-Michel worked at odd jobs, including teaching blind students to swim and dive. Ann-Marie claims the young family often lacked money for even the bare necessities.

Unlike Philippe, who resented allegations that he used his father's fame for his own advantage, Jean-Michel eventually cashed in on his famous lineage by hitting the lecture circuit with slide shows and inexpensive short films about the undersea life. The Captain objected to his son's cut-rate efforts, but Jean-Michel soon averaged a lucrative three speaking engagements a week.

Jean-Michel also organized a travel service, named Project Ocean Search, that arranged three or four diving expeditions each year for rich tourists. Thirty or so participants paid several thousand dollars for the natural experience and the vacation, as well as the prestige of diving with a Cousteau. The eight-day to monthlong excursions explored sunken ships and coral reefs. Jean-Michel attracted a diverse mix of individuals, "some college students, some older people, some world travelers, some who've never been out of their home state. Put all that in a blender," he said, "and it really works well. They learn from one another."

When the senior Cousteau knew that ABC would not renew his contract, he spent most of his time searching for new funds and a new outlet for his films. He eventually turned to Robert Anderson, chairman of Atlantic Richfield, the giant petroleum corporation headquartered in Los Angeles.

Few suspected that an oil company would support an environmentalist, but after the embargo by the Organization of Petroleum Exporting Countries (OPEC), skyrocketing gasoline prices, lengthy lines at filling stations, and allegations of huge oil company profits, major petroleum firms were desperately seeking ways to improve their public images. Mobil, for instance, sponsored the award-winning Masterpiece Theatre throughout the Public Broadcasting Service. Anderson, considered one of the industry's maverick futurists, decided his firm would benefit by being associated with the famous Captain Cousteau.

Anderson agreed to provide a tax-exempt grant to KCET, the public television channel in Los Angeles, for the production of twelve new Cousteau shows over a three-year period. KCET promised to market the hourlong broadcasts to other PBS stations across the United States. The contract identified the Captain and Philippe as coproducers and granted them independence from editorial supervision by Atlantic Richfield or KCET.

The Cousteau Odyssey Series reflected subtle changes in Cousteau's approach to his world. While the ABC broadcasts focused on colorful animals and dramatic adventures, the PBS shows tended to dwell on problems: environmental disasters; lost cultures; human tragedy. Cousteau's narration became more melancholy. No longer did he dream of new worlds and deeper descents. Instead, he sermonized about death and the decline of civilizations.

Cousteau's gloom resulted in part from troublesome world events in the mid to late 1970's. The oil crisis had created economic chaos, and most experts foresaw dire consequences for the end of the petroleum era. Environmentalists repeatedly exposed the destructiveness of industrial pollution. Even President Jimmy Carter spoke of a national malaise.

Personal frustrations also tempered the Captain's enthusiasm. He reached his sixty-fifth birthday and found himself still struggling to raise money for expeditions. He remained an international celebrity, but his wave of notoriety seemed to have crested. Fifteen years had passed since he appeared on the cover of *Time* or been the center of such media attention. Perhaps more significant, Cousteau's recent television shows had been criticized, his creative genius questioned.

Responsibilities for running a far-flung empire also began to wear on him. The Cousteau Society demanded almost constant attention, his diving equipment companies faced challenges as they expanded rapidly, and the Oceanographic Institute in Monaco still exacted at least a day each week from his hectic schedule. The adventurer had become an administrator, a role that conflicted with his free-spirited temperament.

The new television series on vanishing civilizations, although providing an audience for Cousteau's film, demanded more effort than it gave elation. The shows, the Captain said, were "more difficult than those we did with the animals because these things are inanimate objects. The problem is to make them interesting.''

Cousteau didn't reveal his frustration at a press conference in late 1975, when *Calypso* prepared to sail from Monaco for a yearlong archaeology project in the Aegean Sea. He expounded on the many wonders of the sea and explained his plans for locating submerged cities and shipwrecks from all ages. ''We're beginning another major undertaking,'' he declared.

Disappointments, however, seemed to haunt the Captain. Not long after leaving port, *Calypso*'s engine and clutches broke down, leaving the small ship adrift on the open sea. Mechanics worked day and night to complete temporary repairs.

For more than a month Cousteau and his crew hobbled around Greece, searching for ancient wrecks that contained precious bronze statues. They located a few pieces of pottery, but no trace of a well-endowed vessel. The *Calypso* team moved to the Bay of Pylos, site of the Battle of Navarino during the Greek War of Independence, but again discovered little of value.

The Captain then decided to try a sure bet—a famous sunken Roman ship at Andikithira, where, in 1901, sponge divers had discovered a rich assortment of ancient Greek art and artifacts, including several striking bronze figures. The turn-of-the-century recovery operation also located a clocklike mechanism that contained twenty gear wheels, several dials, and inscribed plates. Archaeologists identified the instrument as an astrolabe, a navigational tool used to observe positions of the stars. This major discovery proved that the ancient Greeks had developed advanced mathematics and astronomy.

Cousteau hoped the Andikithira site would reveal other treasures that the early divers had either overlooked or could not obtain with their rudimentary tools. Ever ready with modern technologies, Cousteau employed an underwater vacuum that sucked large piles of debris into collection baskets on the surface ship, and he equipped his diving saucer with a powerful blower that exposed artifacts hidden under the sand. His sophisticated photographic equipment—including a new side-scan sonar system developed by Professor Harold Edgerton—also allowed him to survey the seafloor.

Calypso remained at Andikithira for just one week, and the divers recovered only pottery fragments and three bronze artifacts, including a small statue of an ancient Greek boxer. Nevertheless, Cousteau declared success and developed an hourlong broadcast on the effort, entitled "Diving for Roman Plunder." He concluded the expedition by announcing, "Another handful of fragments have been returned to man's visible inheritance from the past . . . telling of civilizations that have come and gone." Reviewers protested that the Captain padded his show with ponderous interviews, including footage of Greece's secretary-general for culture thanking the Captain for retrieving his country's ancient art.

Cousteau then turned his attention to the sunken ship *Britannic,* larger than the sister *Titanic* and the greatest passenger vessel ever built until the *Queen Mary.* In November 1916 the *Britannic,* which the British had converted into a hospital ship for World War I, suffered an explosion that ripped a large hole in its hull. In less than an hour the ship sank to the bottom of the sea. Thirty people died.

The British Admiralty failed to determine the exact cause of the tragedy. Some specialists blamed a German torpedo; others pointed to a mine. The Germans argued that the *Britannic,* in defiance of its neutral status as a hospital ship, had secretly carried fresh troops; the British denied the charge. Experts also couldn't agree on why a single explosive had destroyed this supposedly unsinkable ship, the hull of which had been reinforced after the *Titanic* disaster. Cousteau promised to resolve the controversies.

The Captain had placed advertisements in British newspapers to recruit survivors of the *Britannic* for his film. The only respondent was Sheila Macbeth Mitchell, an eighty-six-year-old grandmother from Scotland who had been a volunteer nurse aboard the ship when it sank. For Cousteau's cameras she recalled life aboard the *Britannic* and jokingly asked *Calypso*'s divers to retrieve her sixty-year-old alarm clock from Cabin 15. Falco tried to take the sprightly woman in the diving saucer to investigate the wreck, but she developed seasickness.

To film the sunken ship, the Captain employed a Galeazzi submersible decompression chamber filled with a breathing mixture of helium, nitrogen, and oxygen. Three divers descended for only fifteen-minute assignments before returning to the chamber, located 130 feet beneath the surface. They were then hoisted aboard *Calypso* for decompression that lasted a total of two hours and forty minutes.

Cousteau made two dives using the helium mixture to inspect the ship's holds personally. From the brief examination he declared that the *Britannic* had indeed been a hospital ship and that it had been sunk by a German mine. Moreover, he announced that the explosion had occurred near the ship's coal bunker, causing coal dust to erupt. And so, he noted proudly, "The mystery that had shrouded the sinking of the *Britannic* for sixty years was solved at last."

For the final two shows of the first PBS season, Cousteau pieced together clips that he had made while roaming throughout the Aegean and that Philippe had taken above Bimini and Easter Island. He integrated the shots into a two-part special entitled "Calypso's Search for Atlantis."

According to the ancient Greek philosopher Plato, a mighty and advanced empire, based on an island or continent somewhere beyond the "Pillars of Hercules," had virtually conquered the Mediterranean world. Plato described the beautiful capital city of Atlantis as being ringed by canals, filled with temples and palaces, and inhabited by noble and wise people. The empire, "larger than Egypt and Libya," enjoyed fabulous wealth. Over the years, however, Atlanteans became corrupt and warlike, causing Zeus to "punish them that they might be chastened and improve." Shortly after the Athenians defeated the Atlanteans in battle, according to Plato, "there occurred violent earthquakes and floods, and in a single day and night of destruction all the warlike men in a body sank into the earth, and the island of Atlantis in like manner disappeared in the depths of the sea."

Scholars argued about whether Plato's "Pillars of Hercules" were the headlands overlooking the Strait of Gibraltar or the two promontories on the southern coast of the Aegean island of Crete (then called Mycenae), but they all agreed that Atlantis would have been in the Atlantic Ocean or the Mediterranean Sea. Nonetheless, Philippe initially sought clues to the Atlantis legend on Easter Island and Coco Island in the Pacific Ocean.

From the seaplane Cousteau's airborne team also investigated the "Bimini road," a reversed J-shaped configuration—more than six hundred yards in length—which had puzzled scholars since its discovery near Florida in the 1960's. In a long and labored interview atop the floating aircraft, historian and explorer Dr. David Zink told Philippe how the road was probably a megalithic site, such as Stonehenge in England. Viewers learned nothing about who had placed the fifteen-ton stones into a careful pattern, but the Cousteaus declared with certainty that the road had not served Atlantis. They reached similar "conclusions" about the archaeological treasures of the Sargasso Sea and the Azores.

Captain Cousteau eventually concentrated his search for the lost civilization on Crete and its outlying islands: Dia, Pseira, and the volcanic Santorini (more often called Thira). Historians and archaeologists knew that from this region the advanced Minoan culture had dominated the eastern Mediterranean for fifteen hundred years, until its power declined abruptly in the fifteenth century B.C. Evidence for the kind of civilization Plato described, however, was extremely flimsy.

On the barren and uninhabited island of Dia, Falco identified from the helicopter what appeared to be a submerged harbor. Divers located the area and spent two months excavating a plot measuring ten yards by ten yards, using the air lift to extract layers of mud and history. Under ten feet of sediment they recovered ancient Minoan pottery— indications that the harbor had been used as long ago as 2000 B.C. In his film Cousteau pondered whether Dia had been the port and military outpost for the Minoan kings headquartered at Knossos.

Calypso's team then moved to the island of Pseira, on which Cousteau and his helicopter pilot spotted an uneven wall extending a hundred yards into the sea. Divers discovered that this site also contained thousands of jars, pitchers, and vases, which Greek experts again declared to be from the Minoan civilization. The Captain theorized that the area had been another ancient harbor in which a row of ships, laden with goods, had sunk.

At Santorini, the volcanic island that erupted about 1450 B.C., Cousteau toured the excavated city of Akrotiri. Dr. Christos Doumas, the excavation director, slowly guided the Captain through a network of restored streets and houses, spending long moments admiring the ancient frescoes. Cousteau remarked, "The Minoan artists told us of a fragrant world of animals and flowering plants, of playing children and mating birds. But they also revealed a less visible interior landscape—the poised serenity of a golden age of art, an open joy in the senses, the innocence of a civilization that believed it might last forever."

After scores of dives around Santorini, however, Cousteau complained, "There is nothing whatsoever there to be found. Everything is covered in lava and nothing can ever be found." According to the Captain, Plato was simply a clever theoretician who created "a fantasy of Atlantis as his model for a perfect civilization. Atlantis was never a reality, but the myth was carried on after Plato." Still, Cousteau, demonstrating an increased commitment to environmentalism, claimed that the myth of a disappearing civilization contained a critical warning for the modern world: Unless we stop our wasteful ways, our society, too, will vanish.

Critics attacked the pieced-together series. They complained that the Captain burdened his shows with imposed melodrama and that he subjected viewers to such rhetoric as "Our descent into the void" and "For a long instant, I feel that, like Dante, I am on a journey to hell." John O'Connor of *The New York Times* called it a "two-hour television exploration that is at least 60 minutes longer than substantive content warrants. . . . [Cousteau] did not gather enough solid material to justify hour-long productions. And, considering that these fulfill his programming contract for the current season, the obvious padding becomes all the more questionable for public television."

For the first six months of 1977 *Calypso* lay idle in Monaco while the Captain tried to organize a new project. Building on the ecological lessons of his Atlantean expedition, Cousteau eventually convinced the United Nations and the Mediterranean Commission, which he chaired, that *Calypso* should conduct a thorough analysis of the Mediterranean's marine environment in order to measure the impact of pollution and industrial development.

Cousteau shuttled back and forth to European and North African capitals for the permits needed to sample waters throughout the region. Arrangements, noted survey organizers, "took all Cousteau's patience and diplomatic skill." Although several nations limited the areas in which *Calypso* could travel, twelve countries—Algeria, Bulgaria, Cyprus, Egypt, France, Greece, Italy, Romania, Spain, Tunisia, Turkey, and Yugoslavia—assigned scientists to participate in the Captain's activities and to conduct cooperative research projects.

Calypso spent five months making 126 anchorages throughout the Mediterranean and Black seas. At each site dredges collected sediments from the floor, nets captured drifting animal organisms, and probes obtained water samples at various depths. Scientists sent all specimens to the Atomic Energy Institute in Monaco in order to measure concentrations of heavy metals and polluting chemical compounds such as pesticides, PCBs, and detergents.

The resulting broadcast, entitled "Mediterranean: Cradle or Coffin?" effectively presented clips from Cousteau's post-World War II films showing the waters of Veyron near Marseilles teeming with marine life. Three decades later, in contrast, the Captain found a virtual desert. The sea was empty of fish. Plant life and coral had vanished.

Cousteau interviewed fishermen who complained of small catches and medical doctors who warned of the increasing incidence of mercury poisoning, particularly among fishermen for whom fish was a diet staple. *Calypso*'s divers also discovered a scarred seafloor in the waters near a petrochemical complex at Fos-sur-Mer in southern France.

A Mediterranean ecological tragedy—in which a Yugoslavian freighter carrying nine hundred drums of toxic chemicals had been rammed—captured Cousteau's special attention. He wrote an article for *Saturday Review* about the threat that the sunken *Cavtat* posed to ocean life. When several embassies, the United Nations, and a few hundred concerned citizens responded with letters of concern, he decided to focus his next film, entitled "Time Bomb at Fifty Fathoms," on the efforts to recover the poison.

The story's hero was a young judge from the nearby harbor town of Otranto, Italy. Only through diligence did he persuade the Italian parliament to appropriate funds for the state-owned salvage company to retrieve the deadly cargo of tetraethyl lead, an antiknock compound. The judge then threatened to jail the firm's reluctant president if salvaging did not begin within twenty-eight days. On the twenty-eighth day of February 1977, the operation commenced.

The Italians employed saturation diving techniques that Cousteau had perfected during his Conshelf experiments, allowing salvagers to live for several days in undersea habitats to avoid dangerous and time-consuming decompression procedures following each dive. After ten arduous months they safely retrieved the toxic drums.

Despite such industrial pollution, Cousteau concentrated his personal wrath on land developments—port facilities, marinas, roadways, airports, and high-rise apartments—that encroached on the shallow coastal areas which served as the spawning grounds for undersea life. He also attacked real estate operators for draining swamps and marshes and destroying sources of food for thousands of animals and plants. "Like an underwater dust storm," Cousteau observed, "the silt from the advancing shoreline coats every living thing in a smothering cloud, an impartial catastrophe which makes no distinction among the species."

He also directed criticism toward large-scale fishermen who cared more about amortizing their investments than managing a healthy undersea environment. Frustrated with their short-term perspective, Cousteau protested, "Fish are caught systematically on their mating grounds because they gather there, but it is also a sure way to endanger the future of the species."

Reviewers applauded Cousteau's alert to the environmental dangers of toxic chemicals and industrial developments, but they said the television shows on the Mediterranean lacked drama. Environmentalists attacked *Calypso*'s team for not ringing environmental alarms more loudly. Despite the frightening footage of undersea destruction, Cousteau cautiously concluded, "Polluting agents had not yet created a real danger in most parts of the Mediterranean." Admitting that the "gradual disappearance of fish and other marine wildlife was a growing and undesirable phenomenon," he called simply for more research and increased environmental awareness among the Mediterranean nations.

Although his films focused on the Mediterranean, the Captain was increasing his commitments in the United States. His Americanization had actually begun when he and his brother attended New York City elementary schools and Vermont summer camps. The young explorer had received some of his first financial support from the National Geographic Society, and he traveled frequently to the States to speak at conferences or to promote his films and books. By the late 1970's he had appeared on U.S. television longer than almost any American celebrity.

"I am not an American citizen," Cousteau admits. "But as a boy I played baseball on 95th Street in New York City, and I broke a number of windows, with the usual consequences for kids. I came back to the U.S. when I was 16, when I was 25, and from 1951 on, every year. And since 1974, I have been spending almost half my time here."

The Captain, of course, never fully abandoned his French roots. Despite his many years in the United States, he still speaks with a heavy French accent, and French remains his language of choice aboard the *Calypso* and among family. Some critics suggest that Cousteau consciously maintained his French style and pronunciation to add to his mystique. To millions of Americans, he became a daring and dashing foreigner exploring even more foreign lands.

Throughout the early 1960's the Captain grew increasingly frustrated with the land of his birth. When he accepted ABC's television offer in 1967, the French government, ever fearful of U.S. cultural imperialism, canceled Cousteau's research grants. In contrast, the Captain successfully used his notoriety to create a U.S.-based organization with a large membership that supported his efforts.

The Cousteau Society began operations in Bridgeport, Connecticut, in January 1974. It promised to be a nonprofit, educational group that would help protect the environment. Within a year the organization boasted a remarkable 120,000 members, a size that had taken the Sierra Club several decades to achieve. The society soon possessed the resources to supervise all Cousteau expeditions and the operation of *Calypso*. It opened offices in Los Angeles, where Philippe edited film, and in New York City, where a team of writers prepared Cousteau's books.

Administrative affairs, including membership services and direct mail appeals, were handled in Norfolk, Virginia. In 1979 Cousteau also decided to base *Calypso* there since city leaders had offered dock facilities and financial support. The famous vessel, freshly painted and remodeled, left its traditional port in Monaco for the last time in April. It arrived in Virginia on June 3 of that year.

The move to America, although a major symbolic change, did not eliminate the Captain's frustrations. As if symbolically, rain clouded Norfolk's orchestrated arrival celebrations—complete with two hundred spectators, a speech from the mayor, and a forty piece military band playing *"Aye Calypso,"* a song written and popularized by John Denver. Even Cousteau's first U.S.-based expedition—exploration of the sunken *Monitor*—provoked mostly complaints from Civil War buffs who didn't want the first ironclad revolving-turret battleship disturbed. Moreover, a strong current from the Gulf Stream clouded the water and retarded the team's filming efforts.

While his father turned to ecological studies and administrative tasks, the graying-haired Philippe sought dangers and adventures. He volunteered to pilot *Calypso*'s seaplane, its hot-air balloon, its hang glider, and a parachute that billowed up behind the ship. A rope once broke on the parachute, scarring Philippe's face. He also crashed the hang glider into a cactus.

In 1977 Philippe suffered a more serious accident flying a gyrocopter over Easter Island. While he was trying to obtain aerial footage of the mysterious sculptured heads, his engine overheated and failed. The small vehicle, which looked similar to a toy helicopter, crashed near the island's leper colony, smashing Philippe's kneecap. Assistants rushed him back to Los Angeles for surgery; after three weeks in the hospital he spent several months convalescing.

"With that injury, we both came face to face with mortality," Jan recalls. "Before, we had thought we were golden children. Afterward Philippe was in pain 24 hours a day. It changed him a great deal. There was a quietness then, a turning inward."

Philippe eventually returned to his father's expeditions, largely because of his love of flying the converted PBY Catalina. "Philippe would have hooked wings to his back if he could," remembers Jan. "He came alive when he was in that plane."

Built in the United States and used by the British during World War II, the twin-engine flying boat was a reliable and roomy platform from which Philippe shot aerial photographs and reached inland lakes. First introduced to television audiences by the Cousteaus during the 1976 Yucatán Peninsula broadcasts, the *Flying Calypso* had a thirty-eight-hundred-mile range and a maximum altitude of almost twenty thousand feet.

In February 1978 Philippe and fourteen other members of the Cousteau team set out from Nice to explore the Nile, the great river of antiquity that emptied into the Mediterranean Sea. While *Calypso* remained docked in Monaco, they organized an assult by inflatable boats, four-wheel-drive land vehicles, and the seaplane.

The expedition began with an ominous warning. Not long after the *Flying Calypso* reached Africa, the oil pressure in its starboard engine plummeted, forcing Philippe to make an emergency landing in the Nubian Desert.

But after repairs, the young Cousteau spent ten months executing fifty water landings along the river. He obtained striking pictures of the Nile's full four-thousand-mile length, from the swampy headwaters of the Akagera River above Lake Victoria to the delta in the Mediterranean.

Meanwhile, the land team filmed lions, hippopotamuses, and other wildlife of the African bush. Excellent footage revealed birds attacking columns of lake flies and vegetarian bats winging through the sky. The divers, however, couldn't photograph Nile fish because sediments clouded the river; they had to net various species and place them inside a portable, clear-walled tank conducive to photography.

The Cousteau team collected water samples throughout the river and its tributaries. Like other scientists before, they learned that the

Nile's nutrients no longer fed the Mediterranean. Instead, the life-giving properties were being trapped by a growing number of hydroelectric and irrigation projects.

Philippe paid particular attention to the giant Aswan High Dam. Built with Soviet aid and completed in 1971, the massive structure measured half a mile thick at its base, 364 feet high, and more than 2 miles long. It provided flood control, ten billion kilowatts of electricity (then enough to light every Egyptian village), and sufficient irrigation to open more than 2 million acres of the desert to farming. Aswan and scores of other structures across the Nile represented man's most massive attempt to reorient nature.

The dam's blessings, however, were sometimes deceptive. Without the annual floods, the Nile's silt could no longer renew the land; farmers had to add costly fertilizers to obtain the same crop yields. The waters also couldn't wash away the soil's salt, and contemporary irrigation methods brought destructive brine to the surface. The numerous irrigation canals also gave rise to bilharzia, a debilitating tropical disease that attacks vital organs and shortens life. Moreover, the diversion of river water allowed the Mediterranean Sea to erode the fertile Nile Delta, perhaps the richest land in Egypt.

"Today the Nile no longer goes its own way," Philippe reported. "Year by year, like the tiny people of Lilliput trying to chain Gulliver, well-intentioned men try to bind the giant to their wishes." He declared that modern engineers, impatient for quick solutions, cannot foresee the consequences of the changes they impose. "Perhaps we have mastered the river," Philippe concluded. "We have yet to master ourselves."

Reviewers offered mixed judgments on the television special. Cecil Smith of the *Los Angeles Times* declared that "the beauty of the photography is breathtaking." Others complained that much of the broadcast consisted of Philippe's stiff interviews with tribal chiefs and Egyptian engineers. American audiences suffered through an interpreter's cumbersome account of Philippe's French questions and the experts' Arabic answers, a process that *Daily Variety* described as slowing the show to an "editorial crawl."

In mid-June 1979, after several short projects with his father, Philippe traveled to Portugal, where the *Flying Calypso* was being overhauled, in part to fix the oil pressure problem encountered over the Nubian Desert. On June 28 he took the seaplane aloft to check out the repairs. After a short and successful test flight he banked the plane and prepared to land on the Tagus River, adjacent to the suburb of Alberca, not far from the Portuguese capital of Lisbon. It was a clear, sunny afternoon. The flying boat landed with its usual thud on the calm water. It bounced like a skipping stone and began to slow.

Suddenly and without warning the plane flipped over and tore apart, violently throwing the crew forward. Rescuers, primarily local fishermen, quickly appeared and recovered the copilot and six other crew members, who emerged from the wreckage bruised, with a few broken bones, but without serious injuries. No one, however, could locate the cockpit or Philippe.

When she heard the news, Jan, two months pregnant with their second child, flew immediately with Alexandra and two friends from Los Angeles to Lisbon. They stayed at a local hotel. The Captain, Simone, Jean-Michel, and cousin Jean-Pierre were provided a luxurious villa by the local representative of Air Liquide. Away from journalists, they waited for reports from the rescue units. Simone held back her emotions. Jacques couldn't restrain his tears.

While helicopters scouted the river's banks, a barge dredged the bottom near the crash site. After twenty-four hours the team located the cockpit but no body. Portuguese authorities then added to the task thirty skin divers, who were forced by the lack of visibility to grope about blindly in the mud.

Finally, three days after the accident, rescuers telephoned the villa to announce that they had recovered Philippe's severely mutilated body, which had been cut and crushed when one of the plane's two engines slammed forward into the cockpit. Jean-Michel drove to the morgue to identify his brother's remains and later to the hotel to inform Jan.

Police and aviation investigators issued conflicting reports about the cause of the accident. According to one, the hatch for the PBY's nose wheel caught the water and flipped the plane. Others suggested the Catalina struck a sandbank or a submerged object. Everyone, however, agreed that a broken propeller killed the thirty-nine-year-old Cousteau instantly.

The French Embassy arranged a funeral service in Lisbon's St. Louis-des-Français church. Diplomats obtained special permits from the Portuguese Navy to bury the foreigner at sea, as the family had requested. After a short ceremony, officers placed the coffin, draped in the flags of Portugal and France, aboard the warship *Baptista de*

Andrada. Eighteen miles from shore, mariners saluted while friends slid Philippe's coffin into the Atlantic Ocean.

The Captain returned from the burial and made statements to journalists that sounded insensitive. In fact, he seemed more interested in his own schedule and legacy than in the tragic loss of his cherished son. "Nothing is changed in our program," he declared. Cousteau promised that his upcoming expedition would proceed as planned.

"What was a tragedy for my son was a miracle for his copilot," the Captain continued. "The propeller that killed Philippe saved the life of the copilot, who was tossed, uninjured, to the surface. That is fate. We must accept it and go on. I have another problem now. Philippe, of course, was to take over and continue my work when I am gone. There must be someone to run the society. There must be continuity."

But despite this superficially self-centered pronouncement, the loss shattered Cousteau. For several months he retreated from all adventures and public appearances. Diving, he lamented, produced only memories.

"Cousteau lost his future when Philippe died," commented Philippe's widow, Jan. Added Jean-Michel: "It was very tempting to my father when my brother was killed to just say to hell with everything." Simone, however, prevailed upon her husband to pull himself together and ask Jean-Michel to return to the family business and direct the Cousteau Society's operations.

Jean-Michel did not need to be convinced. "The moment I heard about Philippe," he said, "I knew it was time to close ranks, to come together. When my father asked if I would rejoin his work, I said 'I'm in, don't say another word, it's all taken care of.' "

Letters of sympathy, including one from President Jimmy Carter, flooded the Cousteau Society offices. The group's administrators created a memorial fund to collect remembrances.

The society's newsletter also reprinted a letter from Jan: "We shared 13 golden years. I have no regrets for the past, only for the present and future." She gave birth to Philippe Pierre Jacques-Yves Arnault Cousteau on January 20, 1980, almost seven months after his father's death.

The Captain considered making a film about Philippe but abandoned the project. He refused to talk about the tragedy, but he did write a posthumous letter to his son, which he distributed many months later to Cousteau Society members:

Mon cher Philippe:

I will always remember that day . . . when you joined our Conshelf Two expedition. . . . I was too impatient to show you our "Village under the Sea" before it became too dark. Hastily, we submerged. . . . I kept your hand in mine, to guide you. . . . I felt strangely proud, not of what we had achieved, but because our dreams were always shared so intimately.

Three years ago, I found myself sitting near you in the cockpit of your Catalina. . . . I looked at you, my guide in the sky as I had been your guide in the sea—I saw your shining face, proud to have something to give back to me, and I smiled, because I knew that pursuing rainbows in your plane, you would always seek after the vanishing shapes of a better world.

I love you. JYC

For two of the remaining three PBS shows, completed in late 1979 after Philippe's death, a distracted Cousteau simply pieced together previous footage of shipwrecks and undersea mammals. The segment on Clipperton Island, however, reflected the depth of his depression.

Clipperton, a small and secluded coral atoll 670 miles southwest of Acapulco, Mexico, possessed a tragic history. Sixty-four years before Cousteau's broadcast, the island's women had murdered a brutal rapist who had been torturing them. The Captain's investigation of the horrid story seemed to satisfy his fascination with death.

The two-square-mile island was named after John Clipperton, an English sailor found guilty of mutiny and left on the islet with only a barrel of water. The king of France annexed the atoll in the eighteenth century but failed to occupy it. In 1908 Captain Arnaud of the Mexican Army landed on Clipperton with his young bride and a small garrison, prepared to operate the lighthouse and protect his country's claim. His wife soon gave birth to a son, named Ramón.

Throughout World War I and the Mexican Revolution supply ships frequently failed to deliver food and medicines to the isolated outpost, and the residents started dying from scurvy. In 1915 supplies ran out. Captain Arnaud and two other men drowned when their crude boat capsized on the breakers as they tried to reach a passing ship.

The lighthouse keeper, eking out a living on native fruits and fish, stealthily seized all available guns, disposed of the sick and weak men, and began to brutalize the ten women and children. For almost two years he demanded sexual services, raping and shooting a mother and daughter who refused him. He paralyzed the survivors with fear, promising that if sailors ever arrived, he'd kill his harem and throw their bodies to the sharks in order to keep his savagery a secret.

Mme. Arnaud and two other women could tolerate the brutality no longer. On the sly, they stole a pickax and carpenter's hammer. Late one night, after waiting until their tormentor fell fast asleep, they crept into his hut and smashed him to death with his own tools. The next day, ironically, the USS *Yorktown,* sent to check for enemy Germans, rescued the women and their children.

For his television show Cousteau brought back the seventy-year-old Ramón, who dramatically kissed the ground with emotion when he landed in a small airplane. Ramón erected a wooden cross engraved with his father's name, and he pointed to the sites of the tragic events, describing his terror.

Almost a decade before the Captain and Ramón arrived, Philippe explored Clipperton and devised plans to produce a television segment that would reveal the unique ecology of this isolated atoll overrun with boobies and red crabs. His six-week expedition—which included five French, two American, and two Canadian scientists—filmed the abundance of extra-large tropical fish, dolphins, manta rays, and hammerhead sharks that filled the surrounding waters.

The Captain, however, transformed his dead son's footage of pristine bounty into a drama of doom. His own underwater shots only added to Clipperton's grim human tale. The sequences with fish and animals, noted the *Los Angeles Times* reviewer, "almost out-melodrama the human tragedy of the past." Cousteau, for instance, portrayed a school of fish rising to the surface to escape hammerhead sharks, only to be scooped up by the tens of thousands of circling boobies. Onshore, millions of small red crabs waited to grab any fish dropped by the battling birds. And adding to the violence, moray eels wriggled onto land and gobbled expectant crabs.

Cousteau focused most of his underwater attention on the island's freshwater lagoon, filled with decaying fibers from dead plants. In fact, a toxic by-product of the rotting vegetation seared through the divers' suits and masks to burn their eyes and skin. According to the Captain, "My skin was attacked as if immersed in acid. It became intolerable. When we surfaced from the inferno and took our masks off, the bad smell we had carried with us was suffocating. Our yellow tanks were bleached by hydrogen sulfide, the metal parts of our aqualungs were black as coal, and our red eyes leaked tears for the rest of the day."

Cousteau even presented kindly boobies as tragic combatants by filming twin chicks struggling to gain control of their nest. While the mother remained indifferent, the stronger infant battered and pushed aside the weakling, which was carted off and devoured by the crabs. Confronted with nature's lack of mercy, the Captain "thought of the comparable human tragedy that had happened in this very place." He also lamented his own son's senseless death.

Even Cousteau enthusiasts complained of his graphic depiction of violence. "Clipperton: The Island Time Forgot" may be viewed as a continuation of the catastrophic themes Philippe used in his environmental films, but the hourlong special lacked the young son's enthusiasm for life. It would be up to Jean-Michel to raise both his father's spirits and the tone of his films.

Neither the Captain nor Philippe had cared much for administration. The Cousteau Society and the expeditions were run, as one participant described it, "in a spirit of improvisation." The group had trouble raising money on the scale the two Cousteaus wanted. Cost accounting was barely implemented. Streamlining was never considered.

In short, Jean-Michel inherited a financial mess. After Philippe's death the Captain announced, "Now his brother Michel, who is an architect but also a teacher of marine biology and an ecologist, will wind up his own affairs and will join me to be trained to take over. He cannot replace Philippe, but he has other talents." The elder son's most noted skills were administrative, having been honed by years of advance work for his father's expeditions and by arrangements for his own tourist center.

"I started with the watchwords 'More for Less,' " the new manager explained. "I cut the staff by about 20 percent, to 80 or 90. There was a lot of deadwood." With additional cost controls, he also trimmed the annual operating budget by about a hundred thousand dollars.

Jean-Michel's major administrative challenge was to consolidate his father's expedition equipment from Marseilles, the society's membership files from New York, and the film library from Los Angeles. As mentioned earlier, the Captain had decided to base the *Calypso* in Norfolk, largely because a civic association had raised seventy-five thousand dollars to cover his moving expenses and the city provided free dock space for the ship and office space for the society.

Jean-Michel dreamed of creating a grand Cousteau Society headquarters that would include a museum and entertainment center. He convinced several U.S. cities—Norfolk; Miami, Jacksonville, and Ft. Lauderdale, Florida; and Baltimore, Maryland—to compete for the honor. Several local business leaders felt the Cousteau image was so positive that the Captain's mere presence would attract tourists and other oceanographic businesses. "The magnetism of the man is unbelievable," said John Sears, president of a Norfolk bank. "Someone told me that the two most identifiable men in the world were Muhammad Ali and Jacques Cousteau."

When the Captain brought *Calypso* to Virginia in early June 1979, he told the crowd that Norfolk was competing with "two or three" other cities for the center, but that it had advantages because of its proximity to Congress (Washington, D.C., is about 150 miles away) and other oceanographic research centers, including Old Dominion University, the Virginia Institute of Marine Science, the Atlantic offices of the National Oceanographic and Atmospheric Administration (NOAA), and NASA's Langley Research Center. Mayor Vincent Thomas said he was "very excited at the prospect of the headquarters being moved here."

Some Norfolk civic leaders dreamed that a "Cousteau Ocean Center" would be the centerpiece of an ambitious hundred-million-dollar waterfront renewal project. The Captain remained uncommitted, however, claiming that he would consider proposals only if the Cousteau Society didn't have to pay any part of the bill.

For almost a year after *Calypso* arrived in Norfolk, the famous vessel lacked direction. The PBS series, which had confused viewers and critics, was not renewed, and the Cousteaus struggled to arrange a new mission.

While the Captain negotiated with television executives for a fresh series, Venezuelan ministries hired *Calypso* to help local scientists sample the waters around where the Orinoco River empties into the Atlantic Ocean. The team quickly obtained hundreds of water and sediment specimens, and they drilled three-foot-long geologic cores at 110 different stations, delivering enough data, according to Cousteau, to "provide months, if not years, of lab work for the Venezuelan scientific community."

Calypso then sailed to Curaçao in the Lesser Antilles for routine maintenance work, and the crew flew home for an extended break. By April 1980 the celebrated ship again had nothing better to do than remain docked in Norfolk, where it appeared as the star attraction during the town's Harborfest.

Cousteau finally arranged a contract with the National Office of Canadian Film to coproduce two segments on the Greater St. Lawrence Waterway, including Newfoundland and the Great Lakes. The Captain couldn't refuse the generous offer of a million dollars, but he lacked any enthusiasm for the project.

Cousteau spent little time on the expedition, flying in only to be photographed at a few key spots. Jean-Michel tried to take command, but he soon discovered scores of scientists and divers who knew more than he did. The Canadians grumbled about the arrogant Frenchman.

Calypso arrived in Halifax, Nova Scotia, in late June 1980, and the crew filmed a nearby graveyard of sunken ships, interviewed local oceanographers, and searched for whales. They then headed around Newfoundland to locate humpbacks, an endangered species that frequently became entangled in cod-fishing nets.

While the ship received minor repairs at St. John's, the team learned that a humpback had just been entrapped several miles up the coast. They immediately rented a trunk to transport the bulky camera equipment and a Zodiac. Bernard Delemotte and other divers discovered a net stretched like a bridle bit across the mouth of a young whale, whose skin was scratched and bleeding from the ropes. The calf's only exertion was to return periodically to the surface for air.

Cousteau claimed that his divers "risked their lives to save the life of a baby humpback whale and return it to the warmth and safety of its mother," but Canadian cameraman Jacques Leduc later admitted that the crew faced no danger and fabricated the entire "rescue." Delemotte could have quickly cut the rope to free the terrified creature, except that the Captain needed footage for a touching story. The divers, therefore, spent an hour and a half photographing themselves trying to soothe the humpback. The edited film dragged on with tender scenes of Delemotte hugging the young giant and stroking its face, while the narrator wondered aloud if the whale could possibly be freed.

Finally, Delemotte used his knife to liberate the now-exhausted mammal. In what Cousteau suggested was a show of gratitude, the whale dragged the clutching diver on its back for almost a mile before sounding in the open sea.

Rémy Galliano, an electrician-diver who had been with the *Calypso* team for more than a year, was not so fortunate. On a routine dive to explore a three-masted schooner that had sunk in eastern Lake Ontario, Galliano failed to surface. For more than five hours a search party could find no trace of his body. Divers from the Canadian armed forces finally located it on the muddy lake bottom. Doctors reported that the thirty-year-old Galliano died of an air embolism that ruptured his lungs and blocked the flow of oxygen. They suggested that the experienced diver had misjudged his depth in the murky waters and ascended too quickly without exhaling.

The accident put *Calypso*'s team behind schedule, so the crew skipped the planned ceremonies in Detroit and headed directly toward the area of Whitefish Bay in Lake Superior. There they filmed Indian pictographs, caribou herds, and the wreck of the *Edmund Fitzgerald*, a 729-foot steamer that sank quickly in 1975 and drowned its entire crew.

Cousteau, who had been busy with administrative duties in Paris, joined the team in late September, just in time to participate in the rescheduled celebrations in Detroit. His organizers had arranged a flotilla of some four hundred boats to escort *Calypso* down the Detroit River. The Captain and Jean-Michel flew in their helicopter to Hart Plaza in downtown Detroit, where five thousand fans awaited them. Mayor Coleman Young gave Cousteau a key to the city.

On the way back to Montreal the camera crew interviewed several scientists and explored a few more wrecks. The Captain described the expedition's highlight as the display of colorful sea life fifty feet below the St. Lawrence's chocolate-shaded surface waters. These unique shots, however, paled in comparison with his early undersea photographs.

What Cousteau's resulting two two-hour films lacked in quality and drama, he tried to compensate for with technology. Long scenes simply displayed his array of fancy equipment: the helicopter, diving saucer, Hovercraft, Zodiacs, and giant Land-Rovers. Reviewers criticized the Canadian productions, broadcast over many PBS stations in October 1982, as boring and directless. Environmentalists blasted Cousteau for failing to raise critical issues such as acid rain.

Cousteau's rushed films on the St. Lawrence lacked the relative quality of his early works, in part because other adventurers—from the National Geographic Society to David Attenborough—had learned to produce dramatic nature films. But more important, they lacked Cousteau's personal commitment. The Captain had fallen victim to his busy schedule for maintaining an expanding empire. And since Philippe's death he had been uninspired, spending little of his own time on the productions. According to a Canadian working with the *Calypso* team, "It seems Cousteau was content with simply using his famous name to get the film board's million dollars."

Even *Calypso* took a beating in Canada. In fact, the expedition inflicted more damage on the vessel than did any other in its history, including the voyage to Antarctica. On the winter passage back down the St. Lawrence River, floating blocks of ice banged *Calypso* severely. Because the ship rode lower in freshwater, the sharp ice crystals cut deeply into the wood planks above the copper sheathing that protected the hull.

Sailors had begun to make temporary repairs when a violent storm deposited some fifteen tons of ice on the deck and lines, enough to throw the small ship off balance. Windblown spray pelted and froze the radar antenna and wind gauges, and the caulking of the flexed hull popped loose, creating leaks. Finally, a crashing wave ripped a 118-gallon gas tank from its mounts, forcing the frightened crew to slip across the rear deck for half an hour before they could strap the container down.

Even when the storm had subsided and *Calypso* had traveled south to warmer waters, troubles continued. Melting ice rained down on the electric panels in the engine room. The salt water, according to one crew member, "attacked open relays and circuit breakers, causing shorts and threatening to ignite what all sailors fear: a fire." The Captain ordered the damaged ship into a cove above Cape Cod, where industrious engineers cleaned and dried every aspect of the electrical system. *Calypso* limped into its home berth in Norfolk just before Christmas 1980.

CHAPTER EIGHT

Rediscovery

Cousteau desperately needed new funding and an outlet for his films. Bud Rifkin, who had been vice-president of David Wolper Productions during the *Undersea World* series, approached the networks again, this time trying to entice them with shows on the Amazon, the planet's last and least-known wilderness. Grant Tinker, NBC's chairman, expressed interest and invited the Captain to Los Angeles to meet with other executives. But as far as Brandon Tartikoff, the network's programming chief, was concerned, underwater television was dull, and he crushed Cousteau's network dreams. (Ironically, Tartikoff later endorsed *Ocean Quest,* an entertainment-oriented undersea docudrama that featured a former Miss Universe; critics universally panned the unpopular effort.)

When the networks and public television closed their doors, Cousteau's only option was Ted Turner. John Denver, the singer and Cousteau Society promoter, first introduced the Captain to the cable TV magnate. "It was love at first sight," Cousteau later explained. "Ted has the same interest in ecology, in peace, in Third World problems —everything that I'm interested in."

Turner had become a celebrity in his own right. In 1977 the talkative owner of the Atlanta Braves turned the elite America's Cup race into a media event when he sailed *Courageous* to victory. Although he proved to be a talented helmsman who skillfully trained and motivated his crew, Turner didn't conform to the image of the gentleman sailor. Instead, he is remembered for slipping under a table to enjoy a bottle of aquavit at his nationally televised victory press conference. His colorful character, variously known as the Mouth of the South or Captain Courageous, entertained and enthralled the public.

Ted Turner, however, was more than a loquacious sportsman. In an age when the public deified entrepreneurs, he became a cultural hero, having converted his father's bankrupt billboard business into a cable television empire. In fact, the cable industry grew up with Ted Turner. He created the WTBS station in Atlanta and built it into a superstation that beamed his satellite signals throughout the United States. Several years later he established the Cable News Network in a move that challenged the top three broadcasting networks and established twenty-four-hour television news.

Turner had long cared about environmental affairs. The energy crises of the 1970's added to his conviction that the earth's limited resources should be conserved. He gave generously of his funds and television time to promote ecology and safe energy alternatives.

In his youth Turner had watched the Captain's movies and read his books, claiming that Cousteau gave him inspiration. When the adventurer described his plans to explore the Amazon and advocate its protection, Turner simply asked how much money the Captain needed. They agreed upon a six-million-dollar contract to produce four television segments about the world's largest river. For the first time in almost a decade, Cousteau had the money and time to conduct a thorough expedition.

Despite his lack of alternatives, the Captain claimed his move to cable television was a calculated risk on his part. "I'll tell you why we went to the Turner deal," Cousteau explained in October 1981, "because we think that television will go through a revolution anyway. And usually we always have been pioneers. We don't want to stay behind. And maybe our move to cable was a little premature. It's better to do it now than later."

The Cousteaus had recently redirected their filming attention from the sea to the rivers that feed it. They had traveled down the Nile and across the St. Lawrence on journeys that expressed their concern for the planet's fragile and interconnected ecology. "Rivers that used to fertilize the sea with salts and nutrients, like the breasts of Mother Earth," the Captain wrote, "were turned into kidneys soiling the sea with the toxic residues of our burgeoning and shortsighted modern world."

If the Nile was a river of antiquity and the St. Lawrence a waterway of the present, the Amazon symbolized the future, a laboratory to test if man could manage the environment intelligently. Large portions of the Amazon Basin—fanning throughout much of Brazil, Colombia, Peru, Bolivia, and four other South American countries—remained virgin, yet parts were becoming polluted as a result of rapid development.

For Cousteau, the Amazon represented the supreme ecological wonder. The river discharges seven million cubic feet of water every second, enough to fill Lake Ontario in about three hours. The four-thousand-mile-long waterway also is the world's widest, measuring two hundred miles at its mouth. Its basin would barely fit within the continental United States.

The Amazon sustains the world's largest forest, accounting for about a third of the planet's trees, some of which tower to 150 feet. Its dense jungles contain the widest diversity of flora and fauna, including the biggest parrots, rodents, ants, and snakes, as well as most of the world's species of butterflies, birds, bats, and monkeys. The Amazon also hosts more than twenty-five hundred classes of fish, more than the entire Atlantic Ocean.

Superlatives filled Cousteau's description of his own adventure, too. He called the effort "the greatest and most difficult expedition I have ever undertaken," as well as "the most ambitious land-sea-air expedition in history." Promoters billed it as "awesome and awe-inspiring." Failing to acknowledge such events as Sir Edmund Hillary's climb of Mount Everest, Richard Byrd's trek to the South Pole, or Astronaut Neil Armstrong's walk on the moon, they suggested that Cousteau's trip to Amazonia was the "expedition of the century."

Capturing the monumental ecosystem on film did require a massive effort. Well before the expedition commenced in February 1982, society staffers collected facts about navigation, docking facilities, road conditions, medical provisions, customs requirements, and radio frequencies. Over the course of the two-year adventure, the forty-eight-member crew traveled more than four thousand miles, and thirty-five visiting scientists from five different nations joined the expedition from time to time. To explore the vast area, the Cousteaus often needed to orchestrate four teams working simultaneously in three different countries.

Even obtaining permits and visas from the proper authorities required patience and diplomacy. Because some officials accused the *Calypso,* with its sophisticated communications equipment, of serving as a CIA spy ship, the Captain had to visit several capitals to assure heads of state of his peaceful intentions. Moreover, local researchers demanded that their scientists accompany every aspect of the expedition.

In addition to obtaining Ted Turner's financing, fund raisers convinced Italy's IVECO Corporation to donate an amphibious truck and a six-wheel-drive caravan. Amana was persuaded to install two new freezers aboard *Calypso,* and Atlanta businessman George Montgomery provided an amphibious bush plane. COMSAT TeleSystems also contributed a sophisticated shipboard telecommunications system that offered telephone, telex, data, and facsimile transmission capability, with automatic tuning to all 339 satellite channels then available.

The expedition's overall plan appeared simple. During the first phase *Calypso* sailed as far up the river as possible, while a land team, headed by Jean-Michel, located and traced the Amazon's headwaters in the Peruvian Andes. The second phase found *Calypso* returning down the main river at a leisurely pace, entering the larger tributaries for adventures and filming. The land and flying teams recorded unusual animals or human habitations at remote locations.

The television narrator, Joseph Campanella, began the series dramatically: "A single river carries one fifth of the fresh water flowing on earth. Spilling over half of South America, its thousand tributaries have lured Jacques Cousteau into an expedition more complicated than any he has made before. With a unique armada of modern equipment, he will penetrate the largest liquid kingdom on land: the Amazon rain forest."

Cousteau quickly learned how culturally remote Amazonia is from Brazil's metropolitan centers. To gain local acceptance for his efforts, he began the journey by mounting a typical Brazilian bowsprit, called a *carranca,* on *Calypso.* The dragon-headed sculpture theoretically kept evil spirits away from watercraft. Only much later did the crew discover that inhabitants of the upper river thought the six-foot-tall wooden totem was something French.

The Amazon expedition demonstrated the growing influence of Jean-Michel, who promoted a social as well as an environmental focus. The son convinced his father that the television specials should concentrate on the plight of the surviving Indians, the victims of the massive cocaine trade, the consequences of poaching on ecological diversity, the mad rush for gold, and the growth of industrial development in the wilderness. He argued that the team should climb mountains, interview drug traffickers, and generally spend more time on land than under the water.

The Captain, however, didn't totally abandon his quest for unique footage of water animals, a task made more difficult by the dense jungle. A multitude of tiny creatures remained virtually hidden behind the blanket of leaves, vines, and trunks. The infrequent sightings were so brief that cameramen barely had time to focus. They often captured only the rippling water behind the powerful tail of a disappearing caiman or crocodile. The problem led the team's film editor in Paris to complain that much of the footage included only *ronds dans l'eau* (circles in the water).

One animal that the elder Cousteau could record—although with some difficulty—was the pink dolphin, a mysterious and graceful mammal. The dolphin's beak, according to the adventurer, "is abnormally long, javelin-like; from its back rises a low triangular bulge, more ridge than a dorsal fin; its fins and flukes seem disproportionately large; from its head protrudes a rosy melon-size hump."

Cousteau first spotted the colorful animal maneuvering like a gymnast around the jungle's flooded branches. Accompanying Brazilian scientists explained that the creature's unusually flexible body resulted from vertebrae that were more widely spaced than those of other dolphins. One crew member suggested that the pink mammal "hunts through the woods with the dexterity of a jungle cat."

Sounding his typical note of remorse for the "need" to capture wild and intelligent animals, Cousteau rationalized that he had to answer scientific questions about the dolphin's behavior. For several days he dropped divers, equipped with nets, near the mammals, but he watched helplessly as the pink dolphins retreated and escaped under floating grass prairies. Eventually the men cornered a seven-foot female and transferred her to a restraining pool that Cousteau had constructed of wire fence in a small inlet. Two days later the team caught a male.

The two-hundred-pound mammals objected strenuously to their accommodations, slapping Cousteau's divers with their strong flippers. Other dolphins tried to liberate the caged pair.

A Brazilian scientist, Vera da Silva, described for Cousteau the animal's characteristics and habits. Da Silva had observed the pink dolphin in the wild and often in captivity, and the Cousteau enclosure gave him no new scientific information. However, the experience enabled the Captain to acquire colorful photographs of a unique animal.

With his prize footage in hand, the filmmaker removed the fence, allowing the dolphins to return to freedom.

The Cousteaus and their crew, the promotional materials proclaimed, "endured endless danger and discomfort." Debilitating humidity and a profusion of insects seemed to engulf them. When Falco tied his Zodiac to a large fig tree, for instance, a swarm of bees stung him. The Captain grabbed a tree trunk for support, and a squadron of wasp-size ants streamed up his arm. While most of the team suffered from dysentery and insect bites, eight, including Jean-Michel and his wife, Anne-Marie, had to be treated for malaria. Moreover, terrorists targeted both the Captain and his son for abduction.

Still, the group maintained its good humor. One prankster enjoyed positioning rubber snakes in front of his friends' tents in the middle of the night. A biologist, wanting to establish the size of a rare beetle for a photograph, placed the strange green creature on the face of a colleague, who was quickly stung by the insect; the scientist gleefully responded: "This is great! This is how we learn!"

The first major setback occurred when Jean-Michel led the land team to the summit of Mount Mismi, located on the Continental Divide in the heart of the Peruvian Andes. When the six-wheel-drive vehicle became mired in mud, far away from any heavy towing equipment, Jean-Michel tried to rent pack animals from a local farmer in order to transport his bulky photographic equipment. After an hour of coaxing, the farmer finally conceded, only to dump the baggage along the rugged path after his llamas and donkeys were startled by a Peruvian Air Force helicopter that arrived unexpectedly to aid the expedition.

The air force's high tech ferry provided little assistance, however, carrying the group only a short distance before the pilot decided that the thin air prohibited a safe landing and subsequent liftoff. Cousteau's men, sailors used to life on the sea, then trudged for four hours over rough terrain before establishing their base camp. Although exhausted and famished, they couldn't eat the freeze-dried "astronaut" dinner they had packed in because the kerosene heater couldn't sustain a flame in the oxygen-poor air.

The following morning, suffering from altitude sickness and wrenched knees, they struggled for another four hours to reach the 18,363-foot summit. In a symbolic gesture recorded for the cameras, Jean-Michel hurled snow off both sides of the ridge. That tossed to the south would reach the Pacific Ocean, only 100 miles away. The snow thrown northward would become part of the mighty Amazon and eventually empty into the Atlantic.

Jean-Michel also confronted Amazonia's invigorating frontier, where the currency was gold. Perhaps his most memorable photographs were of Serra Pelada, where more than forty thousand frenzied men, coated in mud and dust, swarmed about an open pit in search of mineral riches.

"The scene below us staggered our imagination," noted Jean-Michel in his tape cassette diary. "It was epic, a vision from the age of the Pharaohs, from Babylon. Or from the insect world. Streaming to and fro were thousands and thousands of organisms the color of the soil, marching in endless files that brushed against one another as they poured in and out of the hole, going and coming, disappearing into the dust and emerging from it, swarming in an orderly way like ants excavating an underground nest."

The two-hundred-foot-deep excavation attracted a mixed set of dreamers: fishermen, foundry workers, rubber gatherers, and rice farmers driven by stories of overnight wealth. One former fisherman supposedly found six million dollars' worth of gold in a single day. Another located a gold boulder weighing 2,954 pounds and valued at twenty million dollars.

Gold was discovered at Serra Pelada, so the tale went, in 1978, when a violent storm uprooted a large tree. Nearby farmers noticed that the tangled roots glistened with gold dust. Within a month twenty thousand miners had begun to excavate a giant hole in the mountain. "The digging began," wrote the Cousteau Society's researcher, "each miner slicing his terrace out of the mountainside until eventually, carved into thousands of terraces, the slopes themselves seemed to move, crawling with men packed together like worker termites."

The Brazilian government tried to establish some order by granting each miner a small plot and the right to hire nine other men. Most diggers stayed for years, leaving either wealthy or penniless. About forty men died in the hole, either from riots or mud slides. Jean-Michel lingered for just ten days, enough time to film miners who appeared, in his words, "like the largest crowd of extras ever assembled in history's most expensive cinema fantasy."

Fascination with the gold rush sent the Cousteaus up the Madeira River, one of the Amazon's largest tributaries, to Jirau, an outpost where thousands panned the river's banks. Some fifteen hundred divers also ventured blindly into the muddy brown river to vacuum up the bottom muck, hoping the mud contained gold flecks. The inexperienced excavators faced many dangers, not the least of which was the threat that jealous competitors would cut their air hoses. Those who survived, however, earned an average of thirteen thousand dollars each month.

While a few enjoyed riches, thousands were being poisoned by the gold extraction process. Miners used mercury as a bonding agent to remove gold from other ores or sand; when they burned away the mercury, pure gold remained. But as a consequence, people on the work site breathed mercury vapors, and the entire village ate fish contaminated by waste and spillage. A visiting John Hopkins University scientist estimated that thirty tons of mercury had entered the river and that villagers suffered twice the normal concentrations of the toxic material, accounting for their high levels of serious illnesses.

Gold was not the only resource that attracted men and women to Amazonia. In the mid-1920's Henry Ford had established a 2.5-million-acre rubber plantation in the heart of the jungle in order to secure an inexpensive source of raw material for car tires. The jungle, however, engulfed and reclaimed his plantation. Billionaire Daniel Ludwig met the same fate when he tried to corner the paper pulp market by planting fast-growing trees on massive farms.

The Madeira-Mamoré Railway represented the most striking example of the jungle's power. The 230-mile line was to have carried high-quality Bolivian rubber around impassable river rapids to Pôrto Velho in Brazil, where awaiting ships would travel 3,000 miles down the Amazon and to the world's markets. Construction, however, took forty years and claimed the lives of ten thousand workers, most of whom died from malaria and dysentery. The railroad began operating in 1912, ironically just as cheaper Asian rubber became available and destroyed Amazonia's economy. Today only 27 miles of the track remain. Tourists pay nine cents for a short scenic journey on what cost thirty million dollars to construct.

Such disasters, the Cousteaus learned, hadn't quelled men's dreams of converting Amazonia's resources into riches. International bankers were investing millions of dollars to develop the iron deposits at Carajás, thought to be the world's largest ore reserve. Foresters were slashing tropical hardwoods at such an unprecedented rate that experts predicted half the planet's rain forests would be destroyed by the year

2000. Some of the tropical woods were processed into furniture or paneling, but most logging created farms, particularly for cattle grazing. While acknowledging that the nation was destroying much of its land, many Brazilian economists saw Amazonia's assets as the best means for the country to obtain foreign exchange and reduce its huge debt.

Such intrusions into Latin America's environmental paradise deeply troubled the Captain. But Cousteau, no radical preservationist, believed nothing could stop the frantic search for gold, iron ore, lumber, or hydroelectric power. Occupation of the land, he admitted, was inevitable. In fact, he criticized conservationists in developed countries for demanding righteously that Third World wilderness be protected. "For people who are hungry," he declared, "preservation and conservation can be just so many pretty words." Still, the Captain pleaded for wise management and "limited-development programs that will not endanger the Amazon's colossal but fragile fecundity."

Jean-Michel, sensitive to concerns about his scientific credibility, admitted that his Amazonia adventure needed more substance than four documentary films. "There will be films," he stressed, "and they will ultimately acquaint millions of people around the world with this priceless, vibrant wilderness." But his "most gratifying achievements" were to be scientific.

The *Calypso,* filled with expensive technical and telecommunications equipment, became a working platform for an international team of researchers. While Jean-Michel announced that he provided these assets at no cost to local scientists and institutions, Brazilian officials acknowledged that they would not have granted the necessary permits to the Cousteaus without such reciprocal services.

Calypso's team utilized two methods of data collection throughout the river system. A flow-through sampling device continuously measured the water's temperature, oxygen and chlorophyll context, turbidity, and conductivity. Vertical stations established upstream and downstream from each main tributary calculated the river's contents. Local scientists had collected thousands of water samples before, but the Cousteau expedition allowed them to digitize an enormous amount of new data for future study. The samples also established a baseline review of the Amazon's health in 1982, enabling scientists from the eight countries that share the river system to determine the future effects of industrial and urban development.

* * *

Often in his speeches at universities across the United States, Jean-Michel talks enthusiastically about his Amazon experience, particularly of his encounter with Kukus, leader of the Jívaro Achuara Indians in Peru. In a 1985 address he noted, "I learned perhaps more about leadership from this one man than I have learned in my 46 years of life elsewhere." The young Cousteau claimed to have acquired from the Jívaro chieftain an understanding about the "connectedness of everything."

Europeans had avoided the Jívaros since the sixteenth century, when Spanish expeditions complained about the tribe's poison dart attacks and its practice of shrinking heads. The Jívaros, moreover, were the only American Indians to have revolted successfully—and ruthlessly—against the empire of Spain. After destroying two gold-mining settlements and killing some thirty thousand inhabitants, the fierce warriors poured molten gold down the throat of the Spanish governor.

Jean-Michel hoped to produce a dramatic broadcast by filming the present state of this presumably savage forest tribe. He contacted Luis Uriarte, a University of Chicago anthropologist who had lived among the Jívaros and learned their language, to establish contact with tribal leaders. After weeks of effort Uriarte obtained permission for a small Cousteau team to visit the Jívaro Achuara, one of five separate tribes in the region.

Jean-Michel, busy with administrative duties in Norfolk, couldn't participate in the initial meeting with Kukus in May 1982. Dominique Sumian acted as expedition leader, Uriarte served as translator, and Anne-Marie Cousteau, Jean-Michel's wife, joined the team as its still photographer. She faced initial resistance from the male-dominated tribe but eventually was adopted by one of the leaders and allowed to enjoy dinner with the men.

Kukus, a short, powerfully built man in his late fifties explained that only forty people lived in his village, yet about five hundred from surrounding farms participated in tribal activities. Clothed in a western sport shirt but with long black hair braided down his back, Kukus admitted to having seven wives and an array of in-laws scattered throughout the area.

The Achuara tribe faced numerous problems. "White man's diseases"—whooping cough, measles, and smallpox—had decimated several villages, particularly attacking the young. Thirty-six of Kukus's forty-two children had died since foreigners came in search of oil and other natural assets.

Kukus was equally troubled by threats to his land. To secure their property rights, Indians had to join the Peruvian Army and obtain government identification cards. But the security forces required recruits to cut their long hair, an act Achuara men considered equivalent to emasculation. Without title to the land, the tribe couldn't control intruders who stole the region's resources, especially the trees.

The forests provided the Achuaras with wood for their canoes, thatching for their houses, and herbs for their medicine. During the previous year, complained Kukus, outsiders axed twelve hundred big trees, and continued depletion threatened to rob the tribe of its transportation, shelter, and health.

Three weeks into the team's visit, Jean-Michel arrived in Rubina to admire Kukus's efforts at conserving local resources for future generations. The chief personally had planted eight hundred new trees, pointing to several that he claimed would become canoes. He also set aside a lake to raise paiche, a giant and flavorful fish popular with the villagers.

Kukus, however, couldn't control a major construction project launched several years before by PetroPeru and Occidental Petroleum. The giant companies had located crude oil in an area claimed by the Jívaro Achuara, but the firms refused to share any of the resources, even two barrels a day as Kukus requested. The chieftain, taking Jean-Michel to inspect the pipeline that bisected his land, protested, "Wildlife has fled from our hunting grounds since the pipe was laid and the helicopters began patrolling it."

Jean-Michel left the Achuara leader to pursue other adventures, but near the end of the Amazon expedition he returned to Rubina to fly Kukus to a district land office in Yurimaguas. The Frenchman tried to help the Indian file the papers necessary to establish title to Achuara land, even though he admitted that bureaucratic barriers made the exercise fruitless.

The young Cousteau then decided to organize a meeting for Kukus with President Fernando Terry Belaunde of Peru, hoping that personal contact would win rights for the Indians. Jean-Michel arranged a limousine and a fine hotel room for this chieftain who had never heard the urban sounds of horns blaring and tires squealing, let alone witnessed multistoried buildings and indoor plumbing.

The Peruvian president was cordial, expressing his concern for the native tribes. But it was the Indian who, according to Jean-Michel, made the most eloquent statement, describing the problems deforestation, oil drilling, and military harassment had caused his people. The two leaders, although both in their late fifties, lived in different worlds and faced different challenges. They reached no agreements, and Jean-Michel wondered if President Belaunde could understand Kukus's concerns or if he even had the power to control the incursions onto Achuara land. Still, the young Cousteau labeled the meeting "a step in the right direction."

Jean-Michel won't return soon to the Peruvian jungles, and he knows that despite his access to television and the world's leaders, he can do little to aid the Achuaras. But Kukus remains a powerful image of leadership for him. The Indian chieftain, according to Jean-Michel, knew "his identity was inextricable from the future of his people. His goal was to bequeath a world intact."

Cousteau's first three Amazon specials—entitled *Journey to a Thousand Rivers, The New Eldorado: Invaders and Exiles,* and *River of the Future*—enjoyed an enthusiastic response from the trade press, publications for cinematographers, producers, writers, and film editors. The *Hollywood Reporter* declared: "One expects a Cousteau documentary to be beautifully photographed, despite the dangers and technical challenges of filming in primitive terrain. 'Journey to a Thousand Rivers' exceeds expectations. Almost every frame of this production is exquisite."

Even Simone, usually the quiet and critical force behind the scenes, publicly decreed, "I think it's the best one we did."

The segment on primitive tribes presented intriguing perspectives on Indian cultures, particularly in contrast with the region's advancing technology. The Cousteau team obtained insightful footage of an animated medicine man trying to suck the arthritis from Chief Kukus's hip, a Matisse warrior accurately firing his blowgun at a distance of sixty yards, and the Ansha tribe releasing poison into a river to stun and seize fish.

But despite this sensitivity, the Captain displayed several disturbing contradictions. His film, for instance, mockingly portrayed chatty tourists snapping pictures of an Indian dance. The natives, Cousteau suggested, had been turned into "circus performers in a freak show," while the visitors only wanted "to say they danced with a cannibal." He further condemned the bartering that travelers did to acquire tribal trinkets. But only moments after the film presented these criticisms, it revealed Cousteau's cameramen photographing the turtle dance of another tribe and Raymond Coll exchanging his trademark red cap for the chief's feathered crown.

Cousteau, moreover, disapproved of settlers cutting trees on Indian land in order to clear fields for corn and other crops. The diverse forest, he argued, must be preserved. But the Captain failed to note that his own men had felled a large tree simply because they needed a marker. The local medicine man declared that the destruction prompted spirits of the sacred tree to make a young child gravely ill. Cousteau's crew quickly left the area before villagers could express their anger.

The height of the show's sensationalism occurred when the team visited three confused women who were probably the only survivors of an isolated tribe. Government officials had recently located the women, encouraged them to wear clothing, and taught them how to create fires and use bows and arrows. Cousteau's photographers brought blankets as presents, but the women, labeled as "castaways in time," lacked the ability to communicate. The Indians became particularly frightened when the Captain's seaplane landed on the adjacent river, and they desperately tired to shoo away the modern technology. Rather than provide comfort, the cameramen used the occasion to secure close-up shots of the women's pathetically bewildered faces.

For the concluding hour of Cousteau's Amazon series, Jean-Michel departed dramatically from his father's traditional focus on the undersea environment: He searched for cocaine and obtained unique snapshots of the clandestine world of coca growers and traffickers. What drug trade had to do with fish and coral reefs was hard for many Cousteau admirers to understand. But Jean-Michel had convinced the Captain that cocaine caused "internal pollution of man" and that the vast narcotics business had a profound impact on the future of the river and its people.

The cocaine exploration also offered Jean-Michel the chance to demonstrate that he was more than an efficient manager of Cousteau Society operations. It was to prove, as the society's promotional pieces later claimed, that he had "developed into a true explorer with hard-hitting journalism skills."

Coca had been an obvious part of Indian life throughout the eastern foothills of the Andes for more than four thousand years. Much the way Europeans smoked cigarettes or drank beer, Andean Indians chewed coca leaves to quell hunger or to experience minor stimulation.

Even Jean-Michel joined several farm workers to gnaw on a few leaves. Tribal elders also openly dispensed ground coca powder during ceremonies in which stuporous dancers reveled through lengthy symbolic prayers for good hunting, fishing, and sexual potency.

Cocaine, however, had fostered a vast drug trade in which massive profits sparked murderous violence. Bolivia, Colombia, and Peru supplied most of the illicit narcotic delivered to the United States and Europe.

In September 1982 Jean-Michel decided to venture into the center of this lawless commerce, a town in central Peru named Tingo María, where 95 percent of the population had some connection with the development and distribution of cocaine. Despite warnings from local Franciscan monks not to film any action on the streets or in the jungles, cameramen accompanied a police unit when it sprayed and destroyed a coca field with herbicides.

The young Cousteau appropriately noted the fine line between villain and victim when his team photographed the police arresting two teenage girls at a bus stop for each concealing a pound bag of coca paste in the waistbands of their skirts. Each badly needed the seventy-five dollars offered by drug lords to transport the material, valued at about one hundred thousand dollars after processing. While breast-feeding their babies, the frightened girls were sentenced to ten years in jail.

Nine months later Jean-Michel was in Lima obtaining permits for another filming venture when he received a telegram from the missionaries warning that death threats had been made against the Cousteau team if it arrived again with cameras. Jean-Michel made the upcoming assignment voluntary for his crew, and the self-described "hard-hitting journalist" opted to avoid the personal risk.

Jean-Paul Cornu, Dominique Sumian, and Yves Zlotnicka returned to Tingo María, known by cocaine dealers as the white city, with a special police unit of two officers, seven armed guards, and a U.S. drug enforcement agent. Over a three-day period the Cousteau team received constant protection, including armed escorts in restaurants and bathrooms.

Following a tip, the police drove deep into the mountain forest, abandoned their Jeeps, and hiked for about an hour to reach a recently abandoned processing plant that converted dried coca leaves into the valuable paste. While filming the clandestine factory, Cornu nearly tripped over a ground wire attached to a shotgun hidden in the shrubs.

At the last moment one of the guards pulled him away from the homemade weapon designed to blow off the legs of intruders.

Back in the safety of Lima, Jean-Michel joined in several counseling sessions for addicts trying to kick their habits. To observe those for whom the traditional methods failed, he gained permission to film a controversial surgical operation in which a tiny part of the brain's limbic system was removed, presumably to retard an addict's craving for cocaine. Doctors conducted the radical procedure on a sixteen-year-old boy, identified as "Patient #19," who had smoked coca paste for more than two years and who feared he might commit suicide, as had his addicted brother. Before the patient was put to sleep, Jean-Michel, dressed in a hospital gown, asked the translator to tell the boy, "We are with him. Good luck." Cameramen then recorded the doctors shaving the boy's scalp and cranking a drill bit into his skull.

Although the five-hour operation failed to cure the patient's addiction, it demonstrated to Jean-Michel the "virulence of the cocaine menace." He concluded in his diary: "So radically is [cocaine] contorting the lives of countless people that responsible professionals with the best of intentions are ready to consider, and now even to carry out, such an unthinkable procedure, believing it is the last possible remedy."

The Cousteau group also flirted with the politics of the drug trade. Deep in the Colombian jungle, two team members interviewed an articulate and affluent drug trafficker who considered cocaine a weapon against imperialism. The college-educated thirty-year-old claimed to have never used the drug personally or to be motivated by the immense profits it generated. "I do it to destroy the United States," he declared. "This is war."

The drug runner admitted that money from illicit sales financed guerrilla operations, particularly the four-year battle by the Sendero Luminoso (or Shining Path) against the Peruvian government. As the Cousteaus perceived it, the guerrilla traffickers knowingly delivered "insidious chemical bombs made of white powder, designed to weaken the populace and wear down the machinery of government."

At a January 1985 press conference announcing the premiere of the resulting television show, *Snowstorm in the Jungle,* Jean-Michel stated that while in Amazonia, he had been offered significant sums to transport coca paste out of the country. Traffickers even suggested that plastic bags be nailed to the hull of *Calypso.*

The Captain warned reviewers that "there are no pretty pictures of fish'' in *Snowstorm in the Jungle*. Instead, the show, he said, presented a compelling and powerful portrait of human conflict within Amazonia's vast and often inhospitable frontier.

Some critics, however, found the cocaine broadcast, narrated by Orson Welles, a bit overdone. Commenting on Captain Cousteau's claim that "the Western world may decline" if the war against cocaine is not won, *People* magazine concluded that "the show begins to take on the tone of Reefer Madness and High School Confidential, becoming almost more camp than compelling.''

After routine maintenance following the Amazon expedition, *Calypso* set off for a less ambitious examination of the world's third longest river, the Mississippi. The yearlong journey, the Captain's first filmed entirely in the United States, demanded little of his own time, but it allowed the Cousteau Society to garner free publicity throughout the nation's heartland. Organizers arranged press events in cities all along *Calypso*'s 3,640-mile route, and they convinced the nationally televised *Entertainment Tonight* to produce a segment about the explorations.

Beginning in August 1983, the famed boat weaved its way from New Orleans through a series of locks and dams. The trip proceeded smoothly except that on one quiet afternoon *Calypso* encountered an unexpected current and slammed into a barge owned by the Army Corps of Engineers; the ship lost about fifteen feet of metal scuppers and deck rail.

Rather than focus on life within "Old Muddy," the Captain concentrated on how the river influenced those living along its banks. "The story of the Mississippi is one of wildlife, natural beauty and, of course, its people,'' he reported. "Our film about the Mississippi is a story of the river told by the people themselves.''

Most of the scenes, however, featured the Cousteaus and their crew. Viewers watched as the *Calypso* team helped the Mille Lacs tribe of northern Minnesota harvest wild rice from canoes. The red-capped Captain banged out a tune on Mark Twain's organ at the author's restored home in Hannibal, Missouri. Cousteau and cameraman Louis Prezelin also entertained the team with accordion and guitar at a campsite once visited by Lewis and Clark. And diver Dominique Sumian tried—unsuccessfully—to master the art of logrolling. Such a potpourri of vignettes provided pleasant pictures and information, but not the adventure and drama characteristic of Cousteau's best films.

To provide footage of wildlife, Jean-Michel and government researchers explored the habits of black bears that had been tagged with radio collars. Through the signal they located hibernating mothers, tranquilized them, and dragged the families from the dens to record their weights and blood quality. Jean-Michel interviewed the researchers, cuddled the cubs, and offered an emotional, if incomprehensible, observation: "As I held the young bears, their birth symbolized for me perhaps the rebirth we have come to study."

Jean-Michel also journeyed to Lake Itasca in Minnesota, where the main stream of the Mississippi begins. Because the water was clearest in the winter, he and a small team of divers chopped through the ice to capture the lake's few fish visually. Mostly they filmed themselves swimming with their feet up and their heads down so as to not stir the mucky bottom with their fins.

The Cousteau team, as usual, claimed a scientific purpose to its efforts. Although the Mississippi was probably the world's most analyzed river, Richard Murphy, the society's director of science, declared that his pollution survey was "the first such research covering the Mississippi's entire length." In reality, Murphy and scientists from the University of New Orleans's Center for Bio-organic Studies collected only eleven water samples that were tested for heavy metals and toxic organic compounds. "Our brief survey," he later announced, "did not show a highly polluted river during the three days we took samples."

Even before Murphy's specimens were analyzed, Cousteau criticized environmental "doomsayers" for claiming that it was too late to save the Mississippi. He admitted that industrial wastes, sewage discharges, and barge spills affected the river and surrounding habitats. But he marveled at the wealth of wildlife, and he applauded the efforts of scientists to monitor the progress of bears, Canada geese, and American bald eagles. The Captain concluded, "The Mississippi River is not dead; rather, it is vital, in all the senses of that word, reflecting the power and diversity of the culture along its banks."

The society's promotional materials declared that *Cousteau/Mississippi: The Reluctant Ally* gave viewers "an emotional, informative, and entertaining look at America's largest river." Despite criticism from a few reviewers, the television industry agreed, awarding the two-hour show the 1985 Emmy for outstanding informational special. It was the Captain's first Emmy in more than a decade, his eleventh overall.

* * *

When not producing television shows or managing his various businesses, Cousteau continued to tinker with new inventions. Along with Jacques Constans, who joined the staff after serving as deputy director general of the European Oceanic Association, the Captain developed a device to analyze the microscopic surface layer of the ocean. The Sea Spider, so named for its numerous delicate arms, measures the exchange processes and temperature in the thin interface between the atmosphere and the sea. The team patented the equipment in the name of the Commission of the European Communities, with the Cousteau Society to receive half the revenue from sales.

Most of the Captain's recent engineering efforts, however, have focused on how ships could reduce their energy consumption. Amid the oil crisis, he argued that his Turbosail™ would revolutionize the merchant marine by lowering fuel costs by up to 35 percent. Also motivating Cousteau was his desire "to come up with a successor to our old exploration ship, *Calypso,* which was built in 1942 as a minesweeper. It is time to replace her with a modern vessel better suited for the kind of scientific work and exploration we are doing today."

A variety of wind-assisted designs for commercial ships had been developed over the previous half century, the most efficient being the Magnus effect rotors devised by German engineer Anton Flettner in 1924. Cousteau, however, considered Flettner's device impractical, arguing that he "would not have those rotating drums on my ship. They can turn at 200 miles per hour and cut like a meat slicer." Flettner's rotating cylinders also hindered tacking into the wind because they required reversing the direction of the rotor rotation. To correct these problems, the Captain turned to Lucien Malavard, an aerodynamics professor at the Sorbonne and a member of the French Academy of Sciences who had helped design the Concorde and the Airbus.

Work on the Turbosail began in September 1980, shortly after Cousteau had secured more than a million dollars in commitments from the French Ministries of Industry, the Sea, and Energy. By guaranteeing that the prototype of a fuel-efficient commercial vessel would be made of aluminum, Cousteau also gained financial backing from Pechiney, the French metals multinational. Pechiney bought Cousteau's argument that most oceangoing freighters—those weighing between three thousand and eighty thousand tons—could employ his device. The company acquired the Turbosail license, while Cousteau planned to benefit from substantial royalties.

Ever mindful of his independence, the Captain acknowledged France's financial contribution but publicly decried the Socialists' environmental policy as "terrible." French governments, he declared, "whether they are right or left, try to appear as if they are interested in environmental issues, but they don't give the minister in charge any money or political power." Demonstrating a lack of tact, Cousteau continued, "The minister is like a puppet. If he had any guts he would resign. They don't resign because when you become a minister you have a pension for life."

Malavard and his student Bertrand Charrier, who had written his doctoral dissertation on wind propulsion, experimented with several options in a wind tunnel before developing an aspirated airfoil, a thick-sectioned sheet of metal with a parabolic leading edge and a semicircular after portion. The smokestack-shaped column, aerodynamically similar to an airplane wing, offered propulsion by deflecting air through the cylinder, producing a drop in air pressure on one side and an increase on the other.

The engineers assumed the wind would be only a complementary source of power. They programmed the ship's on-board computer to regulate the diesel engines so that the set speed would be maintained regardless of wind conditions.

Cousteau installed Malavard's forty-four-foot-high nonrotating vertical cylinder atop an existing catamaran hull. He named the sixty-five-foot vessel *Moulin à Vent* (Windmill). After numerous tests in the Mediterranean, he set sail in October 1983 from Tangier, Morocco, for a well-publicized Atlantic crossing. The Cousteau Society planned a massive welcoming ceremony in New York Harbor—complete with fireboats and fireworks—in mid-November.

In early November, however, a heavy storm, with fifty-knot winds and twenty-foot waves, attacked the experimental windship about four hundred miles east of Bermuda. When the six-man crew discovered that welds at the base of the cylinder were stressed, *Moulin à Vent* limped into Bermuda for repairs. Meanwhile, Jean-Michel flew from New York to Bermuda to join his mother aboard *Calypso,* which had sailed from Miami to assist the damaged vessel.

After a minor overhaul *Moulin à Vent* departed from Bermuda and immediately ran into more rough weather. Three days later, on November 17, the experimental mast fell into the swirling sea. No one was hurt, and the windship arrived in Norfolk under the power of its own engines; but the accident proved to be an embarrassing failure.

Cousteau tried to remain upbeat. "We have lost only the hardware," he said. "The brains who have conceived the systems are already at work. Give me a little time and we will do it again." The Captain declared that his second windship would be larger and employ two cylinders. "This is not dream stuff," he concluded. "This is economic reality."

Cousteau was not the only experimenter working on nonconventional wind-propulsion systems. Japanese engineers had developed a prototype cargo ship with two large, rigid sails of canvas stretched over retractable metal frames; the 216-foot, 700-ton *Shin Aitoku Maru* employed a microcomputer to monitor the wind velocity and adjust the sails accordingly. The Wind Ship Company of Norwell, Massachusetts, also announced that it had completed tests of a rotating sail for fishing vessels and oceangoing ships.

Unlike most of his competitors, the Captain raised enough money to experiment with several designs. Sailors had concluded that the catamaran hull of *Moulin à Vent,* rather than the wind-propulsion system, had caused the ship to behave poorly in the Bahamian tempest. "Instead of an experimental platform on a catamaran," said Bertrand Charrier, "we needed at our disposal a real ship conceived for wind propulsion. Only such a boat would open the door to the use of this process by cargo vessels and oil tankers." The team chose a half-catamaran, half-monohull design by naval architect André Mauric.

The new windship, christened *Alcyone,* set sail from La Rochelle, France, in May 1985. The transatlantic crossing proceeded smoothly, except when an unexpected swell swept cameraman Louis Prezelin off his feet, severely spraining his knee. To obtain free publicity and highlight his growing commitment to dialogue between the two superpowers, Cousteau had invited two journalists—Vladimir Krivocheev with Radio Moscow and Len King with Cable News Network—to accompany *Alcyone* on the maiden voyage to New York City and to broadcast daily reports on the ship's progress. His crew filmed the passage for a one-hour television special, narrated by Peter Ustinov and promoted and aired by Ted Turner's WTBS superstation.

On June 17, 1985, *Alcyone* entered New York Harbor for the postponed but still well-orchestrated celebration. Daylight fireworks roared in the East Bay, fireboats bestowed a water display, and Mayor Edward Koch issued a proclamation promoting Cousteau to "admiral." The proud "admiral" told the assembled crowd, "You will understand how moved I am to be received here in such a way with my old faithful ship *Calypso* and my new blond baby *Alcyone*." Noting the trials he endured to reach New York with a windship, he joked, "Ships are like women—difficult to understand. But when you succeed, it's worthwhile."

Cousteau had named his blond baby after the daughter of the Greek god of wind. He related to the crowd the Greek love story about Alcyone and her husband, an "ideal couple." When the man drowned, Alcyone killed herself in order to be with him. The gods, however, took pity on such a love and turned them both into kingfisher birds.

The 103-foot-long *Alcyone* features two 33-foot-high Turbosails as well as a double keel and a catamaran type of stern that enhance both stability and acceleration. The ship is so stiff, in fact, that all twelve crew members complained of seasickness during the maiden voyage. The vessel's on-board computer, which blends wind and diesel power to maintain a constant speed, has reduced the boat's fuel use by up to 40 percent compared with a similar-size ship.

The windship represents the Captain's commitment to positive action. Unlike most environmentalists, who Cousteau thinks "frequently find themselves saying no, no, no," he argues that "a passive attitude is not enough." When the entrepreneur saw a need resulting from the oil crisis, he took the initiative to develop an active and innovative response.

No doubt the venture was motivated as much by potential profit as by a commitment to renewable energy. Cousteau had hoped to make millions by marketing Turbosails to freighter companies around the world, but the drop in oil prices in the mid-1980's quashed his dreams. Despite elaborate sales demonstrations in Europe, the United States, Brazil, and Japan, *Alcyone* remains the only vessel sporting a Turbosail. Still, Cousteau, predicting that a hundred merchant vessels will be using the device by 1990, maintains that his invention "will transform world shipping."

What *Alcyone* has done is transform Cousteau's expeditions. Two ships certainly allow the Captain to expand his filming opportunities. But they've also enlarged his overhead expenses and added pressure to his already hectic schedule, forcing increased compromises in the quality of Cousteau productions.

In summer 1985, at the age of seventy-five, Cousteau launched a five-year around-the-planet adventure that became the focus of twenty hourlong television specials. As with past film series, Cousteau's *Rediscovery of the World* has featured some of the earth's strange creatures, including the snail-eating fly of the Philippines, the five-hundred-pound clams of the South Pacific, and the platypus of Tasmania. Cameramen also have explored a variety of human systems, from the shark worshipers of the Solomon Islands to the high tech ocean farmers of Japan.

The Captain and Jean-Michel, however, continue to move their films to a new formula, one based less on underwater shots and more on sociological issues. "Waters of Sorrow," for instance, portrays how Haitians have disastrously depleted their marine and forest resources. Another segment discusses nuclear war by examining the long-term impacts of U.S. bomb tests decades ago on the Eniwetok atoll in the South Pacific.

"The Rediscovery series has little to do with the behavior of animals," Cousteau says. "It has to do with the behavior of people with respect to the water system."

The Captain hopes the expedition has answered questions of local urgency which have global implications. How have kelp beds off New Zealand, for instance, been disrupted by runoff from large amounts of land devoted to raising sheep? What are the long-term effects of deforestation in Papua New Guinea on terrestrial and marine ecosystems?

Rather than attempt to uncover still-hidden corners of the environment, Cousteau planned "to take a fresh look at the planet man believes he already knows." He proposed to trace the routes of the early ocean explorers—Ferdinand de Magellan, Vasco de Balboa, Hernando de Cortés, Juan Ponce de León, Christopher Columbus, Amerigo Vespucci, and others—and record how the lush Edens they discovered have been affected by natural and man-made activities.

Turner Broadcasting System agreed to underwrite expected production costs that would accelerate from $750,000 per hourlong episode in 1986 to $911,630 in 1990. During the first year of filming, the society received $3 million from TBS but spent only $2.8 million on the Rediscovery series.

With a lucrative contract, Cousteau decided to redesign his diving gear, in part to take advantage of new technologies and materials and in part to update the image of his divers. Engineers experimented with a variety of compounds to produce a lighter but stronger tank for compressed air. They settled on a steel-titanium compound called Vascojet 9000, which will not be made available commercially because it contains a secret alloy developed by the French government. The new tank is smaller but holds about twice the capacity of traditional units, or about thirty-five cubic feet of air pressurized to five thousand pounds per square inch.

Traditional forged tanks had to be relatively thick to compensate for air pockets in the wall that could cause a rupture. In contrast, Cousteau's secret compound is sprayed through the mouth of a rotating mold, a process that ensures that the thin cylinder casing is formed in a uniform layer. The high tech tanks, however, have not been problem-free. One exploded in Norfolk, causing severe damage to the storage building. Cousteau technicians continue testing alternative materials, including a compound of aluminum and resin.

A new helmet incorporates a light in front and headphones inside. Engineers also inserted a small microphone into the regulator mouthpiece, enabling divers to speak among themselves and to talk with their colleagues on the surface. Some diving specialists, however, suggest the Cousteau helmet is dangerous, designed to be photogenic rather than practical.

The team also modified their underwater scooters to include a light and a regulator in the center and compressed air cylinders on each side. The innovation allows a diver to enter the water more quickly, without needing to strap on tanks. The aerodynamic design also increases the diver's mobility, thus conserving his energy.

Cousteau's most obvious change was to introduce suits, helmets, gloves, masks, fins, backpacks, and scooters that are all colored silver. The new wet suits feature a black stripe down each leg and arm. According to the society's promotional materials, "The familiar black-and-yellow suits of the Cousteau team were designed in the sixties, and now the Cousteau Society has plunged into the space-age technology of the eighties."

The Captain claims that the silver equipment reflects light and allows filming in darker waters. But David Brown, a *Calypso* diver and lecturer, discounts any increased illumination and complains that the silver suits only make him look like Flash Gordon.

Cousteau also turned to a modern tool for capturing images. After sixty-two years behind a movie camera, he switched to video. "I do not make this tremendous change without misgivings," he confessed, echoing his concerns in the late 1960's, when he gave up theater films for television. He also admitted to "painful thoughts" about adopting a medium that conveys "increasingly banal" shows and commercials.

But the modification provides the Captain with more flexibility and saves him considerable expense.

"I have never been there before." And so Cousteau justified making Haiti his first stop on the *Rediscovery* expedition.

Haiti, which occupies the western half of the island of Hispaniola, was discovered by Columbus in 1492. Colonized first by Spain and then by France, it achieved independence in 1791. When Cousteau arrived in July 1985, Haiti was home to almost six million people, making it more densely populated than India. It also possessed the dubious distinction of being the poorest country in the Western Hemisphere.

For centuries Haiti boasted lush forests and rich agricultural lands, and its residents enjoyed abundant sugar, coffee, and other cash crops as well as fish from the sea. But Cousteau's rediscovery of the island revealed that Haiti's farmland and seabeds had been ravaged by severe soil degradation. Devoting less than a third of his film to underwater shots, the Captain produced a sociological portrait of a nation depleting its resources at an alarming rate.

Evidence of the country's ecological despair appeared in the outdoor markets of Port-au-Prince, which Cousteau toured with a video camera in his hand and a floppy straw hat on his head. The meager stacks of fuel wood—used by most Haitians for cooking in hibachi-size grills—symbolized Haiti's frightening deforestation. Forests which once covered 80 percent of the land had been reduced to just 7 percent.

A vendor sold uniformly small fish obtained by local fishermen whose hunting grounds were limited by their motorless sailboats and their cultural fear of the deep sea. *Calypso* divers discovered that the inshore waters had been virtually drained of all but the most immature fish. But where the continental shelf sloped downward, they found an abundance of life: large red snappers, giant parrot fish, barracudas, and shellfish.

Other salesmen wandered about with steel tubs balanced on their heads, ladling clean water into cups for hot and thirsty shoppers. Cousteau's researchers learned that only one in five Haitian homes had access to safe drinking water. Because communities lacked adequate treatment and disposal systems, many residents were forced to bathe in filthy streams that transported sewage.

Few vendors offered grains, poultry, or meat, evidence that protein deficiency was widespread throughout the country, largely because deforestation had severely eroded precious topsoil, cutting food production drastically. Thirty percent of all grains had to be imported, and livestock was scarce.

The combination of dirty water and poor nutrition accounted for the advance of malaria, tuberculosis, polio, parasites, and dysentery. One Haitian child in ten died in infancy.

The nation's health problems almost killed one of Cousteau's own. Late one evening the *Calypso* received an urgent phone call by satellite from Port-au-Prince, where the four-man camera crew, including Jean-Michel, had been struck down by a mysterious illness. The ship turned immediately toward the capital city, arriving two hours later.

Calypso's doctor rushed to the hotel, where cameraman Jean-Paul Cornu appeared semiconscious. The diver's hands were numb, his blood pressure had fallen to 70/40, his gums and teeth hurt, and he groaned alarmingly. The physician diagnosed ciguatera, a severe case of food poisoning, possibly caused by the toxic contamination of fish. In fact, the whole crew had fallen sick from the noon meal of barracuda.

After eight hours of intravenous treatment, Cornu's condition began to improve. But for more than a month he and the rest of the team suffered unbearable itching of their hands, feet, and lips.

Cousteau tried to look beyond the health and environmental crises to record "the spirit of the Haitians themselves who, while facing a troubling future, endow the present with an inviolable human grace." To convey the Haitians' enthusiastic mixture of Roman Catholicism with voodoo, he joined fifty thousand pilgrims converging for an annual celebration at Ville Bonheur, a tiny village about forty miles from Port-au-Prince. Cousteau's driver had painted a colorful version of the *Calypso* maiden on the side of his "tap-tap," which crawled up the rocky mountain road with the human procession.

The pilgrims to Ville Bonheur maintained that the Virgin Mary appeared at the nearby Saint d'Eau falls about fifty years before, sitting atop a palm tree. As proof of the miracle's power, believers recounted for Cousteau the story of the skeptical priest who tried to eliminate the vision with his machete—and died a violent death. Faithful also to voodoo tradition, worshipers argued that water is the pathway used by the spirits to travel between their netherworld and the human world. To commemorate these mysteries and bring good fortune to themselves and their loved ones, they bathed and frolicked in the spring-fed waters that cascaded over forty feet.

The Captain joined the Haitians under the waterfall. His admiring staff described the scene in colorful terms: "Celebrity and celebrant were the same, as each was refreshed and renewed in a rite celebrating the source of life—water."

To enhance the Haitians' limited success with enriching the quality of their water environment, the Captain made a personal and well-publicized commitment to the minister of agriculture to help local experts vitalize the bays and coastal areas with aquaculture projects. After the filming expedition, however, Cousteau reduced his grand offer and simply sent two Haitian fisheries specialists to Martinique for a short course in mariculture.

In contrast with Haiti's "waters of sorrow," Cuba's aquatic system, observed Cousteau, was "a sea brimming with wealth . . . a rare abundance of fish in lush coral jungles." Society staff writers claimed that the difference between the two countries resulted from the Cuban belief that "marine resources are assets rather than raw materials, commodities rather than products. The former are used sparingly and managed over time with minimum depletion. The latter, like cash, are dispersed quickly to cover costs."

Calypso arrived in Cuba in late fall 1985 to follow for ten weeks the routes Columbus examined first in 1492 and more extensively in 1494. The early explorer discovered abundant natural resources, and Cousteau learned lessons in wise environmental management.

The Cuban minister of fisheries informed the Captain of his country's strict catch quotas by species and by area. To examine the policy's effectiveness, *Calypso*'s team visited remote lobster-collecting platforms, where fishermen lived for ten days at a stretch, transferring crustaceans from their rafts into natural tanks. Cousteau found that the workers adhered to minimum size regulations as well as the ban on lobster trapping from March through May, the crustaceans' spawning season. "Even if I wanted to catch the small ones," said a local fisherman, "no one would buy them because everyone knows it is against the law."

Society staffers also investigated Cuba's many aquaculture projects, on which scientists bred rare species of sea turtles, manatees, and crocodiles. Government officials, in an effort to obtain foreign exchange, encouraged fishermen to raise for export conch, shrimp, oysters, and a high-protein freshwater fish called tilapia. They also hired former crocodile hunters to capture the reptiles alive in order to provide a breeding stock; in essence, they converted hunters into salaried conservationists.

The Cousteau team confirmed the richness of the country's undersea environment by diving to the *Cristóbal Colón,* a Spanish armored cruiser sunk by the U.S. fleet near the small town of Chivirico during the Spanish-American War. The wreck had become a haven for thousands of fish and seashells, and the water was so clear that photographers aboard *Calypso* could film divers working below. After a deep dive, rare because of damage to his inner ear, the Captain surfaced and proclaimed: "Absolutely *fantastique.* I have never seen anything like it—a ballet of tarpon—everywhere."

With stunning underwater photography, Cousteau's team recorded, for the first time, the strange vertical feeding position of the whale shark, the largest fish in the sea. The encounter began when the helicopter pilot spotted a frothy foam in the middle of the Caribbean. Captain Cousteau arrived at the scene to discover a massive shark devouring a wall of bonito tunas and anchovies, straining the fish from the seawater that flowed into its four-foot-wide mouth. Because the creature rarely feeds at the water's surface, *Calypso* divers rushed into the water to document the giant's extraordinary behavior. Never ones to miss an opportunity to "commune" with an undersea animal, team members grabbed hold of the whale shark's enormous gray-green fin, and they quickly recorded each other joyriding about the surface for the few moments before the titan returned to the depths.

Moreover, cameramen gained rare photographs of "cleaning stations" within the coral reefs. Tiny fish, as if providing a contract service, clustered in a few spots to nip larger fish delicately clean of parasites and damaged skin.

Not to limit the *Rediscovery* series to such underwater scenes, no matter how dramatic the footage, the Captain left the *Calypso* and traveled inland to film an assortment of Cubans at work and play. He visited a cigar factory where skilled laborers shaped tobacco products by hand. He toured sugarcane plantations where workers gracefully slashed the stalks with machetes. And in Havana he filmed a Catholic festival that commemorated the city's founding and an ancient African dance that celebrated the goddess of the sea.

Cousteau also interviewed Cuban President Fidel Castro about a range of topics. Out of his element, the "Captain-turned-diplomat" abruptly asked Castro's opinion of the U.S. Navy base at Guantánamo Bay in southeastern Cuba. The angry president declared that the foreign military installation humiliated his country, and he pulled from his desk a stack of American lease checks that remained uncashed in protest. Later, at the base, Cousteau suggested to the American base commander that Guantánamo offered no strategic value to the United States, and he expressed regret that people had not overcome their territoriality. "I had hoped all along my journey through life," Cousteau explained, "that humans would finally rise above instincts, to achieve a borderless harmony." The U.S. military officer listened politely.

The Captain, enjoying his self-styled role as "ambassador of good-will," also lectured Castro about human rights abuses and appealed for the release of political prisoners. Within three weeks Cuban authorities freed fifty inmates, including Lázaro Jordana.

Almost seven years before, Jordana had lost his job as art professor at the university in Las Tunas because of "ideological divergency." A year later he and his father tried to flee Cuba, but authorities intercepted their boat and sentenced the pair to twenty years in Havana's Combinado del Este prison. For trying to smuggle his prison drawings out of Cuba through the services of a friend, Jordana was locked in solitary confinement for seven months. Upon his return to the main cells, inmates elected him president of a group of dissident writers and artists.

One day, without warning, Jordana received a letter from Jacques Cousteau stating, "I am extremely happy to announce to you that you will soon be liberated, and to wish you good luck in your new life." As a boy the artist had seen the Captain's shows on Cuban television, but the announcement came as a complete surprise. Authorities arranged visas for Jordana to leave Cuba quickly and emigrate to Paris, where he works as an artist.

"Cousteau saved my life, and my father's life, and the lives of all of the fifty people released," Jordana says. "Then he didn't say anything about it. No publicity. I really like that about him." Of the Captain, Jordana concludes: "He's the kind of man who does things —doesn't talk about them—just does things."

While *Calypso* returned to Miami for repairs, *Alcyone* headed toward the southern tip of South America to test its innovative "sails" in the unpredictable winds around Cape Horn. For nearly four hundred years of nautical history, ships had crossed these treacherous waters between the Atlantic and Pacific oceans. Hundred of vessels had foundered under the Horn's violent gales; thousands of sailors had been swept from their decks by the towering seas.

Alcyone, however, arrived when the Horn offered a deceptive calm. So gentle were the waves that crew members put the ship on automatic pilot so they could take pictures of each other passing through the famous channel. They sent the helicopter aloft to record the ship's transit, and two divers even descended with their scooters to complete the first rounding of Cape Horn at a depth of eighty feet.

Jean-Michel directed a small contingent to spend a few days on Horn Island, while he and other divers explored beneath the waters at the "bottom of the world." The land team stayed with two young officers of the Chilean Navy who operated a lonely communications station that tracked passing ships. In the cold and Spartan outpost cameramen watched the accelerating winds quickly turn the sky from warm sunshine to gray clouds to curtains of hail.

Divers found little to photograph within the sea's dark turbulence. Jean-Michel eventually called off the descents because a quickening current beneath the surface carried the team far away from the Zodiac, which itself was pushed in the opposite direction by a stiff breeze.

The rather uneventful passage changed its tone as *Alcyone* headed north along the Chilean coast, where few of the isolated inlets and channels had been charted. As Captain Bernard Deguy negotiated a narrow pass, the sonar suddenly picked up a big rock within eight feet of the surface. Deguy tried to reverse the engines, but momentum sent *Alcyone* into the deceptive boulder, slashing a hole the size of a diving mask in the starboard keel. Water gushed into the hull, rising to within an inch of the cabin floorboards.

While crew members frantically pumped cold seawater from the ship, engineers worked for eight hours to plug the wound. When their initial seal failed to hold, Captain Deguy placed an emergency call to Chile's navy, which dispatched a helicopter with special cement. The temporary patchwork allowed the team to proceed up the coast to Punta Arenas, where shipyard workers repaired the aluminum keel.

Cameramen, of course, filmed the entire incident, knowing that their efforts would add some drama to their chronicle of the Cape Horn expedition. A society writer later noted that the close call "evoked a sobering realization that human technology remains vulnerable to nature's deceits in earth's most remote reaches."

By May 1986 *Alcyone* had climbed the western coast of South and Central America to the Sea of Cortez, also known as the Gulf of

California. The accident caused the crew to miss filming the migration of the blue whales, but the Cousteaus tried to make up for the setback by assembling U.S. reporters to promote their *Rediscovery* series.

The Captain flew in from Paris for the special event, billed to the media as a rare opportunity to spend time with a living legend. The extended press conference turned into a love feast. "This is a dream come true for me," gushed one newspaper photographer as the Captain's lanky figure emerged from his seaplane.

The journalists spent the weekend at a luxurious hotel on Isla Danzante. Throughout the day they toured *Alcyone* and inspected the new diving equipment. Over dinner they reveled in Cousteau's presence and jovial charm, enchanted by his tales of adventure. According to one reporter, "The Captain was part of the scenery, here to provide the fawning reporters with an exotic dateline, to have his picture shot in a hundred post-card poses and to swat the reporters' lobs of softball questions like Reggie Jackson in batting practice with the Little League." The society got what it wanted: a series of lengthy and laudatory feature articles in some of the nation's major newspapers.

After the reporters departed, the crew got down to the business of making another movie, and the long, narrow sea between mainland Mexico and Baja California offered some of the world's best actors. Massive manta rays both flew through the water and leaped into the air. Hammerhead sharks, their haunting eyes protruding from the ends of their flat snouts, circled the cameramen. Dolphins and several types of whales appeared mysteriously.

Jean-Michel also dispatched a team to film the area's bizarre land animals: rattlesnakes with no rattles and bats that ate fish. These men of the sea rode mules awkwardly across the red-rocked desert to an oasis, where they photographed ancient Indian cave paintings of a breaching whale, manta rays, and other fish. After another day on their surefooted transports, the land team returned to the beach in time to record tourists in dune buggies inadvertently killing thousands of grunions that had come to the shore to mate.

The Cousteaus spent considerable time trying to identify other human actions that were causing an environmental crisis within this "land of paradise." They located experts who declared that Colorado River diversions had slashed the flow of sediments and nutrients into the Sea of Cortez. Jean-Michel, after watching fishermen shovel 90 percent of their catch back into the sea as useless wastes, also learned that government subsidies encouraged fishing late in the season, thus disturbing the benthic environment that supported the shrimp and other fish. But rather than work to change the underlying public policies, the Cousteaus argued that their role was simply to publicize the problems.

Calypso, meanwhile, remained in a Miami shipyard. After forty-four years of service, the former minesweeper's two diesel engines had to be replaced. The Captain refused to risk his first Pacific Ocean crossing with worn equipment.

For several months staffers pleaded with motor manufacturers to make a donation, but the society was finally forced to pay almost $61,000 to Cummins Metropower. After a generator set, two reverse and reduction gears, electrical components, propellers, state-of-the-art navigation instruments, and spare parts had been added, the total bill came to $164,912. Cousteau, recognizing the unanticipated expense as a fund-raising opportunity, sent a special letter to society members asking for contributions to renovate *Calypso.* The generous response totaled more than $261,000.

Engineer Jean-Marie France had to remove *Calypso*'s stack and widen the hole to remove the engines that had provided power since 1942. He and his team spent long hours settling the new 500 hp dynamos into their berths and reattaching hoses and shafts.

In July 1986 the sturdy vessel, now with "the courage of new engines," prepared to leave Miami for the Panama Canal, Tahiti, and New Zealand. The Cousteaus arrived in time for the send-off and an afternoon press conference. "Rediscovery is an ambitious name," the Captain declared. "But it corresponds to reality. The discovery of the planet as we knew it in the 19th and 20th centuries is over. We have to follow up and keep up with the changes."

Cameramen recorded Jacques and Jean-Michel walking through a crowd of admirers to reach the refitted *Calypso.* Men, women, and children surrounded the Captain, pressing to shake the celebrity's hand. In what was becoming a major concern of Cousteau Society staff, however, no one seemed to recognize Jean-Michel.

On the way to New Zealand, Cousteau's team filmed a one-hour broadcast on the Marquesas Islands in French Polynesia, where painter Paul Gauguin was buried. The helicopter swooped through deep canyons and around steep mountains, which the Captain described as "flames of stone into the sky" and "cathedrals of lava," while divers on the Zodiac lowered their cameras amid frolicking schools of dolphins. "Because of delays at the shipyard," stated Cousteau, "we spent only three weeks in the Marquesas. That's very short to make a film, but we were lucky."

Focus rather than time was Cousteau's problem in New Zealand. The crew spent four months photographing, but the Captain struggled to provide some continuity for what became a two-hour television show. With film footage in hand, he told a reporter, "There's a limit to what the viewer can assimilate. That's my big problem here—there is so much, it is beginning to be a problem in editing."

The skilled filmmaker never located a theme in the editing room. "New Zealand: Land of the Long White Cloud" ended up as a hodgepodge travelogue on the South Pacific nation. Viewers endured a long and obviously staged welcoming ceremony by the Maoris, the Polynesian tribe who originally settled New Zealand more than eighteen centuries ago. They had to watch tourists watching a geyser. They saw David Lange, the country's prime minister, board *Calypso* and talk briefly to Cousteau. And they tracked the Captain stumbling slowly through the woods while the narrator sternly warned, "In such an enchanted forest, witches and wizards could lurk."

The film also lacked adventure. Relying only upon eerie background music to create suspense, for instance, the Captain warned that glacial peaks were concealed beneath the water's surface near New Zealand's southern tip and that "*Calypso* must glide carefully among silent hazards." But no icebergs became manifest. A few minutes later in the broadcast, fog quickly blanketed the ship, and the eerie music returned. A cameraman aboard *Calypso* recorded Cousteau looking worried about the helicopter's fate, while another in the helicopter showed the pilot appearing equally concerned. But as rapidly as the fog arrived, it rolled away, and the helicopter returned safely to *Calypso*.

The television special, moreover, failed to convey the technical excellence usually associated with Cousteau's work. Viewers, for instance, watched octopuses move in and out of darkness as divers failed to hold their lights steady on the subjects.

While the quality of Cousteau's films varied, life aboard *Calypso* remained jovial. New divers and scientists joined the team, but several key members—including Albert Falco, Michel Deloire, Dominique Sumian, Bernard Delemotte, and Raymond Coll—maintained the sense of goodwill and adventure that the Captain had fashioned over the years. "People are happy, or they go," Cousteau declared. "The *Calypso* is a bird cage with all doors open."

The wardroom, with its ceiling only an inch over six feet high, has remained the center for socializing. The space is cramped, slightly smaller than an ordinary apartment bedroom. A dining table runs from one end to the other.

With a mostly French crew, breakfast aboard *Calypso* is simple and casual. Divers wander in for bread and jam and coffee. In contrast, lunch and dinner are fabulous productions—prepared by a chef who trained at the École Hotelière in Nice and interned at the famous Savoy Hotel in London—that match expensive meals at first-class restaurants.

As an example, one lunch served while the crew filmed off New Zealand began with cauliflower vinaigrette, followed by a course of salmon in sauce mousseline. The main course featured a leg of New Zealand lamb, accompanied by white beans and carrots in a delicate dressing. Wine, both French and New Zealand, flowed freely. Salad, cheese, and fruit served as the first part of dessert. Ice cream, particularly chocolate since the Captain was aboard, topped off the luncheon. After the meal the men sat comfortably in the sun, smoked, drank coffee from large mugs, and watched the sea pass by.

When present, Cousteau checks his watch regularly and expresses outright pleasure when tasks are completed ahead of his detailed schedule. Despite the elaborate plans, he relies frequently on his instincts and whims. Two men are normally assigned to lookout duty and charged with reporting any form of activity that might call for investigation. Although he overstated a little, one diver said the Captain's "insatiable curiosity about everything concerning the sea had communicated itself to the entire crew, and the smallest unidentified spot on the surface was sufficient to warrant a detour."

Cousteau's men have long enjoyed a spirited camaraderie. In the early days, as one wrote in his diary, there were "expressions of [the crew's] joy in being young and water-borne, of being the first to enter unknown fluid frontiers hidden from all human eyes and swarming with life of a different order."

When at sea, the wooden ship is filled with a variety of noises. Even after the crew members retire to their twenty-seven bunks, "beams creak with the stress of each forward lurch, each warp sideward.'' According to Mose Richards, the society's New York-based writer:

> Like a million beating wings, the thrumming of the engines floods the quarters, drenching conversations, vibrating through the wood skeleton itself. Outside, the clash of breaking water sprays and coughs pass the portholes as a ragged percussion. Occasionally a sigh and shudder murmur through the ship, unheard by the anchor crew, the film crew, the guest scientists, who sleep. The sailing crew is awake, however, scanning the horizon and the radar screen for obstacles, checking the chimney for stack fires, looking into the hold for water-bearing leaks. A person reading in a bunk in the maindeck quarters hears occasional steps thump across the ceiling as a deckhand hurries from bow to stern, cuisinière to bridge.

Throughout the spring of 1987 *Alcyone* made its way up the West Coast of the United States, stopping for media and fund-raising events in San Diego, Newport Beach, Huntington Beach, Los Angeles, Ventura, Santa Barbara, San Francisco, Portland, and Seattle. The eleven-person crew discovered both financial resources and undersea riches.

Off California's Channel Islands, cameraman Louis Prezelin uncovered signs of the natural world's resilience. Despite tons of pollution and years of exploitation by commercial and sports fishermen, isolated underwater sites remained home to hundreds of large pink abalone. Prezelin also explored a narrow cave where "zillions of lobsters were clustered like bats."

Along the timber-lined coast of Washington State, the *Alcyone* team photographed red salmon waiting for enough rain to fill the rivers so they could begin their annual migration to the headwaters. The group also "rediscovered" the giant octopuses that Cousteau had filmed more than fifteen years before.

Above Vancouver Island, in the cold waters of Alert Bay in Queen Charlotte Strait, the divers witnessed extraordinary behavior by a group of orcas, or killer whales. A twenty-foot-long female tried to pass a four-foot salmon from her mouth to her baby's, but the playful infant ignored the prize. The frustrated mother eventually released the unharmed salmon, which righted itself and began to swim away. But when the large orca had repositioned her infant, she quickly recaptured the fish and shoved it into the calf's mouth. The pair swam off, leaving

Alcyone cameramen to marvel at the unique but short-lived event. One diver described it as "like watching a car accident; you're not sure what just happened."

In June crew members began a three-month expedition around the Bering Sea, where they encountered natives, industrialists, and environmentalists battling over access to the abundant resources. On one side, the International Whaling Commission had recently created a hunting quota to protect the endangered bowhead whale. Eskimos, however, wanted to manage whale hunting themselves, in keeping with their cultural traditions. They protested that the commission's strict limitation eliminated one of their main sources of food, curtailing their intake of vital fat and protein. After interviewing both camps, Jean-Michel complained, "Native or whales—must there be only one choice?"

For their colorful television show on Alaska, the team photographed the birth of baby fur seals and the sad spectacle of their being clubbed to death by hunters. The cameramen recorded brown bears peeling salmons, like bananas, leaving only clean skeletons to float down the river. And for a human perspective, they filmed amateur gold prospectors shoveling sand through sluice boxes at the annual treasure hunt in Nome.

Jean-Michel arrived in time to be photographed aboard *Alcyone* as it sailed through the Bering Strait, in sight of both the United States and the Soviet Union. Captain Cousteau joined the ship in the Sea of Japan to demonstrate the vessel's sailing systems to Japanese businessmen. *Alcyone,* having completed its first two years at sea, then spent several weeks in dry dock for a complete overhaul and repainting.

Calypso, meanwhile, arrived off Australia's eastern coast in October 1987 to film the Great Barrier Reef. The world's largest coral reef extends over an area of more than 88,000 square miles, along 1,429 miles of coastline. It supports vast schools of sharks, groupers, jacks, and parrot fish. Cameramen paid particular attention to the spectacular mass spawning of coral during the three days that followed the full moon of November. Dozens of species released millions of colorful balls filled with sperms and eggs. The bright beads slowly rose to the surface, in what divers described as an upside-down snowstorm.

In May 1988 the two Cousteau ships rendezvoused in Papua, New Guinea, described by the Captain as "an ecologist's Eden." Cameramen filmed local fishermen using spider webs attached to a long piece of twine that hung below a flying kite, an arrangement that caused the lure to dance across the surface of the sea. They witnessed a traditional shark-calling ritual in which islanders in their outrigger canoes shook coconut shell rattles to attract sharks, which they lassoed with vine hoops. The Cousteau team also spent eight hours in the water with a pair of powerful orcas that circled the small island of Wuvulu and devoured a six-foot manta ray and several large sharks.

Leaving Papua New Guinea in late June 1988, *Calypso* headed for Singapore and two months of routine maintenance. Cousteau joined his ship in October to explore and film Borneo, a hot, humid island with unique plant and animal life. Jean-Michel and *Alcyone* proceeded to investigate the ecology of Eniwetok Island thirty years after a series of atomic bomb tests had destroyed all life and littered the land with radioactive dust.

In 1990 the Cousteaus plan to explore China. The Captain already has signed a declaration of cooperation with Chinese officials to participate in biogeochemical studies of the Yangtze River. As he has done throughout his life, Cousteau predicts his next expedition will be his greatest ever.

CHAPTER NINE

The Environmentalist

Cousteau came to appreciate the politics of environmentalism slowly. American and European conservationists had struggled since the beginning of the century to preserve wilderness areas, but the undersea explorer initially saw little threat to the abundant life within the vast expanse of ocean. Rather than protect the sea, he sought to reveal its wonders to a curious public through films and books and by providing the diving equipment that allowed people to explore it for themselves.

Selfishness was a major factor in the Captain's first conservation campaign. For years Cousteau and his colleagues had dived among the bright coral in the clear waters near Aldabra, a mangrove-covered cluster of islands off the coast of East Africa. When developers threatened to destroy the pristine paradise in the mid-1950's, Cousteau protested: "We had grown so attached to the place that it seemed like a threat to our own property."

To protect his wildlife sanctuary, the Captain proposed to lease the atolls from the British and build a tropical research center reserved for scientists like him. He presented his plan to the regional British governor, who expressed sympathy for conservation but supported development. Cousteau submitted a formal tender for a fifty-year lease, noting his purposes as preservation, tropical research, and the establishment of a meteorological station. He even flew to London to argue his case to the Colonial Office, Lady Clementine Churchill, and the BBC television network.

"The response gave me no illusions that the islands would be spared," he admitted, "but at least I had put up a fight for the coral sanctuary." The British government eventually rejected Cousteau's bid in favor of the establishment of hotels and other commercial ventures on the atolls.

In 1957, when the Captain became director of the Oceanographic Institute, he convinced Monaco's Prince Rainier to set aside the sea area in front of the museum as an experimental farm. In this Marine Biotron, Cousteau, being then more a tinkerer than a conservationist, proposed to "manipulate the submarine environment, establish artificial housing, plastic kelp, machine-made currents, unnatural photosynthesis, and chemical nutrition, to check against neighboring control areas of undisturbed nature."

Before the Biotron could be established, however, Monaco dumped tons of rocks, gravel, and sand on both sides of the area in an attempt to expand its territory with landfills. The resulting dust and mineral debris that settled onto the site killed most of the delicate marine organisms.

In 1959, after having suffered two conservation setbacks, Cousteau confronted a new and ominous threat. To reestablish the institute as a center for scientific dialogue, he had agreed to sponsor the International Atomic Energy Agency's conference on the disposal of nuclear wastes. As host but with little knowledge of or interest in radioactive rubbish, Cousteau planned to deliver short welcoming remarks and to sit politely through a few speeches before returning to his office.

The second professor to talk, however, delivered a bombshell. He argued that energy demands of the exploding world population required the rapid development of atomic power. Such expansion, he continued, would entail dumping nuclear waste in the ocean, "even at the cost of closing the sea to all human use, including navigation."

A stunned Cousteau couldn't fathom the notion of restricting ocean exploration or travel. By the end of the conference he had convinced the assembled scientists to establish an international center at the Oceanographic Institute to study the effects of radioactivity on the sea.

About a year later, in October 1960, a leading French regional newspaper reported that radioactive wastes from the Marcoule nuclear power station near Avignon were soon to be dumped into the Mediterranean Sea. As if polluting Cousteau's precious Mediterranean were not sufficiently blasphemous, the paper quoted atomic commission officials claiming that the dump site had been "chosen after studies by such oceanographers as V. Romanovsky and Cdt. Cousteau." The adventurer fumed at the unauthorized use of his name and the affront to his reputation.

The next morning Cousteau called Dr. Vsevolod Romanovsky to deliberate their response to the atomic commission's actions. The respected scientist agreed to write protest letters to the newspaper and the government, noting that he found the "experimental dumping" to be premature.

Cousteau then demonstrated a keen understanding of media relations. Worried that atomic commission representatives might pressure the newspaper to block any expression of protest, he waited to file his complaint until late on Sunday, after the managing editor had gone home. He reached a young assistant, who, facing a deadline, had little time to consult with senior editors, let alone government ministers. Cousteau dictated a statement that his organization had never studied atomic waste disposal and that the selected site presented enormous dangers to surrounding French towns. Prevailing currents, he claimed, would contaminate Mediterranean beaches with radioactivity.

The newspaper's morning edition carried Cousteau's entire statement, and twenty journalists, sensing a growing conflict, greeted the Captain when he arrived for work at the institute. With a grand gesture, the protester escorted the media into his spacious office. In the midst of a lively and animated discussion, Cousteau accepted a telephone call from an atomic commission representative.

"How dare you!" the bureaucrat snapped. "My minister is very angry. I am warning you on his behalf to keep quiet from now on."

Cousteau, greatly enjoying the drama playing out before the reporters, responded firmly, "I don't believe that a minister of France would single out anyone for the sort of treatment you gave me." He hung up the phone and continued his press conference.

Later that afternoon the commission announced that the dumping would occur in ten days. Cousteau marked his calender "D [for dump] Day, Minus 10." Clearing his schedule, he began to organize.

On D day minus nine, dumping opponents gathered at the Oceanographic Institute to produce mimeographed statements for the press and to dispatch speakers to chambers of commerce, trade unions, tourist agencies, fishermen's syndicates, and any other group that would be affected by the sea's contamination. The following day Monaco's Prince Rainier appealed—unsuccessfully—to French President Charles de Gaulle, and Toulon's city council, in a raucous public meeting, demanded that the French government call off the dumping. On D day minus one, citizens of Nîmes gathered on the railway tracks to block the waste train from arriving at the Toulon port. No trains ran on D day.

As public pressure continued to mount, French ministers invited Cousteau to Paris for discussions. The Captain agreed that dumping could be necessary in the future, but he demanded that additional studies be conducted to determine the impact of radioactive poisons on the sea. As the French Senate began to debate the issue, the atomic commission quietly canceled the dumping operation.

The victory, of course, was not Cousteau's alone, though he later claimed most of the credit. The mayors of Nice and Menton and senators and deputies from Marseilles and Toulon argued strenuously against the dumping plan as well. Hundreds of citizens devoted thousands of hours to raising a public protest. Still, the Captain provided effective leadership. He had recognized a threat to the sea and acted decisively to stop it.

Cousteau, many years later, still savored the 1960 campaign against France's nuclear dumping as his finest environmental accomplishment. He boasted, "It was one of the very rare victories against the nuclear lobby."

The early 1960's were heady years for American conservationists. They preserved pristine lands in national parks and predicted that an enlarged federal government would manage new technologies to increase both economic efficiency and environmental quality. Enveloped in the optimism of the Kennedy administration, Interior Secretary Stuart Udall declared that "the swift ascendancy of technology has made the scientist the surest conservation symbol of the '60s. His instruments are the atom-smasher, the computer, and the rocket—tools that have opened the door to an ultimate storehouse of energy and may yet reveal the secrets of the stars." In words that would shock today's environmentalist, Udall described nuclear power as "the supreme conservation achievement of this century" because it fashioned an "almost self-renewing source of energy."

Such optimism did not last long. Rather than solve environmental problems, technological advances after World War II greatly increased the generation of pollutants. In the thirty-year period from 1940 to 1970, for instance, annual phosphate output from fertilizers and municipal sewage increased more than sevenfold to almost three hundred million pounds per year, seriously degrading surface waters.

Rachel Carson recognized the growing crisis and switched tactics. Having preceded Cousteau with lyrical and informative books about the ocean, she produced in 1962 the seminal *Silent Spring*. Calling her time "an age of poisons," Carson documented the threat that the indiscriminate use of phosphates, pesticides, and other pollutants posed to both humans and wildlife. Confronting brutal attacks from business leaders, the soft-spoken writer ignited an international campaign against pollution.

The conservative community of Santa Barbara never expected to convert Rachel Carson's concerns into a national protest. But on January 28, 1969, an oil platform off California's Pacific coast exploded and spewed some 235,000 gallons of crude oil into the city's harbor and along a thirty-mile stretch of unspoiled beach. For several weeks the national media filmed retired residents and college students collecting dead birds and fish that had been trapped in the tar. They interviewed normally apathetic citizens demanding that pollution be controlled. They editorialized about the dangers of wanton economic expansion. The Santa Barbara disaster, they concluded, marked a turning point in the public's attitude toward nature, and it gave birth to a new political actor: the environmental activist.

The gravity of ecological problems cannot totally explain the rise of modern environmentalism. Pollution had been more lethal in many communities a few decades before. For instance, the 1948 air pollution calamity at Donora, Pennsylvania, claimed forty lives but did not elicit strident calls for new regulations. In the late 1960's, however, the growing belief that public needs must be placed above private interests fueled the ecology movement and converted it into a political force. Unlike conservationists of an earlier era, the organizers of Earth Day in 1970 had little interest in managing natural resources efficiently in order to promote economic growth. In fact, they questioned the very purpose of technological development and business expansion if the results were pollution and ecological imbalance.

The rapid advance of antipollution activism caught most social prophets by surprise. As late as 1968 experts at the Brookings Institution in Washington, D.C., didn't even list ecology among the most pressing issues facing the country. But just two years later Earth Day touched a responsive chord as more than twenty million people participated in teach-ins and ecology fairs. Memberships in the five largest citizen-based environmental groups jumped by four hundred thousand, a 33 percent increase in 1970 alone. Activists harnessed this heightened public interest to pass landmark legislation designed to clean the nation's air and water, create the Environmental Protection Agency (EPA), and regulate all major government projects that affect natural resources. "Love Your Mother"—a reference to Mother Earth—became the slogan of the day.

While environmental activism advanced in North America and Europe, Cousteau spent most of the 1960's promoting industrial projects. *Calypso*'s divers, for instance, helped lay natural gas pipelines in the western Mediterranean, and they conducted extensive surveys for Tunisian and Italian natural gas firms. The team also periodically exploded undersea bombs to help scientists locate mineral resources beneath the seafloor, even though such seismic refraction destroyed wildlife and vegetation.

Cousteau, moreover, agreed to help a Marseilles aluminum company locate an "acceptable" deepwater dumping site for its polluted wastes. Despite vehement protests from fishermen and marine biologists that the firm's red mud would kill everything on the ocean bottom, Cousteau selected a six-thousand-foot canyon. The Captain estimated that the toxic discharges wouldn't fill the gorge for at least a hundred years, but he couldn't guarantee against leaks. Ironically, he defined his lack of certainty as "an unexpected scientific bonus" because it would require researchers to observe over time how "turbidity currents behave and how far the mud spreads on the abyssal plain."

Cousteau marks the turning point in his environmental consciousness as the manned landing on the moon in July 1969. *Calypso* had dropped anchor off the island of Unalaska when Neil Armstrong and Edwin Aldrin took their giant steps for mankind. The ship's log noted that while two men looked back toward the blue planet, Raymond Coll was piloting the minisub some five hundred feet beneath the sea.

The satellite pictures of the earth conveyed more clearly than any environmentalist's treatise the fragility and wonder of life. Several years later Cousteau declared, "We can see for ourselves that the earth is a water planet. There is a limited amount of water on our globe—no more, relatively speaking, than a single droplet of water on an egg—but nonetheless, the earth is the only known planet to be washed with this vital liquid, so necessary for life. The earth photograph can drive a second lesson home to us: It can finally make us recognize that the inhabitants of the earth must depend upon and support each other.

The dust of distant planets has been baked and doused with chemicals in the desperate quest to discover life, but we have discovered only that we are alone in the solar system and perhaps in the universe.''

Unlike most environmental activists, however, Cousteau did not alter his deep faith in technology. Wise management, he claimed, could harvest the sea's abundant resources and still protect the ocean's bountiful diversity.

Cousteau labeled his approach "ecotech," a combination of ecology and economics. "Both sciences," he said, "have the same duty: the art of harmoniously managing our household, the water planet earth. Both can do little without the help of technology, and technology goes wild without economic and ecological controls." Although they never came to pass, the Captain proposed to create chairs in ecotechnics at several universities around the world, assuming the professors would develop practical antidotes to environmental problems associated with development.

Cousteau may have once argued that the government spent too much money on the space program and too little on undersea projects, but the astronauts' photographs moved him to picture space exploration as the "midwife to the birth of a new global consciousness." The benefits of space-based technologies became increasingly clear to Cousteau. "Space engineering today is essential to oceanographic research," he said in 1980. "Teledetection and the probing of instrument-equipped buoys by satellite are going to make most of the old oceanographic research techniques completely obsolete."

As important, Cousteau recognized the benefits that could be derived from cooperating with the space establishment. During the next decade he convinced NASA and NOAA to sign several contracts and to contribute an array of sophisticated electronic equipment to *Calypso*.

Not long after *Calypso* returned from Antarctica, Cousteau expanded his environmental advocacy, largely in response to an international crisis that began when Egyptian troops crossed into Israeli-occupied Suez and closed the Suez Canal. Spurred by Arab unity against Israel, Sheikh Zaki Yamani, Saudi Arabia's oil chief, convened a meeting of OPEC, on October 17, 1973. The oil ministers agreed to increase petroleum prices 70 percent, to $5.12 a barrel, and to cut production 5 percent each month "until the Israel withdrawal is completed . . . and the legal rights of the Palestinian people [are] restored.''

Within days Saudi Arabia had slashed production 20 percent and announced a total embargo on oil to the United States and the Netherlands, Israel's key allies.

Although Arab cutbacks accounted for less than 10 percent of the world's supply, pandemonium ensued. By November 1973 the price of oil on the spot market had increased from approximately $3 to $17 a barrel. Fearful of shortages, motorists waited hours in gasoline lines that circled filling stations and spilled out onto the surrounding streets.

Prompted by the twin challenges brought on by the energy and environmental crises, the Captain launched the Cousteau Society, a nonprofit membership-supported organization, in January 1974. He dedicated the U.S.-based group (and later the Fondation Cousteau in France and the Cousteau Society of Canada, both established in 1981) "to the protection and improvement of the quality of life." The society, he promised, would assume the role of "a global representative of future generations."

The Undersea World television series enabled Cousteau, he once boasted, to reach more viewers in one evening than the most successful movie of all time, *Gone with the Wind,* had in fifteen years. Still, the Captain had more grandiose objectives in mind. Educating the public and influencing policy makers, he declared, demanded something greater than a one-time exposure to ocean life on television. It required a coordinated campaign of publications, classroom materials, articles in popular magazines, lobbying, and lectures. It demanded an ongoing organizational structure.

"We are explorers, believing that humanity must better educate itself about the exquisite and inexorable mechanisms of life on this planet—and how those mechanisms can be interrupted," declared one of the society's early papers. "We are communicators, using words and pictures to educate living and future generations about our biological home. We are advisers, representing a kind of international 'State Department' for the quality of life, trying to educate the world's most powerful decision makers about the ecological ramifications of their decisions."

Creating an educational and advocacy group represented a major shift for Captain Cousteau. "I am entering a new phase in my life," he admitted. "I have been a fighter against the elements. Now I am a fighter against the system when it is wrong."

The political system, according to Cousteau, often tilted off-balance. "There is sufficient evidence that world leaders are systematically lying about environmental and energy matters,'' he said. The Captain proposed to talk directly with presidents and legislators but, when necessary, to go over the heads of the "conventional decision makers whose actions have frequently put selfish interest before environmental concerns." He promised to use his new group to mobilize public support for wise management of global resources.

Although the Cousteaus maintained decision-making control over the society's operations, they invited a group of scientists and celebrities to join a Council of Advisers. Perhaps the best known were singer John Denver, activist Dick Gregory, and science-fiction writer Ray Bradbury. Scientists included biologist Andrew Benson of the Scripps Institution of Oceanography; electronics inventor Harold Edgerton of the Massachusetts Institute of Technology; nuclear physicist Henry Kendall of the Massachusetts Institute of Technology; toxicologist Gabriel Nahas of the Columbia University College of Physicians and Surgeons; neurochemist Elie Shneour of Biosystems Associates; and ocean engineer Edward Wenk, Jr., of the University of Washington at Seattle. Attorney E. Allan Farnsworth of the Columbia Law School and environmentalist Hazel Henderson, then with the Princeton Center for Alternative Futures, also provided guidance and bolstered the new group's credibility.

The Captain integrated many of his operations—including the television shows, the expeditions, and the operation of *Calypso*—under the newly formed Cousteau Society. As a nonprofit organization the society and its activities were exempt from U.S. taxes. The group paid the Captain no salary, but it covered his substantial travel and business expenses. Cousteau continued to receive a generous stipend from the Oceanographic Institute in Monaco as well as royalties and fees from his numerous business interests.

The organizational structure allowed Cousteau to capitalize on his celebrity status and transform his loyal viewers into regular contributors. After the first year the society had grown to 120,000 members who paid an average of twenty dollars each, providing the Captain with a large and stable source of financing.

Cousteau initially attracted members by doing what most other citizen-based groups do: mailing mass solicitations to supporters of like-minded organizations. His form letters talked about *Calypso*'s adventures and the threats facing the undersea world. They described the society's planned advocacy of "our Water Planet" before influential leaders in government and industry. They argued for more research into the intricate elements of "our fragile water-dependent ecosystem," and they offered a subscription to a newsletter entitled *Calypso Log*. The letters also appealed for support: "Because the money you give now may literally help to save the world. Save it, not only for ourselves, but for our children and their children."

The group paid particular attention to the next generation. It claimed environmental goals would never be fulfilled until we effectively educate the children of the world. In 1981 the society began to communicate with young readers through a full-color sixteen-page magazine. *Dolphin Log* described *Calypso*'s adventures and displayed facts, photos, and games intended to interest and teach young people about the oceans and ecology.

The Cousteau Society also outlined a "Bill of Rights for Future Generations" that called on individuals and governments to "prevent irreversible and irreparable harm to life on earth and to human freedom and dignity." Each generation, it advocated, had "a right to an uncontaminated and undamaged earth."

That right, the Captain and his new group declared, required the rapid development of safe solar energy. Cousteau calculated that the United States needed to spend one trillion dollars over a fifteen-year period to harness power from the sun, wind, falling water, ocean, and plants. He joined *Calypso* at a sunrise celebration at the United Nations on Sun Day, the May 1978 international event to promote renewable energy. But launching a trend that increasingly disturbed environmentalists, the Cousteau Society failed to promote the Captain's budget proposal before policymakers.

The group did organize a series of eight Involvement Days, carnivallike conferences on the ocean environment that promoted Cousteau's celebrity and highlighted his ideas. The regional U.S. gatherings featured scientists, public figures, and scores of booths displaying solar energy and organic farming technologies. As with similar festivals in the late 1970's, a large number of participants, particularly teenagers, came to hear the musicians; at the Ventura County Fairgrounds in California in October 1979, Graham Nash, David Crosby, Stephen Stills, Poco, and Jackson Browne performed to an enthusiastic audience.

California Governor Edward G. "Jerry" Brown joined the Captain and Albert Falco at a wine and cheese reception following the Ventura event. Reflecting Cousteau's renown, the governor concluded his remarks by saying, "Let us not forget that of all the people in government, the impact on people's awareness about the oceans and their integral part in our fragile life support system have had less impact than one person—the person standing next to me—Jacques Cousteau.''

Today Cousteau, through the society's large membership and his personal access to millions of television viewers, is the most visible champion of the seas. But despite Governor Brown's accolade, the Captain has failed to become an environmental leader. In fact, he distances himself from ecology advocates, refuses to join political coalitions, and avoids direct lobbying. Rather than attack the political system, as he proposed to do when the society was founded, he ignores it. Rather than mobilize his members to solve social or environmental problems, he has decided simply to identify the challenges in his films and books. And rather than advocate policy alternatives, the Cousteau Society has become primarily a film production company.

Cousteau has rejected many of the positions taken by major environmental groups. When activists decried the destruction of the planet's ozone layer, for instance, the Captain argued that the protective gases had not noticeably diminished. When they protested about accelerating nuclear contamination, he noted that his work with the International Atomic Energy Agency detected no increase in the radioactivity of the oceans. And when asked about the fate of the seas in general, he said, ''The majority of scientists see no hope. In this they are more pessimistic than I.''

Unlike most ecologists, the upbeat Cousteau doesn't focus blame for environmental deterioration on industrial pollutants. ''After diving extensively and taking hundreds of measurements,'' he said, ''we began to realize that the drop in animals—vertebrates and invertebrates—which feed upon the meadow that is the ocean was much bigger than could be explained by chemical pollution.'' He believes the decline results primarily from ''mechanical destructions,'' including dynamite fishing, fishing in spawning grounds, river diversions, and landfills on marshes. ''The ocean floors are being scraped,'' he declared. ''Eggs and larvae are disappearing. In the past the sea renewed itself. It was a continuous cycle. But this cycle is being upset. Shrimps are being chased from their holes into nets by electric shocks. Lobsters are being sought in places where they formerly found shelter. Even coral is disappearing.''

Cousteau also broke with environmentalists over nuclear power.

Rather than join the call for a moratorium on reactor construction after the Three Mile Island accident in 1979, this advocate of technology requested "vastly increased monetary investment for nuclear research." Even the Captain's concerns about atomic power focused less on radioactive contamination than on the equipment's poor economics and the frightening "potential for dispersal of bomb-grade materials among unstable governments and terrorists." He remains a staunch supporter of nuclear-fusion development.

Cousteau has faced particularly harsh criticism from ecology activists for his work on Mururoa, an island in French Polynesia that the French military has used since 1956 as a nuclear test site. The French Defense Department, sensitive to charges that the blasts are injecting dangerous radiation into the environment, invited the telegenic Captain to observe a test blast and study its effects on the marine habitat.

Calypso entered the atoll's lagoon twelve hours after the underground explosion on June 21, 1987. For the next five days, divers roamed the waters with Geiger counters to survey the coral, and crewmen aboard the ship collected samples of water, sediment, and plankton, which Cousteau sent for evaluation to the French Atomic Energy Commission and the Marine Biogeochemistry Laboratory of the Graduate School of Education in Paris.

The Cousteau Society concluded that "the waters of the lagoon displayed only infinitesimal traces of radioactive elements, primarily cesium and plutonium, well below allowable proportions. . . . It was reassuring to discover that the Mururoa test site is not contributing in a more severe way to the degradation of the surrounding environment."

Environmental activists, including Greenpeace, were bitterly disappointed. Instead of the condemnation they expected, the Cousteau Society produced what one observer called "a whitewash." Tahitian activist and anthropologist Bengt Danielsson, referring to Cousteau's expedition as "a guided tour," criticized the Captain for not having a medical doctor examine the effects of radiation on neighboring islanders, for neglecting to examine the suspected relationship between the destruction of Mururoa's reefs and the alarming rate of ciguatera poisoning among Polynesians, and for failing to inspect deep fissures in the atoll. Danielsson's lengthy letter to Cousteau declared, "You are out of your depth."

The Captain, in turn, has criticized most environmental activists for blocking technological progress. "Instead of simply being negative," he wrote, "they need to offer constructive counterproposals. It requires a lot of imagination, but it contributes to the protection and improvement of life in a constructive manner.''

Cousteau claims to have "no politics," but his antigovernment pronouncements border on libertarianism. As a lover of personal freedom he detests restrictive ideologies, and he fears political coalitions may constrain his actions.

The Captain's political recalcitrance also results from his distaste for personal confrontation. He arrogantly believes his film images and written words present sufficient wisdom to convert anyone to his point of view. The give-and-take of debate only frustrates him. He sees himself above the fray.

Cousteau Society writer Mose Richards depicts Cousteau's lobbying approach by recounting his February 1977 trip with the Captain to Houston for one of the Involvement Days. Richards tried to warn Cousteau that reporters in America's petroleum capital would not appreciate his views opposing offshore oil drilling. "We may become entangled in an unpleasant fight," Richards cautioned. But the Captain responded simply, "We don't want to fight with anyone. We just want to change their minds."

Cousteau, of course, holds strong opinions, and his quick wit does periodically sting his opponents. Once the sponsor of spearfishing competitions in the Mediterranean, the Captain now admits such sport was a stupid act done "because I was baffled by the familiarity of the fish." Noting his change of heart, he recently called recreational anglers "perverts." Of hunters, he said, they're "working to diminish the quality of the race. I would commit suicide if I were a hunter."

Cousteau's comments prompted hundreds of angry letters, an exchange society staffers describe as an "unfortunate controversy." They claim the group doesn't have a policy either opposing or promoting sport fishing. The Captain's complaint, they say, is against large-scale commercial operations that deplete fishing grounds around the world. Trying to avoid further attacks, group officials argue that "while our motives may not coincide, the Society and most sport fishing groups have the same goal in mind—the continued abundance of marine species." Yet *Field and Stream* editors, representing sport fishermen, remain disillusioned with Cousteau, calling him "egotistical," "autocratic," and "as isolated from reality as a dictator after 30 years of rule."

Leaders of the major environmental groups are confounded by mixed feelings toward the Captain. On the one hand, they admire, and almost envy, his ability to educate millions about environmental issues and to gain an audience with almost any nation's president. Yet they lament that the filmmaker rarely mobilizes his resources to influence policies that would help protect the ocean environment. Some complain that Cousteau talks a nice line and presents pretty pictures, but never delivers real change.

Enviromentalists also charge that practices aboard Cousteau's ships sometimes contradict the Captain's ecological rhetoric. In Papua New Guinea, for instance, *Alcyone* crew members, relaxing on deck with beers, casually tossed their empty cans into the pristine waters. Trash is such a problem that the Cousteaus recently wrote a memo to their crews: "These two ships consistently pollute by dumping trash in the sea. This contradiction must stop. Garbage is no problem—it is fish food. Plastic is very bad. . . . Cans and bottles are not as bad, but they are trash, and, philosophically, we cannot throw them at sea."

Cousteau flirted briefly with French electoral politics in 1978, when he campaigned for several ecology candidates in the parliamentary elections. In 1981, after the St. Lawrence expedition and before the Turner television contract was signed, he seriously considered an offer to run as the ecology party's candidate for the French presidency. Environmentalists hoped that Cousteau's popularity would sweep in an ecology slate, yet they worried that he was too cautious, too inexperienced in the art of political exchange and compromise, and too unwilling to cooperate with broad coalitions of interest groups. Still, French newspapers featured the possible nomination in headlines and editorials for more than two weeks.

Cousteau's friends, most of whom objected to the idea, say he went off by himself for several days to contemplate the career switch. They remember that he took with him only a copy of Plutarch's *Lives* and letters from supporters. Years later the adventurer-filmmaker says he never seriously considered becoming a politician. The role, he claims, would have been too restrictive. The Captain believes he can be more effective working outside the political system.

Environmentalists have alternative views of Cousteau's refusal. Some insist that the Captain simply made a careful examination of the political possibilities and decided that he lacked the resources to win. Others say he despised the banter of political coalitions. Notes Brice Lalonde, then leader of Amis de la Terre, France's Friends of the Earth, and now the country's environment minister: "Cousteau wasn't comfortable with our approach. He didn't want to be limited to one political party."

Although the Captain decided against elective office, the Cousteau Society claims to have a "significant impact" on policy debates within the U.S. Congress. The group's organizers boast of the Cousteau's "critical testimony" on the Ocean Dumping Act before a subcommittee of the House of Representatives. But *Calypso Log*, the society's newsletter to its members, devoted less than one page to the subject over a four-year period, and an informal survey of officials in Congress and at NOAA suggests that the Cousteaus and the society had little influence on the legislation. Several congressional aides said they never hear from the Captain or his members.

When confronted with such criticisms, Cousteau asserts that the society's political effectiveness can best be determined by how his films and books have created "an abiding affection for the undersea world and a powerful curiosity about nature among people everywhere."

Researchers at Ohio State University tried to evaluate this claim by measuring the impact of a Cousteau broadcast on the audience's knowledge and attitudes. They assembled 250 television viewers to watch "The Warm-Blooded Sea: Mammals of the Deep," a 1982 release featuring colorful footage of gentle whales and dolphins. A pretest determined the participants' knowledge of and attitudes toward the ocean. The researchers distributed similar questionnaires immediately after the show and again two weeks later.

Regarding increased knowledge of the ocean, the broadcast proved to be successful. The participants' average score rose from 46.5 on the pretest to 71.7 on the delayed posttest. Thus, even after two weeks, viewers remembered a substantial amount of information from the Cousteau special.

On the issue of changed attitudes, however, the film had no impact whatsoever. The immediate posttest indicated a slight positive shift toward environmentalism, but within two weeks the participants' outlook had reverted to what it had been previously.

Cousteau Society staffers examined the results and proclaimed their effectiveness. "It's good to know [that the Cousteau films] may be having an effect," they declared in *Calypso Log*. "We are intrigued, we are moved, and, it turns out, we are probably educated."

The independent researchers, however, couldn't offer such a rosy conclusion. The Cousteau broadcast did convey some information about the ocean, but it failed to shift people's attitudes toward ecology or to encourage citizen actions that would protect the environment.

Ecology advocates may complain about the Captain's tame methods, but most forget that the Cousteaus produced a hard-hitting television series about urgent environmental crises. It failed miserably.

Just after ABC canceled its contract and before Atlantic Richfield agreed to sponsor *The Cousteau Odyssey Series* on PBS, Philippe and the Captain produced six half hour specials documenting man's rape of the land and sea. *Oasis in Space,* with its dour list of subjects, represented a daring departure for the Cousteaus.

The first segment, aired on PBS stations in February 1977, showed a pulp mill in Canada dumping mercury-laden wastes into a stream used for bathing and drinking by local Indians. The Cousteaus illustrated the consequences of such industrial pollution by juxtaposing Canadian scenes with graphic photographs of the deformed victims of mercury poisoning in Japan's Minamata Bay.

The shows mixed such alarming footage with pronouncements by environmental and social pundits like Barry Commoner, Margaret Mead, and Robert Heilbroner. Philippe conducted most of the interviews, asking scores of basic questions as if he were an innocent young student interested in the planet's problems.

"*Oasis* indulges in no cosmeticizing," said one reviewer. "Those interviewed speak plainly and candidly, and the documentary footage bears out their comments."

Philippe, who served as executive director, developed the series' title while working on a project with NASA. After analyzing satellite pictures of the planet, he concluded, "Our earth stands alone, an oasis in an otherwise barren universe."

Funding for the accusatory broadcasts proved elusive. "We had counted on corporate sponsorship of the shows," said Philippe. "But when they found out what we really had in mind, they all pulled back. No one industry wanted any part of indicting another." That left only a $126,000 contribution from the Public Broadcasting Service. The Cousteaus decided to add about $300,000 to the effort from the society's accounts. "It was that important," declared the Captain.

The shows may have presented urgent themes, but they garnered a very small audience. Most critics said the series lacked the adventure of Cousteau's previous efforts. The footage told no stories and showcased few colorful animals. The interviews, while candid, appeared stiff and sluggish.

The Captain concluded from the setback that few people wanted to watch depressing commentaries on the planet's destruction. He vowed to return to a television formula that delivered information about the environment in a more entertaining context.

Cousteau, of course, did not totally avoid advocacy, but he tended to concentrate his efforts on relatively noncontroversial issues. The society, for instance, devoted substantial attention to the startling and mystifying mass strandings of marine mammals. At Cape Cod in November 1982, some 65 pilot whales surged above the high-tide mark and died in the marsh. At Casey Key, Florida, more than 150 spinner dolphins beached themselves; volunteers tried to carry the one hundred-fifty pound mammals back to the surf, but the confused dolphins turned around and again rammed into the shore. Similar phenomena have occurred with seals, sea lions, sea otters, and manatees.

Numerous causes—parasites, disease, disorientation, or pollution poisoning—have been advanced, but no one understands why marine mammals strand themselves. Many of the animals appear to be perfectly healthy.

When possible, researchers have collected tissue samples from the hearts, brains, blubbers, muscles, and organs of the beached mammals in order to identify evidence of disease or parasites that might explain the strandings. In the late 1960's Dr. James Mead, curator of mammals at the Smithsonian Institution, began collating and disseminating these data. Under the Marine Mammal Protection Act of 1972 and the Endangered Species Act of 1973, the National Marine Fisheries Service provided funds for scientists to systematically obtain such basic biological information. By 1982, when the Reagan administration curtailed funds, the network had assembled data on 13,072 stranded cetaceans, providing unique information on the demographics of marine mammals and some of the only intelligence on rare species such as the beaked whale.

Cousteau wrote a special appeal to his supporters on behalf of the Marine Mammal Stranding Network. The response allowed him to contribute twenty thousand dollars and a computer system to the Smithsonian Institution's research and tracking efforts.

The Cousteau Society claims proudly that because of its contribution, "valuable information can be collected in an organized way, evaluated, and disseminated to help answer questions about the ocean and its residents, to determine what impact man may have on this system, and ultimately to understand how best to manage these resources." The group published numerous articles in the *Calypso Log* on the strandings, and it printed colorful posters that were placed in lifeguard stations and coastal schools, giving a phone number people could call when a marine mammal was found on the beach.

The Captain also spent some of his own time promoting the Law of the Sea Treaty. The lobbying effort on this key environmental issue illustrates Cousteau's ability and approach.

President Harry Truman had fired a major salvo against the concept of a global ocean commons when he proclaimed in 1945 that national sovereignty extended to the resources of the continental shelf. Other nations quickly followed suit, claiming jurisdiction over areas as much as two hundred miles from their shores. The Geneva Convention of 1958 added to this notion when it declared that the high seas belonged to no nation and that no international authority could exercise control.

In 1970, however, the General Assembly of the United Nations adopted the Declaration of Principles Governing the Sea-Bed and the Ocean Floor, and the Subsoil Thereof, Beyond the Limits of National Jurisdiction. The preliminary document, the first internationally accepted set of rules affecting the oceans, proclaimed that the riches of the sea are "the common heritage of mankind . . . [and] shall not be subject to appropriation by any means by States or persons." The General Assembly also voted to convene a comprehensive Conference on the Law of the Sea in 1973 to define precise regulations for resolving oceanic disputes.

Cousteau endorsed the UN's goal of a global ocean commons for future generations. He envisioned an "ocean constitution" that would be "parallel with the global nature of the sea." This international authority, he said, should "set safety, health, and general ecology guidelines over coastal regions as well as the high seas."

Achieving a comprehensive treaty, however, proved to be complex and contentious. Needed were consensus priorities for the many and often competing uses of the world's oceans, including fishing, commercial shipping, naval defense, oil and gas drilling, future mining of the deep seabed, oceanic research, and dumping of wastes.

The 1973 OPEC oil embargo set back the global negotiations because the United States and its industrialized allies became increasingly wary of international cartels controlling vital raw materials. As the American position hardened against the initial cooperative ideal, developing countries began to proffer their own vision of a world authority that would redistribute the planet's undersea wealth. They proposed that the mining companies of industrialized nations be required to supply the capital and technology needed by this international authority to harvest seabed minerals.

The heated debate dragged on well past the original 1973 deadline into the 1980's, with the Captain objecting to the Reagan administration's Truman-like advocacy of "exclusive economic zones" which would give coastal nations virtual property title for all resources—from fish to oil—extending two hundred miles from shore. "What we are trying to do," Cousteau explained, "is to slightly modify the concept of exclusive economic zones into zones of responsibility. But in order to do that we would have to create a world ocean authority. Not only for the open ocean, but also for the continental shelves. This world ocean authority could set global rules of management of the ocean accepted by every nation. And then every coastal nation would be responsible to implement these rules in the so-called economic zones."

Cousteau's rare lobbying effort for his "zones of responsibility" was predominantly personal. Believing in the power of his one-on-one presentations to world leaders, he did little to organize his members or to mobilize public opinion through speeches, books, or movies. He was the only environmentalist to gain an audience with President Reagan, who stood virtually alone among world leaders in his opposition to the Law of the Sea Treaty and environmental regulations. The Captain described his June 1981 White House luncheon as "cordial and satisfying."

Cousteau arranged similar sessions with French President François Mitterrand and West German Chancellor Helmut Schmidt. Recognizing that Third World countries distrusted initiatives proposed by industrialized nations, he also encouraged Mexican President José López Portillo to introduce environmental amendments at the United Nations.

In April 1982, despite the Captain's efforts, the United States, Israel, Turkey, and Venezuela refused to support the Law of the Sea Treaty, scuttling the measure's implementation. Cousteau concluded sadly, "The ending of the Law of the Sea negotiation process, once such a sign of hope and cooperation, seems to indicate an intensification of competition and divisiveness, where technological and military power will substitute for cooperative policies and respect among nations.''

Jean-Michel, a trained architect who designed environmental displays aboard the *Queen Mary,* has encouraged his father since Philippe's death to direct the society's efforts more toward educational projects at museums and entertainment parks. He has proposed the construction of Cousteau Ocean Centers around the world that would combine exhibits, rides, and multimedia presentations.

"Television is the most superficial way of reaching people," Jean-Michel argues. "Books are a little more in depth. A museum is the broadest and deepest way I can think of to transfer a message.''

Norfolk officials tried to entice the Cousteaus to locate their first center along the city's waterfront. It would be, predicted the *Virginia Pilot,* a ''mecca for sightseers as well as environmentalists and oceanographers.'' No doubt Norfolk also needed some centerpiece that would help revitalize a downtown that in the late 1970's alternated between isolated high-rise buildings and swatches of desolation.

Local support for Cousteau's plan was not unanimous. The *Times Advocate,* another Norfolk newspaper, wrote: ''The Cousteau Caper is just another one of these frantic attempts by so-called civic leaders to graft on some form of glaring gimmick they feel is going to 'save' and 'restore' public interest in Norfolk's presently bombed-out downtown desert. They'd spend a million dollars having Indira Gandhi walk nude on a tightrope across the Granby Mall if they felt it'd bring a dozen shoppers back to Smith and Whelton [the main downtown intersection].''

Still, the city council approved a twenty-million-dollar grant in 1979 to help build the Ocean Center, provided that the Norfolk museum would be the Captain's headquarters and that the Cousteau Society would put up five million dollars of its own. The city's commitment seemed to generate others. James Rouse, the celebrated architect who revitalized harbor markets in Baltimore and Boston, expressed interest in a Norfolk venture, and local investors began planning an office complex across the street from the proposed museum.

Feasibility studies suggested that almost three quarters of a million people would annually tour the Ocean Center. Rather than display live fish and marine mammals, which are expensive to catch and maintain,

Cousteau proposed to suspend plastic models from the museum's ceiling. Through films and "sophisticated illusion techniques," visitors, according to the society, would enjoy "a personal adventure to explore the mysteries of the undersea world of Jacques Cousteau." Tourists also were to experience "a cycle of emotions: awe at the beauty and majesty of life; fear at the threats to this life unique to our planet; and finally, hope for the future in realizing their own personal potential to make a difference."

Norfolk's mayor initially voiced enormous enthusiasm about his city's association with the Captain, even though Cousteau rarely visited the society's administrative offices. Noted Mayor Vincent Thomas: "If he's on television saying that the *Calypso* is actually out of Norfolk, he's probably doing more for us than if he's actually here."

By 1986, however, Thomas had become anxious and angry. Little progress had been made on the Norfolk site, and local businessmen traveling across the country learned that Cousteau Society staffers had been promoting Ocean Centers in cities from Florida to California. Plans were even being developed in landlocked Denver, St. Louis, and Phoenix and overseas in France, Australia, and Brazil.

More disturbing to the Norfolk City Council was the society's continued refusal to contribute its five million dollars toward the center's construction. According to one journalist, "The attitude seems to have been that Norfolk was darned lucky to have such a great man as Jacques Cousteau willing to associate his name with such a second-rate city." In May 1986 bitter council members finally withdrew their support.

"I'm disappointed," responded the Captain. "They don't know what they're missing. We'll do it somewhere else."

Jean-Michel turned his architectural attentions to Paris, where he inaugurated the Parc Océanique Cousteau (Cousteau Ocean Park) in summer, 1989. To develop the educational entertainment facility, he had formed a related but separate organization, Cousteau Centers, Inc., which borrowed almost eight hundred thousand dollars from the Cousteau Society to launch its operations.

The Ocean Park's three expansive levels of displays are located in Les Halles, the chic underground shopping area that was once the central marketplace for fish, vegetables, and meat. Only two short blocks from the Pompidou Center and one of the most visited areas in Paris for both tourists and natives, Les Halles provides an ideal location for an environmental education center. Its steel and glass design blends gracefully with France's classic Commodities Exchange Building, which sits atop Cousteau Ocean Park.

High tech exhibits allow visitors to "rocket" into space and then "ride" through the water planet's depths. The voyage to the bottom of the sea provides, according to promotional materials, "the most realistic experiences achievable of hidden environments previously seen only by scuba divers and explorers in bathyscaphes." A project spokeswoman adds that the play-oriented tour takes about one and one half hours to enjoy.

Visitors also meander through an animated life-size blue whale to appreciate the mammal's pulsating heart and other internal organs. Children frolic in a marine jungle gym covered with carpeted sharks; the intent, says Jean-Michel, is to demystify the sleek, scary creatures.

The Ocean Park's theater is equipped with a forty-five-foot screen and the latest film projection technology. Cousteau's team spent more than a year with a sophisticated 35 mm camera to assemble the special film, which features orcas, dolphins, and silver-suited divers using their scooters to perform an underwater ballet in the waters off Costa Rica's Cocos Island. Participants leave the exhibit hearing the Captain's appeal that everyone should "protect what they love" as well as remember that "the destiny of future generations is in our hands."

While exhibits at the Paris Ocean Park perpetuate Cousteau's traditional focus on the undersea environment, the Captain's priorities are changing. He first expressed his concern for the environment by trying to preserve an island. Later he attacked plans to contaminate the Mediterranean waters near his home with radioactive wastes. For most of his career he tried to harness technology to manage natural resources efficiently. In the early 1980's, however, Cousteau shifted his attention to social issues. He declared that environmental protection makes sense only if "we defuse the threat of an atomic war; we better share the resources of the world; we overcome the population explosion; and we effectively protect and decently educate the children of the world, our only hope for the future."

Cousteau has reduced protecting the environment to a distant fourth priority, well behind attaining peace, curtailing poverty in the Third World, and educating children. "The interaction between people and the aquatic system of the world," he explains, "introduces more and more sociological problems into our marine explorations."

The Captain's shift from ecology to world peace has, in his view, been a logical and direct transition. The space photographs that advanced his environmental thinking eventually moved him to concentrate on man's responsibility to preserve all life on the water planet. In 1986 he addressed the first conference of the Association of Space Explorers, a unique group of twenty-five astronauts and cosmonauts whose voyages changed their lives and personal philosophies. Encouraging space travelers and oceanauts to work together for peace and ecology, Cousteau spoke of "a moral gateway that exploration has given to humanity." He declared that both fliers and divers have "the conviction that our nations' disputes are ridiculous and that we must get along with each other once and for all so that mankind can begin a new adventure into the universe."

The focus of the Captain's films also is shifting away from undersea creatures and toward mankind. Influenced substantially by Jean-Michel, this new Jacques-Yves Cousteau has spent more time examining peace initiatives in Costa Rica than enjoying the dolphin's grace and beauty. "Protecting dolphins and whales," he says, "would be of no avail if nuclear war reduced the Earth's crust to ashes."

CHAPTER TEN

The Poet

Cousteau's silhouette is forceful and lean. His head has been compared to that of an ancient stone sculpture: half man, half bird, mythic and eternal.

Cousteau's face actually shelters two distinct personalities. The gaunt cheeks, hooked nose, and large-lidded eyes present a solemn, almost sad countenance. But when the Captain smiles, his cheeks crinkle, and his eyes roll upward in mischievous wonder.

Cousteau's ideas are equally diverse, spanning the gulf between the practical and the visionary. He invented the useful aqualung, but he writes surrealistic poetry. He is a successful executive, but he believes business is inconsequential compared with the life of a pelican or a dolphin. Over a meal his conversation ranges from French wine to whale communications to nuclear war to the phenomenon of the sun rising and setting each day.

Cousteau claims his desire to "have fun" has integrated his life's activities. "I was playing when I invented the aqualung," he declares. "I'm still playing. I think play is the most serious thing in the world. When I see someone who becomes serious and announces his work as a great discovery, I burst into laughter."

The Captain displays his playful intellect frequently, and each of his colleagues seems to have a favorite tale. Ghostwriter James Dugan remembered a particularly tense planning session for an early submarine device. After listening passively to the discussion for several minutes, the Captain announced: "Well, I think it will work and perhaps bring valuable information, but the important question is, 'Will it be fun?' ''

Cousteau has tried to realize as many of his own impulses as possible. In his eyes the perfect life is for a man to be "pushed by his instincts, needs, pleasures, drives, and to play without measuring the consequences.''

In his more practical and self-centered moments, however, the Captain admits that this "ideal" life-style is not for everyone. He argues that if too many individuals practiced such freewheeling ways, the planet's beauty and ecological diversity would vanish. Yet he maintains that special and creative men—like him—shouldn't be restrained by governments or rules.

Much of the Captain's career, in fact, has been spent searching for freedom. Goggles delivered the young naval officer to the vast freshness of the undersea world. The aqualung liberated him from reliance upon surface assistants. And the diving saucer enabled him to descend to the farthest reaches of the ocean.

Diving also offered Cousteau a supernatural escape. "From birth,'' he explains, "man carries the weight of gravity on his shoulders. He is bolted to earth. But man has only to sink beneath the surface and he is free. Buoyed by water, he can fly in any direction—up, down, sideways. Underwater, man becomes an archangel.''

To describe his quest for total freedom, Cousteau outlined what he feels are the world's three basic philosophies. First is the philosophy of the stones, which is based on stopping time. In this approach, which the Captain claimed never to have accepted for himself, you "build estates and acquire things in the hope that it will last and make you immortal.''

The second philosophy, one which Cousteau abandoned in the early 1970's while he filmed the ABC television series, is of the lovely but short-lived rose. "You take full advantage of the instant,'' he said, "trying to make each instant beautiful and fruitful. You are ornamenting yourself to produce and to die, but the trouble with this approach is that it's also very vain.''

The third and the Captain's ultimate state is of the wind. "You just blow wherever you want; it doesn't matter. You don't need ornamentation; you just need the current of air. You are organized nothingness. That's what we are, carefully organized nothingness.''

Cousteau, however, does differentiate between positive and negative nothingness. "I prefer to blow in palm trees or a field of flowers than in cement," he admitted. "I prefer to do things that give pleasure."

Cousteau ranks Bertrand Russell as his idol, someone he describes as a complete man who embodied the philosophy of the wind. "Russell's work for me," he says, "is the fantastic combination of a great scientist, a good writer, a human character who loved women, life, and who had the courage to go to prison for his ideas." The Nobel prize winner, who died in 1970, was jailed while campaigning for nuclear disarmament. He also lost teaching positions because of his outspoken agnosticism and his alleged advocacy and practice of sexual promiscuity.

Russell's religious arguments greatly influenced Cousteau. "The whole conception of God is a conception derived from the ancient Oriental despotisms," argued the philosopher. "It is a conception quite unworthy of free man." The Captain, in response to questions, expresses a similar distaste for religious worship, calling it debasing rather than ennobling.

Russell also taught Cousteau to avoid sentimentalizing history and to live for the moment. "A good world needs knowledge, kindliness, and courage," declared Russell. "It does not need a regretful hankering after the past or a fettering of the free intelligence by the words uttered long ago by ignorant men."

Most important, the British scholar, although primarily noted for his work in mathematical logic, convinced Cousteau that logic would not satisfy his thirst for truth, that the inspiration guiding poets brings them nearer to reality than anyone else. The Captain has declared:

When I reason, when people reason, they come most of the time to logical absurdities. I find poets closer to the truth than mathematicians or politicians. They have visions that are not only fantasy. They have visions that are, for some reason they cannot explain, an inspiration that guides them and brings them by the hand, or by the pen, closer to the truth than anybody else in life. It's the light. It's the star we should be guided by. Poetry, and poetry under all its forms. Poetry in anything you are doing. The only remedies to the logical absurdities are utopias.

Cousteau's pragmatic side, however, argues that these visions must be "reasonable utopias." He has spent much of his life proposing ways to adjust the human community so that men and women don't harm others or future generations. "I think the only usefulness of people today," he said in the mid-1980's, "is to make sure they are able to pass along to future generations an inheritance that is as good as what we've got, and maybe better."

Critics scoff at some of Cousteau's specific proposals. At his seventy-fifth birthday party, for instance, the Captain declared that he "would devote all of his remaining efforts" to transferring 1 percent of the world's military budget to a vast exchange of children. "Imagine a world where all seventh graders would have to spend a year on the other side of the fence," he demanded. "It would not only be a great opening for their minds, but it would be a formidable barrier against war." One skeptical politician chuckled and said no one would seriously consider such a plan.

Many of Cousteau's television fans would be startled by his private thoughts on subjects such as marriage, which he defines as an archaic device that "people use to avoid facing the fact that we are all solitary and perishable." And love, he maintains, is simply "a drug to blur the truth that a couple is not a couple but a juxtaposition of two alone individuals."

Fans also would not recognize the dark thoughts that frequently appear in Cousteau's personal log. "At times," he recently wrote, "I find myself flirting with the morbid idea of lassitude. The constant breakdowns, repairs, delays, empty me of resolve. And in the bilges of my mind, I deeply resent anybody and anything which interrupts our dream of action, of protecting the seas and water life. Even the necessity of drydocking for repairs becomes adversity."

Even though Cousteau relishes his star status, he aggressively protects his privacy. His personal life, he declares firmly, "is no one's business but my own." When reporters press him for details, he grows testy: "I don't want you to know if I drink coffee or tea or have adventures with my secretary. . . . Out! This is my life. It's my privacy. Hands off!"

The Captain particularly avoids questions about his marriage. For almost four decades, he and Simone have spent little time together, largely because she's remained aboard *Calypso* while he traveled around the globe. On the road Cousteau is an acknowledged flirt who likes to chat up and charm young women, and they seem to be drawn to the glib celebrity. He's been known to arrive at a new location and immediately ask, "Are there beautiful women here?" Some society staffers suggest Cousteau maintains a typical Frenchman's appreciation of the opposite sex.

In an age when tabloids report the personal habits of celebrities, Cousteau's revealed indiosyncrasies are not that revealing: He is a connoisseur of wines, his favorite being the French Côtes du Rhône; he enjoys tea rather than coffee; he avoids dairy products and animal fats, especially in hamburgers; he occasionally smokes small, foul-smelling cigars; his breakfast usually consists of dry toast with orange marmalade; he claims never to read novels, finding fiction to be a writer's egotistical display; he gets his rest from ten-minute catnaps in taxis and on planes; he exercises each morning, often completing a hundred push-ups; he spends a lot of time flying but never feels safe in airplanes; he hates mountains, finding them "oppressive things"; his close friends call him "Pasha" (the Old Man).

What is clear is that millions idolize Cousteau, not merely because he is a charming celebrity but because he embodies that yearning we have to live by our impulses. The Captain projects a sense of eternal youth.

Friends who have known Cousteau for many years say he possesses a special "control" over nature. The weather clears on his command. Fish perform. The coral appears to part so *Calypso* can pass through.

Few associates attribute Cousteau's achievements to supernatural forces, and none deny the Captain's many setbacks when he films in the wild. Still, they maintain that Cousteau has more luck—or what they describe as magic—than any other person they know.

Shooting nature scenes requires a tremendous amount of patience. The sea must be clear and calm. Enough light must be available to expose film adequately. The animals must accept the presence of divers and execute their required scenes. Even Cousteau admits that the process is an emotional roller coaster of expectation and frustration: "We can spend three months waiting on *Calypso,* unable to do any work, and then suddenly the weather turns perfect, the animals are there, and the film can be picked up in 24 hours."

Still, Cousteau's presence often seems to minimize the frustration. According to Jan Cousteau, Philippe's widow, "He always brought good weather. It may have stormed for days, the boys were playing bridge, Monopoly, Scrabble, getting restless. Then the Captain came and the sun shone. When he left, the bad weather often returned."

Cousteau senses this magical quality, and he doesn't mind showing off to strangers. Sara Davidson, writing for *The New York Times Magazine* in 1972, recalled her first meeting with Cousteau when he invited her for a swim during a thunderstorm. "It is dark as night and I am shaking with cold," she remembered. The Captain looked up at the black sky and announced that the sun would shine soon. Davidson chuckled at the absurd prophecy. "There is no one in sight," she wrote, "no sound but the rain and the tinkling of metal on sailboats. A minute later, the water is lit up as if by a klieg light."

Luis Marden, a *National Geographic* correspondent who often accompanied *Calypso*'s early expeditions, also witnessed Cousteau's remarkable abilities. Near Assumption Island in the Indian Ocean, Marden had spent days underwater trying to photograph the blast from a miniature volcano, presumably caused by the spout of a hidden animal. He lay on his stomach for endless hours, his camera trained on an individual cone, only to have nearby volcanoes explode. Whichever one he selected remained dormant. Cousteau finally dived to see what was keeping the cameraman busy and frustrated. The Captain examined the scene for a moment, pointed his forefinger at a nearby sand cone, and flipped his thumb like a trigger. The pyramid erupted. Back on board, Cousteau credited his feat to "fantastic luck," but Marden claimed more profound powers were at work.

No doubt much of Cousteau's "control" over nature simply results from his having carefully observed the sea and its creatures for so many years. He has acquired a sense of the animals' habits, and like other experienced sailors, he has learned to "read" ocean waves and currents. Still, *Calypso*'s crew maintains that the Captain's talents are unique. Acknowledging his biased perspective, Philippe once noted, "I have known highly skilled seamen who make use of echo-sounding equipment as they would a precise and impersonal instrument, but I feel sure that, to my father, it is something much more than this. He had guided us precisely to the spot we were searching for, with as much sureness as if he were actually walking on the sea floor, with no hesitation whatever, using the ship and the elements themselves as a virtuoso might use his favorite instrument."

Cousteau's communion with the sea has evolved. He recalls that at the age of three or four "water fascinated me—first floating ships, then me floating and stones not floating. The touch of water fascinated me all the time, but the real interest in the ocean came when I was already in the navy. I turned to the navy as a career, in the beginning, because of my love for water and because of my desire to travel and see the world.''

At age twenty-six, after suffering the automobile accident that almost paralyzed his arms, the young officer turned to swimming for recuperation. The physical exercise, however, became a spiritual journey when he placed his goggled eyes beneath the sea's surface. Underwater his body became weightless, free of earth's gravity. He could float with liberty throughout what he described as the ''embracing medium.''

''The spirituality of man cannot be completely separated from the physical,'' Cousteau wrote after one of his early dives. ''But you have made a big step toward escape simply by lowering yourself under water.''

Cousteau's mystical experience, of course, blended with the sheer adventure of opening up a new world—the undersea world—to man. He remained for many years on the cutting edge of that exploration, with the experiments and the revelations providing an intoxicating thrill. Much of Cousteau's early public appeal, in fact, resulted from his obviously joyous enthusiasm for the experience of discovery.

By the early 1960's Cousteau sought practical results from his otherworldly adventures. ''Undersea exploration is not an end in itself,'' he declared. ''The privilege of our era, to enter this great unknown medium, must produce greater knowledge of the oceans and lead to assessment and exploitation of their natural resources.''

The leader of the Conshelf expeditions imagined man colonizing the ocean floor, tapping its resources to lengthen life and memory, to retard aging, and to cure illnesses. ''Organic anesthetics can be extracted from marine animals, eliminating the need to introduce synthetic chemicals into our bodies,'' he predicted. ''Cephalotoxin is a poison found in the saliva of the octopus that hinders the coagulation of the blood. Elecosin is also found in the octopus's saliva; it may one day be used to control high blood pressure.''

Some twenty years later Cousteau joined environmentalists in condemning the exploitative destruction of the seas. He still imagined raising fish for food, mining minerals from the seafloor, and extracting energy from the ocean's waves, but he no longer promoted permanent colonization. The Captain claimed that humans remain aliens underwater and that the undersea environment ''is not ours.''

* * *

Cousteau's environmental perspective may have evolved over the years, but his dedication to self-promotion has remained constant. Since the age of thirteen, he has placed himself in front of his own cameras and recorded his actions and thoughts in scores of books. Still, he exhibits a charming humility before strangers. A young reporter once exclaimed that the Captain had become a true international legend. Cousteau's response was short and quick: "Bull!

"If you begin to believe in yourself," Cousteau continued, "you're sentenced to become a joke. We're nothing, none of us."

Even in reflective moments, Cousteau argues that introversion and egomania result only in hollow pleasures. "We enrich our own souls when we reach out to enrich the souls of others, to gather and appreciate and absorb not the manufactured wealth of society but the natural wealth of the universe," he wrote in the society's newsletter. He submits that "self-extension" is the only route to happiness and that it can be achieved through creation (such as writing and filmmaking), knowledge (such as science and expeditions), and love.

Cousteau is no isolated individualist; he relishes his relations with colleagues and friends, and he operates the *Calypso* and the expeditions as team efforts. Although he clearly directs activities and enjoys his own suite aboard the ship, he shares meals, thoughts, and honors with his crew.

"The history of the *Calypso* is important to me for its scientific importance and its technological value," the Captain declares, "but above all it is a story of human adventure. I can more easily recall the person with whom I did something than remember what I did."

Regardless of the grueling work, the long hours, the lack of family life, and the dangers, Cousteau has had no trouble attracting divers, sailors, engineers, and scientists to the *Calypso*. Many, as the Captain admits, were "sensitive men, men who have not found happiness or peace in leading an ordinary life." Some sought adventure and exploration; others pursued solitude and meditation.

The crew came from diverse backgrounds. Mechanical engineer Armand Davso was a street cleaner in Marseilles when he first saw Cousteau's early films. Albert Falco, who has been at Cousteau's side for thirty-five years, was a champion spearfisherman, known for having killed fish with everything from sewing needles to curtain rods. André Laban, an early diver, was trained as an engineer and a chemist. Cameraman Louis Prezelin performed rescue dives for the French Air

Force, while sound engineer Guy Jouas served in the French merchant marine.

Participants have been selected for their ability to fit in with the rest of the crew. They must withstand pressures imposed by nature, mechanical breakdowns, and, according to the Captain, the "stress from too much to do, too far to go, too little time." For three-month stretches, they often work seven days a week and twelve to sixteen hours each day. "We lose about one person a year," Cousteau says, "but people who are accepted and cherished by their friends will stay, maybe 20 or 25 years. It's like a transplant, an organ transplant. It is rejected or accepted. That's the way we make our team."

Camaraderie dominates everyday life aboard *Calypso* and *Alcyone,* and mischief seems to be its most obvious expression. Guy Jouas, the sound and electronics engineer who has been with Cousteau for more than two decades, is the team's most noted prankster. He once tied all the crew members' belt loops together; when he issued the call for all hands, his colleagues jumped up from the dinner table together and abruptly fell into a heap. During the Canadian expedition Jouas glued Jean-Michel's cold-weather boots to the deck, enabling the crew to enjoy a hearty laugh as the young Cousteau rose from his chair and sprawled forward headfirst. For Jean-Michel's forty-ninth birthday, Jouas produced a cake in the shape of a humpback whale; the design included a tube, filled with confectioners' sugar, that ran from the whale's blowhole to a foot pump on the floor; when Jean-Michel leaned over to examine his present, Jouas delivered a full charge of white powder into the birthday boy's face.

The Captain has often shared credit willingly with his companions. He clearly conceptualized and developed *The Silent World,* but according to Louis Malle, a successful filmmaker today, "Cousteau was graceful enough to give me credit as co-producer of the film. I was only 23, and it gave me a wonderful start on my career. I have kept a passion for documentaries from my days with Cousteau and *Calypso.* I cannot forget that I was lucky enough to work with Cousteau. I learned a lot from him. Those years are really my golden years of filmmaking."

Armand Davso, the first engineer aboard *Calypso,* proudly remembers when a visitor asked Cousteau how he produced such beautiful films. "That's easy," replied the Captain, "it's because Armand made me the best cameras in the world."

Despite the apparent humility, Cousteau views himself as special, apart from the common man, and "chosen." He declares, "When one person, for whatever reason, has a chance to lead an exceptional life, he has no right to keep it to himself."

The Captain and his family, in fact, believe they have a unique mission to witness and report on the wonders within and the challenges to the planet's water system. At times the Cousteaus have assumed this task as if it were a noble burden. Philippe once wrote:

We were akin to those knights-errant who traveled across the world and returned to tell the king the news of the Holy Land or of Mauretania. We were different in the sense that we would bring the story of our adventures not to a solitary king, but to millions of people. When one thinks of it, however, the task becomes enormous. We could imagine each of our future viewers, and knew he would be hoping that we brought back accounts of things that were beautiful, true, and intellectually rewarding. Each of them was investing some degree of confidence in us, and this implied a heavy responsibility. We could no more deceive this confidence, this patience, this need for information on the marvels of the deep than we could have abandoned a blind man we might have been guiding across a busy street.

Cousteau's perspective may be filled with vanity, but he says straightforwardly, "I'm not interested in achievements. I'm interested in having an interesting life myself and sharing it with the public on television."

Still, as the Captain approaches his eightieth birthday, he is being showered with awards for his lifetime contributions to science, television, and film. Both the United States and France delivered their highest honors to Cousteau during his seventy-fifth year. France awarded him la Grand Croix dans l'Ordre National du Mérite (the Grand Cross of the National Order of Merit), and President Reagan bestowed the Presidential Medal of Freedom at a White House ceremony.

In November 1987 Cousteau was inducted into the Television Academy's Hall of Fame along with Johnny Carson, Jim Henson, Bob Hope, Eric Sevareid, and the late Ernie Kovacs; his citation reads, "With his underwater TV explorations, he unlocked the ocean's colorful treasures from the depths of obscurity to the eyes of the world above sea level." Later that same month he traveled to New York to receive the Founders Award from the International Council of the

National Academy of Television Arts and Sciences; the prize recognized the Captain's presentation of television programs to more than 115 countries and at least 250 million homes worldwide. Shortly thereafter he was welcomed into the Television Movie Awards Hall of Fame.

In 1988 Cousteau joined a select group with Sir Edmund Hillary and Jane Goodall to receive the National Geographic Society's Centennial Awards for "special contributions to mankind throughout the years." His name also was placed on the United Nations Environment Programme's "Global 500 Roll of Honor for Environmental Achievement." And he was recently elected to *L'Académie Française,* the elite guardians of French culture and literature.

Like few others, Cousteau has maintained his celebrity status for decades. In 1953 *The Silent World* became an international best seller. In 1969, a year after *The Undersea World* series began, opinion surveys identified the Captain as one of television's most popular personalities. In 1985 a *Good Housekeeping* magazine poll found Jacques Cousteau to be one of the world's ten most admired men. In 1989 Cousteau claimed that each of his documentaries reaches a half billion people —one tenth of the planet's population.

Even *Calypso* has become an international symbol that evokes delight and enchantment. While cruising up the Mississippi River, it was greeted by thousands of well-wishers lining the riverbank, sometimes in the pouring rain. The admirers waved until the small ship passed out of sight, expressing thanks for the years Cousteau had transported them out of their living rooms into worlds they would never have seen or could barely have imagined.

Captain Cousteau is one of the rare Renaissance men of the twentieth century. In addition to his noted filming, writing, and engineering achievements, he plays the piano, paints, composes poetry, and comments on international affairs. He speaks English and German fluently, understands Spanish, and reads Russian.

Cousteau has met and entertained the world's political and cultural leaders. "I'm pretty good with presidents," he claims. He has also maintained lengthy correspondence on aesthetics with various artists. Pablo Picasso, for instance, accepted the Captain's gift of black coral, revered in many Middle Eastern cultures. "After his death I met his wife," Cousteau remembers, "who told me Picasso had the coral in his hand when he died. He liked to touch it, to feel its smoothness with his fingers. That was moving for me."

Both a pragmatist and a dreamer, Cousteau has been able to connect seemingly unrelated facts and to communicate his concepts clearly to a wide audience. "While the world looks at life through a microscope," observes Jean-Michel, "my father looks at it through a macroscope."

The Captain has consistently sought intellectual stimulation. He once described his explorations of the undersea world as "inspiriting." He didn't mean spiritual or religious, "but a life full of daily inspiration like that to which man has risen as a result of creative developments in his past—the Greek concept of the ethos, the High Renaissance, the 18th century revolutions."

Although best known for his films and television broadcasts, Cousteau gained significant stimulation from writing scores of books. Most publications reported on his adventures or offered information about various undersea animals. Several—including *The Silent World* and *The Living Sea* (1963)—enjoyed critical and popular acclaim. In recent years, society staff writers—primarily Mose Richards in New York and Yves Paccalet in Paris—have converted the Captain's ship logs into manuscripts on his odysseys; Cousteau simply polishes the drafts, using his red pen to rewrite sentences.

On three occasions, the Captain has tried to present his comprehensive vision of the world. Not surprisingly, the multifaceted author developed complex amalgams of ideas and data.

In the late 1970's Cousteau convinced Doubleday & Company, a large U.S. publishing firm, to advance approximately two hundred thousand dollars for the development of *The Cousteau Almanac,* billed as "an inventory of life on our water planet." The Captain and Philippe jointly conceived the book as an extension of the Involvement Days at which they had arranged diverse displays on the environment. The book, according to original plans, "would be an almanac—lively and witty, but a solid reference as well. It would be a browsing book, filled with maps, lists, lore, cartoons. It would carry short articles and statistics about virtually every major environmental issue in the world." The book, in essence, was to convey the interconnectedness of all the planet's living systems.

After developing a detailed outline, the Captain turned the project's management over to Mose Richards, a talented editor who hired a team of twenty-five writers and researchers and solicited articles from approximately sixty independent authors. Cousteau visited the society's New York City office every few months to check on the book's progress and to offer his latest insights and suggestions (some of which, such as the proposed chapter on lovemaking, were ignored by the staff). The staff team spent about eighteen months trying to reflect the breadth of Cousteau's interests.

The final document "is about the entire world," said Richards. "It is a planetary inventory of living, an attempt to help people find their place in the great global organism of which we are part, in its flows and circles, and in the sweeping developments that are changing it rapidly in our age." The 838-page book, completed after Philippe's death, included some of the features of a regular almanac, such as statistics on population, incomes, and per capita energy consumption. But it also presented short profiles of futuristic bicycles, disappearing species, and energy-efficient buildings. Moreover, it encouraged citizen action by profiling "wavemakers" and by suggesting tactics for organizing political campaigns.

"It's a monument of data on uncorrelated things," boasted the Captain. The heavy and complex book was popular in France, but it sold only forty thousand copies in the United States, far below Doubleday's original estimates.

In the mid-1980's Cousteau decided to create another massive compilation of thoughts, this one to be titled the *Peace Almanac*. "It will not be what people think," he explained. "It's going to discuss scientifically the importance and role of violence in evolution and the selection of species."

When the Captain proclaimed his idea for the book, "everybody just rolled their eyes," said Richard Murphy, the society's staff scientist. "Then he gave an outline to me, and here we are, doing it! The guy is an unbelievable mover."

Cousteau turned the project over to Elisabeth Barbier, an editor working out of the Fondation Cousteau offices in Paris. Progress was slow, largely because the Captain managed to speak with Barbier only three times over a two-year period. The Cousteaus also couldn't agree on a definition of peace. The Captain and the French-based editors wanted to focus on North-South issues, while Jean-Michel and the U.S. staff expressed more interest in East-West relations. While Cousteau continues to explore peace issues, his son canceled the book project in summer 1988, claiming he could not locate a commercial outlet.

Cousteau's third writing project, being done in concert with Susan Schiefelbein, a former editor for *Saturday Review* and a longtime Cousteau ghostwriter, will be the Captain's "book of ideas." It's been in the works for almost a decade, and Cousteau still occasionally writes notes to Schiefelbein about the manuscript, but he isn't sure it will ever be finished.

The proposed treatise will present Cousteau's views on the future, illustrating the wandering insights of his creative and unorthodox mind. According to Schiefelbein, it will be "a conversation about life, an application of what he's seen to social issues."

Speaking about a future scenario that might be included in the publication, Cousteau said, "After all the dangers of the Bomb and starvation in the Third World have come to pass, finally, by gene manipulation, we achieve the eternal. People don't age. They die only by accident. Then what should they do? They recreate evolution from the beginning! They create a super zoo with every possible mutation as part of a favorable environment, and we get back to where we are now! Finally, they communicate with other civilizations that are developing, and they all end up eternal. Then they decide not to fight anymore—no more star wars. There's a big meeting, and it's like Olympus because they're gods—and you're back to the original Greek concept of the gods on Olympus ruling the world! So that's how I see the future of the universe."

CHAPTER ELEVEN

The Legacy

Can the Cousteau Group—the collection of sixteen corporations around the world engaged in oceanographic research, marine engineering, manufacture of diving gear and gases, production of films and television specials, and ecological education—survive without Cousteau?

Replacing the Captain will not be easy—for anyone. Turner Broadcasting's promotional materials call him "the world's greatest explorer." Hyperbole aside, Cousteau has remained an international celebrity for almost forty years. His inventions have changed the way we view the world. His films and television shows have transported several generations of viewers to exotic and faraway places, and his books have educated millions about the wonders beneath the sea. He is clearly one of the great men of the twentieth century.

After Philippe died, Jean-Michel, now fifty-one, became the heir apparent, and Cousteau clearly hopes his elder son will continue his work. But despite Jean-Michel's interest in explorations and educational projects, the son lacks his father's creativity, charm, and charisma.

Society staffers, dependent upon the Captain's legendary status for support, have done their best to make the two Cousteaus "interchangeable." Over the past several years Jean-Michel has been given a high profile in all television shows, books, and newsletters. Promotional photographs feature both men. Sometimes the society even downplays the Captain's activities in favor of his son's. The February

1988 issue of *Calypso Log*, for instance, carried six pictures of Jean-Michel and none of Cousteau.

Jean-Michel was not initially groomed to be the prince of his father's undersea world. While his younger brother, Philippe, worked by his father's side to learn the family moviemaking business, Jean-Michel resigned himself to handling administrative tasks for *Calypso*'s early expeditions. He wasn't ignored by the Captain, but he certainly wasn't favored or promoted. The elder son lacked his brother's flare and angular stature. A bit overweight and stooped, he could not compete with Philippe's dynamic presence. While Philippe struggled to become a star, Jean-Michel sat behind a drafting table at architecture school.

Jean-Michel acknowledges that he can't create poetry like his father or even his brother. The little writing he does for *Calypso Log* is often overdone. Consider his philosophic observation in the December 1985 issue: "We are part of a vast, rich, multi-hued, and complex work, a tapestry interwoven with life where every individual is part of a larger pattern."

Cousteau tried to use his son's design talents, but problems often seemed to plague Jean-Michel's equipment. With the squaloscope, for instance, Jean-Michel tried to allow divers to observe and study sharks in a confined area. His rectangular box enclosure measured twelve feet by nine, with vertical bars about six inches apart on the sides, and with four transparent plastic domes on the roof through which cameramen were to film the captive creatures. The first two sharks that followed the fish bait into the squaloscope, however, twisted the weak aluminum bars out of shape and escaped. More troubling, the second pair died of asphyxiation because the small space restricted their ability to swim and pass sufficient amounts of water over their gills.

Jean-Michel also developed an ill-fated cage intended to protect divers. Named La Balue in honor of the unfortunate Cardinal la Balue who was imprisoned in an oversize birdcage by Louis XI, the Plexiglas structure should have enabled cameramen to film freely in the open ocean without fear of shark attacks. Jean-Michel, however, failed to realize that sea currents would jar the box; as a result, divers were jerked around uncontrollably.

Despite these setbacks and shortcomings, Jean-Michel has assumed a major role within the Cousteau organizations. While clearly capitalizing on his father's notoriety, he is intent on making his own mark.

Jean-Michel has overseen, for instance, vast improvements to the *Calypso Log,* which began as a bimonthly bulletin in July 1974, shortly after the society was formed. Philippe became editorial director in March 1979 and shifted the informal update to a quarterly magazine with a glossy cover and color photographs throughout. In late 1980, after his brother's death, Jean-Michel asked society writer Mose Richards to spruce up the *Calypso Log*'s ponderous style. The elder son assumed the position of editorial director in March 1981 and promptly upgraded the design, adding more white space and stylized headlines. And to demonstrate his new prominence in the organization, he placed three pictures of himself in his first issue.

Although less scientifically inclined than his father, Jean-Michel has increased the society's scientific work. He continues the Captain's tradition of carrying researchers aboard *Calypso* on expeditions, but he goes farther in promoting an oceanographic image. The society's annual reports now highlight papers by staff biologists Richard Murphy and François Sarano, and the group advertises Project Ocean Search as an opportunity for novices to cooperate with professionals on biological and archaeological inspections. Preserving the planet's ecological treasury, Jean-Michel argues, "begins with the inglorious, day-after-day analytical toils of scientists."

More sensitive than his father to criticism of the society's credibility, Jean-Michel has counterattacked by claiming that Cousteau films have "generated financial support for scientific research." He suggests that the international success of the Captain's work has engendered widespread curiosity about the undersea world. "Without the documentaries," he declares, "there would not be sufficient funding to create the kind of ecosystem-wide studies to which we are also committed, funding that is not subject to the limited viewpoint or self-serving approach that can apply when the support comes only from government agencies or vested commercial interests. In a sense, as the Cousteau Society sets out to translate science for the public, we are also finding ways to support it."

The son also wants to change the image that Cousteau operations are open exclusively to men. During *Calypso*'s early years, Simone made sure other women neither threatened her prized position as the ship's only female resident nor skewed the ship's harmonious all-male dynamics. The Captain involved a few female scientists for short assignments because they were competent and photogenic, but he maintained a patronizing attitude toward women. Even with Simone,

Cousteau once declared that her role was to do "everything the men cannot do, from tending to curtains and penicillin reserves to hearing the problems of the sailors."

Jean-Michel has appointed several women to senior positions, but most are the wives of current society officials. In essence, he has converted the fraternity into an extended family. His own wife, Anne-Marie, snaps the organization's still photographs. Pam Stacey, wife of Richard Murphy, the vice-president for science, edits the *Calypso Log*. And Susan Spencer-Richards, wife of chief writer and producer Mose Richards, used to solicit equipment donations from corporations. Still, women remain virtually excluded from frontline filming and diving jobs. "We are really considering changing our views about that," claims Jean-Michel.

Money has long been a sensitive topic for Cousteau, and his finances are obfuscated behind layers of organizations and corporations. He claims to possess almost no assets, feeling "much freer having practically no money for myself," but he was able to make a personal, no-interest loan to the society for a quarter of a million dollars. He takes no salary from the nonprofit group, but colleagues suggest his annual fees, stipends, and royalties from other Cousteau businesses, as well as his pension from 27 years in the French Navy, total more than two hundred thousand dollars. A connoisseur of French wine and fine food, he enjoys traveling first class on both commercial airplanes and his own ships.

During congressional testimony in 1983 the Captain defended his objectivity by pronouncing, "We are completely self-supported, and we do not receive any government funds from any country." But Cousteau conveniently forgot that France initially supported *Calypso*'s activities, that the Greek government helped sponsor his 1976 archaeological studies among the islands of the Aegean, that the Venezuelan government financed his 1979 exploration of coastal waters, that the Canadian Film Board paid for his St. Lawrence expedition, and that NASA contracted for a handful of missions over the past decade. He also failed to mention that France recently contributed more than a million dollars to help design and construct his wind-powered ship, *Alcyone*.

Although an effective fund raiser, Cousteau dislikes making personal appeals for money. He will sign form letters asking millions of strangers for support, but he refused to appear on television urging viewers to contribute a twenty-dollar membership fee. In a society commercial, the Captain would only say, "Please join me," while a narrator made the actual pitch for funds. Jean-Michel has no such hesitation.

In fact, perhaps the most important difference between father and son is Jean-Michel's commercial orientation. Jean-Michel refers to the Cousteau Society as the company. He openly discusses the challenge of covering *Calypso*'s $8,000 a day operating costs and of meeting the payroll for 135 employees in New York, Paris, Los Angeles, and Norfolk. Recognizing the Captain's lifelong struggle to raise money, he diversified his money-making ventures from travel services to comic books to amusement parks.

Before returning to the family business after Philippe's death, Jean-Michel had established his own tourist agency, which placed well-to-do amateurs with marine scientists on dives in beautiful locations. Although his father and other *Calypso* divers disdain the encroachment of tourists on the planet's pristine sites, Jean-Michel has used the Cousteau Society to expand Project Ocean Search, now in its sixteenth year. He aggressively promotes the tours—often utilizing two full pages of *Calypso Log* as advertisements—with high-minded goals: "Education is the only means by which to appreciate the true values embodied in the ocean. It must be dramatic education, indepth, in order for the human race to restore its ties with the environment. It must let the environment speak eloquently for itself."

Project Ocean Search began on scenic Hilton Head Island, South Carolina, and subsequent tour groups frequented resorts on Wuvulu Island, north of Papua New Guinea, and Catalina and Santa Cruz Islands, off the coast of Southern California. For the past nine summers Jean-Michel has organized eleven-day sessions on Moskito Island (named after Indians, not insects) in the British Virgin Islands. The privately owned island, which stretches one mile long and half a mile wide, delights divers with its healthy reefs and abundant marine life. When they're not underwater, the travelers can hike good trails to cliffs that offer outstanding views of the sea. Participants relax at an exclusive resort, Drakes Anchorage, and enjoy the island's lush foliage, scalloped bays, and talcum white beaches.

Moskito has become a retreat for underwater archaeologists. Early pirates and sailors used the region's calm waters as a passageway to the Caribbean. But the nearby reefs were deceptive, and confused captains littered the seafloor with their shipwrecks, now the playgrounds for Ocean Search participants.

Jean-Michel convinced the University of Southern California's College of Continuing Education to offer academic credit for the Club Med-style adventures. Promotional brochures say the program allows "a hands-on, educational experience of the marine environment, an experience full of activity and new approaches to solving ecological and resource management dilemmas." Accompanying pictures suggest the participants enjoy a great deal of swimming and sunbathing. One of the instructional workshops promises to have student-tourists sit waist-deep in water on a secluded beach and read aloud *Moby Dick* or other great books about the sea.

The commercialization of the Cousteau name has been extensive. Cousteau comic books are published in France, and Jean-Michel is searching for a U.S. distributor. The Revell toy company created a thirteen-inch model of *Calypso,* complete with two divers, a helicopter, antishark cage, diving saucer, Zodiac, minisub, and camera sled. The society markets its own cards of undersea lore—much like baseball cards—to children on a subscription basis.

The organization even sells a sixteen-inch porcelain sculpture of a humpback whale for a whopping $1,850. In advertisements the society answered its own question about why the group commissioned such a costly item: "Because in works of art and in symbols of commitment, it's the quality that counts. . . . Very rare things are very precious— like the humpback whale."

For several years the society devoted two pages of its twenty-four-page newsletter to advertisements of Cousteau sweat shirts, calendars, and T-shirts (including one promoted as "summertime chic for ladies"). In late 1986 the editors admitted that they had "agonized at taking two full pages in the *Log* to offer merchandise items." But since the service brought in almost half a million dollars of revenue, society managers were not about to abandon it. They adopted a "compromise": Every issue now contains a four-page advertising insert, allowing two additional pages of information as well as two more pages for promotion.

The Captain does set a few limits on his son's marketing plans. He refused, for instance, to grant approval for a look-alike doll with the famous red cap and a removable diving suit.

To attract members to the society, the Cousteaus send approximately 6.5 million pieces of "junk mail" each year to supporters of like-minded organizations, such as the Sierra Club, Environmental Action, and the Union of Concerned Scientists. Fewer than 1 percent of the recipients respond favorably, a typical response rate for nonprofit groups. Unlike most organizations, however, the society spends almost $450,000 more each year on such direct mail than it receives in contributions from new members. Where the society makes its money is on renewals, the annual donations of existing contributors. In 1987 the group raised $5.4 million from existing members, more than five times what it paid to solicit those funds.

By early 1989, at the society's fifteenth anniversary, membership had increased to almost 246,000, more than ten times the original number in 1974. The Fondation Cousteau in Paris boasts an additional sixty thousand. Cousteau claims his goal is 500,000 members.

Jean-Michel pays particular attention to his wealthy supporters. To the five thousand Friends of *Calypso* who contribute monthly, he sends periodic updates, and he plans to distribute regular "videologs" that provide intimate insights into the expeditions. He also encourages rich members to bequeath part of their estates to the Cousteau Society. Staffers recently convinced one supporter to provide a no-interest $1.2 million loan, and a British admirer to donate a 160-foot oceangoing luxury ship, valued at $1.3 million.

To keep in touch with his members and earn additional income, Jean-Michel travels across the country delivering lectures and slide presentations. In 1984 he gave 127 addresses. But as his administrative tasks have increased, he has turned over most speaking responsibilities to David Brown, a former student with Gloucester's Cetacean Research Unit who was hired to be the society's lecturer. In 1988 Jean-Michel spoke at only eleven institutions, while Brown traveled to forty-two.

The pair's speaking schedules are organized by a professional booking agent in Washington, D.C. To hear Jean-Michel deliver an hour and a half lecture, a college or other organization must pay seventy-five hundred dollars, plus all travel expenses. Almost twenty-five institutions have placed their names on a waiting list, suggesting that Jean-Michel could be booked for the next five years. When asked why the Captain doesn't lecture, the agent explains that the senior Cousteau has no inclination to go on the road and that some audiences complain of his hard-to-understand French accent.

In 1985 Jean-Michel signed a contract with Paquet Cruise Lines to provide slide and film presentations aboard luxury tours of Caribbean and Alaskan waters. In 1987 he also agreed to join Sun Line Cruises' *Stella Solaris* to South America, and in 1988 the ships of Royal Viking Line became hosts for Cousteau Society lecturers. The son of the famous explorer speaks and shows his father's movies. Sun Line offers Cousteau Society members a 5 percent discount on the cruise fares, and it sends a matching amount as a contribution to the society.

Jean-Michel enjoys experimenting with alternative fund-raising methods, too. He recently launched the society into the world of direct television marketing with sixty-second commercials that encourage the viewers of Cousteau specials to call a toll-free 800 number to join the society. He has also organized art exhibits on Maui, Hawaii, and in Monterey, California, from which part of the proceeds are donated to the group.

Despite Jean-Michel's fund-raising successes, the society does not conform to the standards set by the National Information Bureau, a New York-based rating service for foundations and philanthropic in-dividuals. The bureau, which favors low fund-raising expenditures and outside directors who objectively oversee operations, complains that the society spends approximately 25 percent of its income on fund raising and that some board members, including Jean-Michel, receive compensation from membership contributions.

The Cousteaus, moreover, face severe financial challenges, not the least of which is a growing feeling among executives at Turner Broad-casting that the Cousteau Society's overhead costs—burdened with operation of two ships full-time, employment of large crews, and enjoyment of a first-class life-style—are exorbitant. In fact, production costs for each of Cousteau's hourlong shows total almost nine hundred thousand dollars, three and one half times more than those developed for Turner by the National Audubon Society and 80 percent above those by National Geographic. Despite the high costs, Cousteau's broadcasts earn no larger a market share than do the other nature documentaries. Turner, long a fan of the Captain's, will probably not cancel the contract. But society staffers worry about their continued access to television.

The Cousteaus also fret that maintaining two boats often demands unexpected costs. In early 1988, for instance, Typhoon Roy tore *Al-cyone* from its anchor chain and set it adrift into the island of Guam. The ship became entangled in a ton of old, rusty World War II cables, damaging the propeller, shaft, and hull. In March, fuel bubbles and steam gushed from *Calypso*'s pressure safety cap, requiring technicians to spend four sleepless days and nights checking and cleaning the engines. Another blow came in April when *Calypso*'s communications equipment failed. Parts, as well as a satellite technician, had to be flown from the United States to Papua New Guinea.

Most of Jean-Michel's commercial ventures are associated with the Cousteau Society, where he manages an annual budget of almost twelve million dollars. But he is becoming more active in other Cousteau businesses. In fact, Jean-Michel is not averse to using the nonprofit society to promote the family's profit-making ventures. He recently allowed U.S. Divers, the corporation the Captain chairs, to offer a one-week all-expense-paid trip to a Cousteau Society expedition for the winner of a promotional drawing. To encourage diving equipment sales, customers were told they would "dive with either Jean-Michel or Captain Cousteau (possibly both)."

Jean-Michel also represents U.S. Divers and its parent company, Aqua Lung International, at trade shows to promote diving equipment, including the silver wet suits developed for the *Rediscovery* expedition. He even appears in advertisements for the company, which with its subsidiaries in France, Italy, and Japan, boasts sixty million dollars in annual sales. Moreover, he oversees licensing arrangements with the several other companies that market his father's inventions, including the Paris-based ÉnAIRgie S.A. which promotes wind-energy projects that use the systems developed for *Alcyone*.

No one doubts Jean-Michel's organizing skills. At an early age he handled the endless logistical tasks associated with sending *Calypso* and twenty-five men around the world. More recently he supervised the complex and successful Amazon expedition. Of his son's talents, the Captain admits, "He beats me in one thing—he's a good administrator."

The administrator, however, struggles to be the visionary his father is. Jean-Michel focuses his public speeches on the current generation of world leaders, arguing that they possess abundant technical tools but lack examples of how to use those resources to improve the planet. The absence of leadership models, he claims, is one of the greatest challenges facing the world today.

Jean-Michel doesn't seem entirely comfortable with his own leadership of the Cousteau Society, sometimes suggesting that his brother might have done a better job. "With the death of Philippe we've lost a talent I don't have," Jean-Michel admits. "Philippe was full of poetry and dreams, he was a beautiful story-teller, a talented filmmaker. His world was in the air. How can we reinstate that perspective? I am not a balloonist, not a pilot. I'm an ocean person. The society will always be marked by his absence.''

Jean-Michel's role models are his father and Kukus, the Anchuara Indian chief he met in Amazonia. Cousteau, according to his son, is more than a brilliant filmmaker and inventor; he thinks long term about the water planet's survival. Similarly, Kukus invests in wood and water supplies for his tribe's future generations.

The Captain, however, both influences and overwhelms his son. According to Jean-Michel, ''My father has achieved almost everything. He's a discoverer, adventurer, explorer, a catalyst. He is an hour, a week, or a year ahead of the next guy.''

Of the Captain, Jean-Michel continues, ''He's my boss, my father, and my friend. It's a fantastic relationship in many ways. It's like having private tutoring all your life.''

That family schooling began early, when Cousteau took his young sons for long walks on dark nights to view not just one constellation but the entire universe. ''I remember my father as a philosopher,'' Jean-Michel says. ''He would show us the stars and tell us what life could mean.'' Jean-Michel recalls spending his school vacations aboard *Calypso,* helping the crew clean the deck, paint, cook, and grease engine cogs. He became, because of his father, ''one of the divers privileged to view a world whose beauties were only then becoming known to us.''

After Philippe's death the Captain created a new position at the society as vice-president for communications, allowing Jean-Michel to upgrade the newsletter, create a lecture series, and expand Project Ocean Search. A few years later Cousteau promoted his elder son to be executive vice-president of the society, a position in which his administrative talents have blossomed.

Jean-Michel may be assuming more authority, but the passing of power from one generation to the next is not a smooth process. Father and son have developed a complex pattern of collaboration and tension, in which their obvious affection seems barely to mask their ignitable tempers. Jean-Michel, however, acknowledges his place. ''There's a sailor and a sub-sailor,'' he says. ''I'm the sub-sailor.''

The son differs from his father in many ways. While Cousteau imagines poetic utopias when he considers the planet's future, Jean-Michel seems trapped within his role as a manager. ''My commitment,'' the son says flatly, ''is to focus on management of our world ocean resources, to bring them public attention, and to try to suggest better ways to handle them.''

David Brown, the society's lecturer, suggests the differences are more than stylistic. Recalling his job interview, he says, ''Jean-Michel really grilled me on my philosophy of life: Would I respond [to audience questions] in a Cousteau-like fashion? Then he left and his father came in. He was real mellow, looking at my slides. Jean-Michel was really pinning me down; the other guy was just dreaming through.''

Other staff recognize the father-son contrasts and express concern for the society's future. ''Zheek is a poet,'' says one inside observer. ''He really has a special angle and infuses his spirit into everything. The question is whether Jean-Michel can keep it all going. He has different interests, and while he's good as one of the guys, he's less inspired, less odd.''

Another, complaining that Jean-Michel lacks his father's vision and humor, predicts disastrous internal problems for the organization when the son assumes full command.

When the Captain dies, Jean-Michel will no longer be able to rely upon his tutor, boss, and role model. He must assume responsibility not only for organizing the society's details but for providing its artistic inspiration and social commitment. In short, he must lead, not only administer.

Jean-Michel will not be alone. He and his father have assembled a talented and diverse team of divers, writers, and cameramen, several of whom have worked with the Cousteaus for more than three decades.

Armand Davso, for instance, has remained intensely loyal to the Cousteaus since 1952. ''The Captain has taught me many things,'' he says. ''I was a sweeper in Marseille [*sic*], and he made me an engineer. If I hadn't met him, no one would know that I exist. I will continue working with him as long as he needs me.'' Davso is actually the longest-serving Cousteau team member, surpassing his friend Albert Falco—who introduced the street cleaner to the adventurer—by just one week. Since the early 1950's, when the talented engineer created Cousteau's first underwater cameras, Davso has continued to perfect the team's photographic and life-support equipment.

Albert Falco, the stocky ''right-hand man'' featured in most Cousteau films, began free diving in 1939, at the age of twelve. He became a champion spearfisherman who throughout World War II relied upon his undersea talents to provide daily food for his family. When Cousteau publicized his archaeology project in 1952 at Grand Congloué Island, Falco left his office job in Marseilles and volunteered. Bébert, as he is nicknamed, displayed an uncanny understanding of the sea's creatures, rare strength and agility underwater, and dependable steadiness in crises. The Captain appointed him to be the first pilot of the diving saucer and the first oceanaut (along with Claude Wesly) to live within the Conshelf I undersea habitat. Today the experienced and reliable Falco coordinates many of the diving and filming projects.

Raymond Coll joined the Cousteau team as a diver-handyman in 1954 and has been an underwater cameraman since 1971. The taciturn Coll relishes the silent world. "I continue to dive because of the beauty," he declares, "but also because I like to be in a quiet place. Sometimes when I pilot the diving saucer I turn everything off to observe the beauty around me quietly."

Dominique Sumian met the Captain in 1966 after serving in the French Navy as a frogman. The six-foot-three-inch Sumian is the largest and strongest member of the team. And according to Cousteau, Sumian possesses rare versatility: "He is an experienced professional diver, a mechanic, a carpenter, a plumber, a licensed truck driver, a skilled sailor; he is trained in first aid, and of great importance, an excellent chef." Once very close to Philippe, he recently coordinated logistics for Jean-Michel and the Amazon land team. In addition to his strength and stamina, Sumian maintains a deep compassion for animals. Other crew members joke about the husky sailor's stopping his truck along a busy road to collect and care for injured birds, and rather than swat houseflies with a rolled newspaper, he catches them in his huge hands and sets them free outdoors.

Louis Prezelin became a rescue diver for the Cousteaus in 1969, a task he had performed for the French Air Force. He convinced the Captain to introduce him to photographic equipment and techniques. Encouraged by his progress, Prezelin left the Cousteaus for a few years to study cinematography at the Brooks Institute School of Photography in Santa Barbara. Today Prezelin strives to create images that make television viewers believe they are part of the diving team. "You have to join the action," he explains. "It's a tricky technique to pull back from an approaching animal underwater. It's as if you were on land and saw a herd of wild horses galloping toward you. You'd have to see them coming and join them as they go." To perfect his filming method, the hardworking Prezelin often practices in a swimming pool by placing a small bug about an inch away from his camera lens and tracking it through the water. Like the Captain, he rejects using the viewfinder because "it's like walking down a busy sidewalk with a telescope in front of your face the whole while. You bump into trash cans, signs, lampposts, whatever."

Mose Richards is one of the newer American-born aides who, since 1973, has put his creative and lyrical mark on many of the society's productions. As the Captain's chief U.S. writer Richards coordinated the 838-page *Cousteau Almanac,* created a more professional style within the *Calypso Log,* authored *Jacques Cousteau's Amazon Journey,* and wrote the script for *Snowstorm in the Jungle.* Before joining the Cousteau Society, he was a television news reporter and a writer-producer of documentary films. Mose was actually born Fred Richards, but his participation in a summer beard-growing contest in Pismo Beach, California, led friends at Stanford University to label him "Moses." The name stuck when a producer suggested "Mose" would be more memorable on film credits than "Fred." (Richards's mother still calls him Freddy.)

Jean-Michel recruited Charles Vinick in May 1981 to help improve the society's management. The two met when Vinick, the director of the special programs associated with the University of Southern California's College of Continuing Education, arranged for participants in Project Ocean Search to receive college credit. Having also served as director of human resources for TRW, Inc., Vinick became the society's director of corporate affairs, responsible for raising money and expanding membership.

But perhaps the most critical team member remains Simone. His mother, says Jean-Michel, "has been *Calypso*'s guiding spirit. The crew's confidante. The friend." He pauses. "Maybe she's the real captain behind the scenes." Eight years younger and significantly shorter than her lanky husband, Simone has been the team's inexhaustible worker, serving as supply officer, nurse, assistant cook, sonar specialist, and whale watcher. Although she has diligently avoided the spotlight, La Bergère, according to crew members, maintains the spirit of purpose and camaraderie aboard *Calypso.*

The fiercely independent Cousteaus may have gained a financial resource when they formed the Cousteau Society, but they also acquired supporters who force them to answer questions about their operation. With a chuckle, the Captain admits that several adult society members have written to him about the propriety of the nude Calypso appearing on the group's logo. The design by French painter Luc-Marie Bayle portrays the well-endowed enchantress of Odysseus swimming freely beside a dolphin. "The woman is naked," society writers tried to explain. "Yet in an age of diminishing diversity, not only in numbers of species but in cultural options, she evokes images of a gentler time in the history of mankind's relation to the seas. Calypso detained Odysseus against his will. We have freely given *Calypso* our attentions. She is, especially now, an ironically proper and most beautiful, albeit naked, symbol of the best of us all." Evidently the Fondation Cousteau's members throughout France have not complained.

More critical, some members, having joined in response to environmental appeals, object to the Cousteaus' focusing the society's energies and resources on drugs, nuclear war, and other social concerns. Ignoring such protests, Cousteau plans to devote more and more attention to peace issues and a massive international exchange of children. He maintains that environmental protection is his fourth goal, well behind peace, the third world, and education.

"Today, social problems swallow the world," the Captain states. "One of The Cousteau Society's main priorities is to contribute to the establishment of lasting peace, because if this planet is going to be completely turned to ashes, it's no use to protect it. . . . We are ready, all of us, to dedicate our energy to contribute, even modestly, because even though this Society cannot completely modify the world, we can contribute to actions that are aimed at those four goals."

While Jacques and Jean-Michel usually refuse to cooperate with other organizations, they've become active members of Ted Turner's Better World Society, which fosters awareness of global issues that affect all life on earth. They've traveled several times with the group to Moscow, and Jean-Michel flew with Turner to Nicaragua for a two-hour meeting with President Daniel Ortega. The Better World Society's contingent advocated a peace park that would run along Nicaragua's border with Costa Rica, from the Atlantic to the Pacific. "It would be a buffer zone for nature and for human beings as well," Jean-Michel suggested diplomatically.

To promote dialogue on world peace, the Cousteaus also produced a half hour special on Costa Rica, which four decades ago abolished its army and redirected the national budget toward educating its young and protecting its environment. *Island of Peace* featured Jean-Michel's interview with President Oscar Arias Sánchez, winner of the 1987

Nobel Prize for peace, as well as footage of the national celebration commemorating the army's demise. Broadcast by TBS in late June 1988, the video, according to the Captain, "introduced a people who have managed to establish peace within their borders, to guard that tradition, and to shun engagements in conflicts beyond their borders."

Although society staffers suggest the Captain's genius and charm will always attract broad-based support, no matter what projects he pursues, most members, according to a recent survey, don't believe the organization should simply be a support group for Cousteau's films. In fact, fewer than 40 percent of the contributors take time to watch old Cousteau specials on their local channels, and only a quarter view the newest shows on Turner's Cable network.

The Cousteaus, despite their growing personal interest in social rather than oceanographic issues, recognize that individuals join the Cousteau Society because of the Captain's image as an undersea explorer. They, therefore, continue to write direct mail appeals that focus on dolphins rather than nuclear war. The group, as a result, faces the dilemma of having attracted supporters interested in issues that its leaders no longer rank as priorities.

Colleagues who have known the Captain for many years attest to his diverse talents as a filmmaker, adventurer, and friend. According to Frédéric Dumas, coauthor of *The Silent World*, "When I met Cousteau at twenty-eight years old, he was as he is today [in 1985]. He has not changed. What was always dominant in Jacques was his extraordinary charm. Not only does he have a bright intellect, but he hypnotizes everyone. He is irresistible."

Filmmaker Louis Malle reports, "I always loved working with Cousteau because he has a great sense of humor. It has always been difficult for me to work with people who take themselves seriously. Cousteau always had this sort of funny attitude about everything."

Albert Falco, the star diver of so many Cousteau films, enjoys fond memories of the bond between the two men. "I am in my sixties," he says. "When I see my sailor's bag next to me, it is absolutely full. All the memories, all the adventures lived through. Thanks to Cousteau."

But even some of Cousteau's closest supporters believe the Captain is spread too thin and moving too fast. "When I picture him, I see him leaving great piles of paper everywhere," says Ruth Dugan, an old friend and widow of Cousteau's primary ghostwriter during the early adventures. "I have always felt that if he stayed in one place long enough to let some of the questions be answered, he might be able to do more. What he seems to be doing is running away from piles."

Others complain that the Captain's vision has been distorted by so many years behind and in front of the camera. Since the age of thirteen he has recorded his life on film or videotape, becoming increasingly concerned with his image. Rather than experience adventure, Cousteau has sought to record his explorations, and he doesn't recognize that his camera changes the nature of his efforts. "It isn't possible to be participant and recorder at the same moment," wrote syndicated columnist Ellen Goodman. "The camera distorts vision, reducing the experience to the size of the lens. It distorts time, capturing the present so that in the future you can enjoy the past."

Everyone, however, agrees that the Captain translated his remarkable charm into a fund-raising asset that has attracted research grants, an oceangoing vessel, television contracts, and about 300,000 individual supporters worldwide. His spell convinced a Puerto Rican woman to return the sea lion Christobald to *Calypso,* the prince of Monaco to hand over his museum, and the rulers of the world's nations to open their doors.

Sometimes, however, the charm seems calculated. At a 1986 press conference to promote his television series, the Captain was asked why he was so aloof. "I live in my ivory tower," he revealed. "Nobody ever sees me. When I appear, of course, it's rare." Then he added with a smile, "What is rare is expensive."

Everyone also agrees that Cousteau's life has been filled with accomplishments. He has contributed to the invention of scuba diving equipment, underwater vehicles for exploration, artificial islands, deep-saturation industrial diving, and the utilization of satellites in oceanography. His movies have won three Oscars, while his television shows racked up eleven Emmys. He has authored or coauthored more than eighty books, including *The Silent World,* which was translated into almost two dozen languages. Having spent a lifetime exploring the planet, he has become the world's best-known living adventurer.

The Captain, however, has allowed himself to rest on these laurels, drowning in his own legend and frequently accepting compromises in the quality of his productions. He has created a filmmaking and book-writing bureaucracy which he has failed to oversee and manage. Between the Antarctica adventure of the mid-1970's and the Amazon films of the mid-1980's, Cousteau's productions lacked focus and drama. The films and books seem to have been put together more to fulfill contracts than because of love and art.

Parts of the Amazon series demonstrate that the Captain can still convey a sense of awe and wonder toward the environment, but most of the recent *Rediscovery* broadcasts again reveal the constraints of Cousteau's rushed schedule. Unlike his outstanding early films, recent segments fail to present story lines that capture the viewer's attention; without coherent themes, they become mere travelogues rather than commentaries, adventures, or documentaries. It is ironic that the Captain is being showered with international awards at a time when his creativity is adrift in the sea of corporations and projects that have become the Cousteau empire.

Another generally accepted conclusion about Cousteau is that after decades of producing nature films, he is one of the planet's leading environmental activists. Cousteau Society publicists promote that image by claiming "he's rescued countless endangered species and exposed the ecological dangers which are making mankind an equally endangered species." They further assert that "Cousteau's investigations of the world's ecological systems have set the standards for many of today's conservation efforts." But behind the carefully constructed legend, it's clear that the Captain's only major environmental victory occurred almost three decades ago, when he helped block the dumping of radioactive wastes in the Mediterranean.

No doubt Cousteau's films and books have increased the public's knowledge of the undersea world and the threats to it. But the Captain promised to do more to protect the environment, and he has not delivered. He said he would mobilize widespread public support for resource management, but the Cousteau Society's 246,000 members have not been organized into a political force. He pledged to become "a fighter against the system when it is wrong," but he avoids political controversies and refuses to attack unenlightened politicians or polluting corporations. He committed himself to "present the case of our Water Planet to hundreds of influential leaders in government and industry" as well as to "support vital exploration and research projects," but his actions lead to elaborate journeys and movies rather than new laws or scientific insights.

All membership organizations that advocate for the environment consider part of their mission to be public education. But except for the Cousteau Society, the others also seek more tangible results: the purchase and preservation of a tropical rain forest; lawsuits to stop toxic discharges; research to counter industry propaganda; legislation to adjust public priorities. Cousteau has harshly criticized environmental activists, despite their clear accomplishments, for not proposing positive alternatives. In fact, other than his advocacy of the Law of the Sea Treaty and his development of a windship to help combat the oil crisis, it is the Captain who has not promoted technological alternatives and policy options.

As the 1990's approach, pollution increasingly threatens the planet's environment. Fossil-fuel combustion is depleting the stratospheric ozone, causing what appears to be a greenhouse warming of the earth. Garbage and medical wastes are washing up on beaches. Acid rain is killing forests and fish. Toxic contaminants are leaching into our drinking water. More movies won't solve these problems; creative and dedicated leadership will. If he changed his tactics, Captain Cousteau, with his access to the world's presidents and command of an international audience, could be in the vanguard.

"I have made friends with death," says the Captain. The vibrant adventurer has certainly brushed against the Grim Reaper several times: in 1936, when he crashed his father's Salmson on a foggy mountain road; in 1940, when he went into convulsions after descending too deeply with an experimental oxygen tank; in 1947, when he virtually collapsed from carbon monoxide poisoning at the bottom of the Fontaine-de-Vaucluse; in 1955, when he beat back frenzied sharks with his camera.

"I have accepted death not only as inevitable but also as constructive," Cousteau explains. "If we didn't die, we would not appreciate life as we do. So it's a constructive force."

He tries to avoid using the word "death," preferring the concept of being switched off. "I pray God to be switched off in action," he declares.

Cousteau has never been particularly sturdy, and he has been consistently underweight. As a child he suffered from enteritis and anemia. His periodic attacks of neurasthenics still produce nervous tension and malaise. And he remains susceptible to high altitudes, undersea pressures, and cold water.

The Captain continues to dive, but an accident in 1979 damaged his left ear. Rather than rest when his ears were stopped up and irritated, he pressed on and ruptured a membrane. He now suffers from vertigo.

"It's very disagreeable, because you don't even know where up and down are," he explains. "You lose all sense of direction. You have to close your eyes."

It now takes Cousteau four or five days to adjust his ears to the pressure of deep water. Because he often arrives at his ships for only brief periods to be photographed for the films, his dives are rare. His most recent deep descent was on the Cuban expedition in the fall of 1985. Before attempting even shallow dives, he must use a nasal inhaler containing Albuterol to clear his wind passages.

Still, for a seventy-nine-year-old man who has confronted more than his share of accidents and trials, Cousteau is in great shape. He credits his good health to luck or divine compensation for his childhood illnesses. But Cousteau does take care of his body, exercising a half hour each morning. He eats plenty of vegetables, tries to vary his diet, and takes vitamins. He also avoids doctors. While claiming to have suffered a score of broken bones, he has not had a checkup or medical attention of any kind since a hernia operation in the late 1970's. Before that, he says the last time he saw a physician was after the automobile accident in 1936 that left him paralyzed for eight months.

The Captain maintains an incredibly full schedule, even for someone half his age. Although he resigned the Oceanographic Institute's directorship in late 1988, he still travels constantly to supervise the production of four documentaries each year, to guide large environmental organizations on two continents, to tinker with new technologies, and to manage an international array of businesses. Simone, complaining of her husband's endless activities, admits she has suffered nightmares that Jacques, feeling bored without enough to occupy his time, might begin a job as a night clerk at the Hotel Royalton in New York City.

Cousteau remains an adventure seeker at heart. In January 1986, after the *Challenger* disaster, he wrote a letter to President Reagan expressing personal sympathy for the astronauts and praising the President's decision to continue the shuttle missions. "As a token of my deep solidarity," Cousteau concluded, "I wish to express my sincere desire to take part in one of the next shuttle flights."

Friends say that the Captain, despite his on-the-go life-style, is basically a calm and reflective man. Over the past decade he has focused his thoughts increasingly on the future.

At his seventy-fifth birthday gala at Mount Vernon, for instance, Cousteau spent a great deal of time introducing his grandchildren, appealing to the next generation to carry on his work. He told Fabian, Jean-Michel's son, then aged seventeen, that he should "be prepared" to take over the Cousteau enterprises. Fabian, now a college student, is an avid diver who has joined his father on the *Rediscovery* expedition, but society staffers believe the young Cousteau has interests other than directing the family businesses.

Céline, Fabian's younger sister and a high school student in New York City, displays brilliant blue eyes and her grandfather's mischievous smile. The Captain joked to Céline, whose hair was cut short on one side, "Maybe when you have cut your hair properly, you will remember that a girl is just as good as a boy." He drew applause from the liberated crowd by saying that Céline should play a role in the Cousteau dream, too.

Cousteau cried during the middle of his address when he mentioned "the great absence tonight—Philippe." Philippe's children, nine-year-old Alexandra and "little Philippe," then aged five, also sobbed. After all the speeches they and their grandfather shared a long and sorrowful hug.

The Captain usually avoids reflecting on the past. He candidly concedes, however, that his stimulating career demanded sacrifices. "I have a good wife and a good son, and I'm not complaining," he says. "But if I had it to do over again, I would not get married. It's impossible to be an adventurer and a bureaucrat at the same time, and if you get married, you should be a bureaucrat and have a stable job. I have tried to save the relationships in spite of my activities, but I could have done better."

The sea, to which Cousteau did devote his attentions, also delivered frustrations. "From the very first," he acknowledges, "my sense of wonder at the sea has alternated with a sense of revulsion." He admits to having been often attracted by a different kind of life, yet he gave himself over, body and soul, to undersea discovery. "My motive in seeking out new sites to explore, in diving even deeper, in staying below even longer, in filming, in fighting, was, certainly, the satisfaction of my curiosity about the sea. But it was also an emotional, almost sexual need. . . . I was biologically drawn to the sea, but I knew very well that I would never succeed in possessing it totally."

Of his life's accomplishments, Cousteau admits taking "my pride from a wild love for life, from an insatiable curiosity, from the fascinating challenges of discovery, from my complete obliviousness to the impossible. And I know humility when I stand terrified before horizons which unceasingly recede as we approach, and before the loneliness of our species in the universe."

Cousteau finds most self-examination to be a waste of time. He condemns those who write autobiographies as people whose own art and accomplishments are not as important as their actions and habits. He doesn't even review his own movies or television shows. "When I finish a film," he says, "I never look at it again, even when it is broadcast. It is finished, dead."

But as far as he is concerned, his own life is anything but over. Although Jean-Michel is clearly being groomed to inherit the Cousteau empire, the Captain shows no signs of retiring. Even Jean-Michel concedes, "My job is to allow my father to be as efficient as possible, to take all the boredom of details off him, and give the world another 20 years of Cousteau."

Approaching his eighth decade, the Captain seems to have lost little of his enthusiasm for life. His step is no longer sure. He slumps. Large bags puff below his eyes. His skin is weathered and brown, and he has had to wear glasses since 1960. But there's no doubt he remains young in spirit.

Ever curious and optimistic, Cousteau still dreams. He wants, for example, to build and launch *Calypso II*, a more sophisticated research vessel. He would love to compose the music for one of his films. He talks of flying in the space shuttle. The Captain pauses at the end of such suggestions, laughs, and says, "You know, I think I'll do it all."

Cousteau's only enemy is time.

Acknowledgments

Writing is often a solitary activity, but I have enjoyed the cooperation and help of many individuals. Several deserve special mention. Leona Schecter, my literary agent, provided guidance and advice. Bruce Lee and John Harrison of William Morrow shepherded the manuscript through several edits, providing perceptive suggestions. Robert Spaulding energetically gathered information and conducted interviews in France. My deepest thanks go to my wife, Diane MacEachern, for her support, critical reviews, and encouragement.

This is not an authorized biography. Although numerous Cousteau associates provided information and insights, the Captain did not cooperate with this project. In fact, his lawyers have tried to block the book's publication. I hope, however, that Cousteau and other readers will find the manuscript to be fair and balanced.

Notes

INTRODUCTION

13. Observations made by the author at Cabrillo Beach on September 15, 1986. Present were Captain Jacques-Yves Cousteau, Jean-Michel Cousteau, Cousteau Society writer Mose Richards, Cousteau Society administrator Charles Vinick, and cameraman Louis Prezelin.

I. THE LIVING LEGEND

16. The narrator's observations—"Divers are true spacemen"—from *The Silent World*, released in 1956.

17. "I've spent life amazed by nature. . . ." *Jacques-Yves Cousteau: The First 75 Years*, broadcast by Turner Broadcasting System in June 1985.

17. "The ideal is to own nothing." *Calypso Log* (June 1985).

17. Claims of being "the world's greatest explorer," of making "earth-shaking discoveries," and of having "rescued countless endangered species . . ." from *The World of Cousteau: A Captain's Logbook*, published in 1985 by Turner Broadcasting.

18. "I warn the hostess. . . ." Sara Davidson, "Cousteau Searches for His Whale," *New York Times Magazine*, September 10, 1972.

19. Cousteau Society staff members call Jean-Michel a "sweetie." Interview with Mary Paden.

19. Cousteau Society staff members say "it's hard to work for a living legend. . . ." *Ibid.*

19. "I told [Ronald Reagan]. . . ." *Jacques-Yves Cousteau: The First 75 Years.*

20. "[Adults] have lost the ability to see what they're looking at. . . ." *Calypso Log* (June 1985).

II. ON THE ROAD

23. Quotes about Eugene Higgins from his obituary in *The New York Times* on July 30, 1948.

23. "My parents were moving. . . ." Turner Broadcasting System, *Jacques-Yves Cousteau: The First 75 Years.*

23. "When I was four or five. . . ." *Calypso Log* (June 1983).

23. "They triggered my mind to become a naval officer. . . ." *Calypso Log* (September 1980).

24. Mr. Boetz "didn't like me very much . . ." *Calypso Log* (June 1985).

24. "I worked very hard. . . ." *Ibid.*

24. "Boys thereby gather cynical impressions. . . ." Jacques-Yves Cousteau with Frédéric Dumas and James Dugan, *The Silent World* (New York: Harper & Brothers Publishers, 1953).

25. "I was fascinated by the hardware. . . ." David Crook, "The Captain Won't Settle for Anything but Adventure," *Los Angeles Times,* June 15, 1986.

25. Early film clips were edited by Turner Broadcasting for a promotional broadcast entitled *Jacques-Yves Cousteau: The First 75 Years,* released in June 1985.

25. "My early movies weren't much good. . . ." *Los Angeles Times,* June 15, 1986.

26. "He surfaced a minute later. . . ." Nancy Hicks, "Cousteau's Philosophy Helps Get Him Another Medal," *New York Times,* October 25, 1970.

28. "It was two o'clock in the morning. . . ." *Calypso Log* (June 1983).

29. "It was a test for me. . . ." *Ibid.*

29. "Sometimes we are lucky enough to know our lives have changed. . . ." *Silent World.*

29. Cousteau described his first experience with goggles as seeing "wildlife untouched, a jungle at the border of the sea. . . ." *Time* (March 28, 1960).

32. Pierre-Antoine's book about Jews is entitled *L'Amérique juive* (Paris: France, 1942).

33. "I did all I could to reinforce the impression." *Silent World.*

34. "Simone and I wept by the radio. . . ." *Silent World.*

34. "I have never found sea water that was warm enough for me." Jacques-Yves Cousteau with James Dugan, *The Living Sea* 54 York: Harper & Row, 1963).

36. "Verne, like many great poets, led the way for science to follow." Jacques-Yves Cousteau, *The Sea of Legends: Inspiration from the Sea* (New York: World Publishing, 1973).

38. Good histories of underwater diving and photographic equipment include: Philippe Diolé, *The Undersea Adventure* (New York: Julian Messner, 1953); Rachel Carson, *The Sea Around Us* (New York: Oxford University Press, 1951); Jacques-Yves Cousteau, *Man Re-enters the Sea* (New York: World Publishing, 1974); and Dimitri Rebikoff, *Free Diving* (New York: E. P. Dutton, 1956).

38. "In testing devices in which one's life is at stake . . ." *Silent World.*

39. Cousteau complained that "the darn things runs wide open. . . ." *Silent World.*

40. "I experimented with all possible maneuvers. . . ." *Time* (March 28, 1960).

40. "Now I flew without wings." *Silent World.*

40. Dumas had "a queer feeling of beatitude. . . ." *Ibid.*
41. "I like it [nitrogen oversaturation] and fear it like doom." *Ibid.*

III. THE FIRST MENFISH

43. Pierre-Antoine's comment—"sealed under a permanent avalanche of incendiary bombs . . ."—from his book *Les Lois de l'hospitalité* (Librarie française, 1959).
44. Jean-Pierre Cousteau's comment—"Relations between the brothers . . ."—from Axel Madsen, *Cousteau: An Unauthorized Biography* (New York: Beaufort Books, 1986).
44. "A dead ship is the house of tremendous fish and plant life. . . ." *Silent World.*
45. The wreck was "a fine movie studio." *Silent World.*
45. "It was quite lifelike. . . ." *Ibid.*
46. "At 15 feet red turned to pink. . . ." *Ibid.*
47. "Stupefied by the sight. . . ." *Ibid.*
48. The diver had to "train his camera . . ." *National Geographic* (September 1952).
48. The darkness "would flower for a long instant. . . ." *Silent World.*
48. The father "gave another lecture on the theme that the sea was a silent world. . . ." *Ibid.*
49. "For reasons of their own, women are suspicious of diving. . . ." *Ibid.*
49. "I deeply regret the lack of time I've had with my sons." Susan Schiefelbein, "The Cousteau Clan," *Dial* (July 1982).
49. The Undersea Research Group "neglected no opportunity to make ourselves known as a powerful bureau of the *Marine Nationale*." *Silent World.*
50. "We were aware of the dangers and limitations of diving. . . ." *Silent World.*
50. Describing early dives as "insane," Jacques-Yves Cousteau and Philippe Cousteau, *The Shark: Splendid Savage of the Sea* (Garden City, N.Y.: Doubleday & Company, 1970).
51. Cousteau noted "the divers would look at each other and wince at the lunatic idea." *Silent World.*
51. "The intoxication was there, flooding my entire being. . . ." *Ibid.*
51. "I was sufficiently in control to remember. . . ." *Ibid.*
52. Dimitri Rebikoff's comment from his book *Free Diving.*
52. The hydrologist's comment about the spring at Vaucluse from Philippe Tailliez, *To Hidden Depths* (New York: E. P. Dutton, 1954).
54. The cleric "had come no doubt to be of service in a certain eventuality." *Silent World.*
55. Maurice Fargues's question—"What do I risk?"—from *Silent World.*
55. Philippe Tailliez's statement—"Suddenly I felt my breath quicken"—from *To Hidden Depths.*
56. The crew "made a subjective comparison of cognac narcosis and rapture of the Fountain." *Silent World.*
56. Frédéric Dumas's declaration—"It was extraordinary that we did not stay in

that cave"—and Captain Cousteau's response from *Jacques-Yves Cousteau: The First 75 Years*.

57. "I mentally composed a report to my superiors. . . ." *Silent World*.

58. "We were merely scratching at history's door." *Ibid*.

58. Cousteau described "the finest antishark defense ever devised. . . ." *Ibid*.

59. The effect "was rather like a preposterous underwater birdcage. . . ." *Ibid*.

59. "I reached for objects, saw my hand fall short. . . ." *Ibid*.

60. Cousteau felt he looked "like a beast of burden. . . ." *Silent World*.

60. "The warm and cold layers meet with the precision of wood veneers." *Ibid*.

60. Cousteau learned that "pressure changes become progressively easier on a diver the deeper he goes. . . ." *Ibid*.

61. Cousteau marveled that dolphins were "faster, and infinitely more maneuverable, than the best machines that human ingenuity had yet been able to devise." Jacques-Yves Cousteau and Philippe Diolé, *Dolphins* (Garden City, N.Y.: Doubleday & Co., 1974).

61. Cousteau concluded "that here, some 50 miles from land, the dolphins knew the precise azimuth of Gibraltar. . . ." *Ibid*.

62. Dolphins are "the most attractive and intriguing form of marine life." *Ibid*.

62. The dolphin possesses "a keen look, slightly melancholy and mischievous. . . ." *Ibid*.

63. The whale is the "monarch of the sea." Jacques-Yves Cousteau and Philippe Diolé, *The Whale: Mighty Monarch of the Sea* (Garden City, N.Y.: Doubleday & Company, 1972).

63. Cousteau launched the harpoon "without feeling the slightest twinge of conscience. . . . We still had much to learn. . . ." *Ibid*.

IV. CALYPSO

66. Conversation between Cousteau and Noel Guinness reported in *The Living Sea*.

67. "Beyond the more obvious adventures. . . ." *Calypso Log* (June 1985).

69. Cousteau declared an "almost militant insistence . . ." *The Living Sea*.

69. "She can take it!" *Ibid*.

72. A crew member's question—"Poor vintage century?"—from *The Living Sea*.

73. "I wanted to translate the underwater world and to share it with people." *Calypso Log* (June 1985).

73. "When I first dive down the water is clear and very blue." *Life* (November 1950).

73. "The best way to observe fish is to become a fish." *National Geographic* (October 1952).

74. "Fish do not like to go up or down. . . ." *Silent World*.

74. "What do fish do all day long?" *Ibid*.

74. "The more we experience the sea the less certain we are of conclusions." *Silent World*.

74. "It is not the reality of the sea as we have known it with naked ears." *Ibid.*

74. "The monsters we have met seem a thoroughly harmless lot." *Ibid.*

75. Cousteau noted "the extraordinary vitality of sharks." *Silent World.*

75. "Spearing rays has no further interest for us." *Ibid.*

75. "I never planned to write it at all." *New York Times Book Review,* February 22, 1953.

75. James Dugan described as "a writer of great wit and enormous curiosity." *Calypso Log* (June 1981).

76. The review—"Awe and beauty are two sides of wonder. Therefore, this volume is truly wonderful."—reprinted in Cousteau Society brochure.

76. Conversation between Simone Cousteau and the oil executive reported in *The Living Sea.*

77. "The super-tempered cutting mouth was crumpled like a paper napkin." *National Geographic* (August 1955).

77. "We located the oil. . . ." *Calypso Log* (June 1985).

78. Louis Malle's statement—"We had to make the underwater cameras ourselves . . ."—from *Jacques-Yves Cousteau: The First 75 Years.*

79. The narrator's announcement—"This is a motion-picture studio sixty-feet under the sea . . ." —from film entitled *The Silent World,* released in 1956.

80. "The animals would race along the length of the whale's body. . . ." *The Ocean World of Jacques Cousteau: Quest for Food* (New York: World Publishing, 1973).

80. The sharks' feeding frenzy was "terrifying and nauseating to watch." *The Shark.*

80. The men "were overcome with the hatred of sharks. . . ." *The Living Sea.*

81. Reviewer Bosley Crowther's comments—"surely the most beautiful and fascinating documentary of its sort ever filmed"—from *New York Times,* September 25, 1956.

81. Crowther's additional comments about the film's commentary and colors, as well as his conclusions, from *New York Times,* September 30, 1956.

83. Albert Falco's notation—"Fortunately, I was already on the platform, holding the loaded harpoon gun"—from *Dolphins.*

84. Falco's additional notes—"Canoe and I left the animal alone for a few moments . . ."—*Ibid.*

84. "At one-thirty in the afternoon, the dolphin was dead." *Ibid.*

85. The mission provided "much valuable information on the reactions of dolphins. . . ." *Ibid.*

86. "Pierre was the smart one, much more than me." Reported by Jean-Pierre Cousteau in *Cousteau.*

86. Cousteau described as diving's "patron saint. . . ." *Time* (March 28, 1960).

86. "Diving is the most fabulous distraction you can experience." *Ibid.*

87. President John Kennedy's description of Cousteau as "one of the great explorers . . ." from *National Geographic* (July 1961).

87. "For me, this is much more than a personal award." *Ibid.*

V. CONSHELF

88. The *Bulldog* naturalist's declaration—"The deep has sent forth the long coveted message"—from *Man Re-enters the Sea*.

89. Cousteau's description of Auguste Piccard as an "elderly scientific extremist" from *Silent World*.

89. Cousteau's description of Simone as "a Navy wife with a self-disciplined attitude toward my activities" also from *Silent World*.

89. Simone's plea: "No one ordered you to go." *Ibid*.

91. Cousteau's prediction that future designs would take men "to the basement of the world." *Ibid*.

92. Dr. Harold Edgerton compared the effort "to photographing birds on a foggy night from a balloon." *The Living Sea*.

93. "Request special aircraft at Konakry . . ." *Ibid*.

93. Cousteau's declaration that "robot oceanography is getting nowhere." *Ibid*.

94. Cousteau argued for "a radically new submarine, something small, agile." *National Geographic* (April 1960).

95. "We have no idea what the gray blobs are." *The Living Sea*.

95. The saucer turned "as whimsically as the fish." *Ibid*.

95. Cousteau described the saucer as "a scrutinizer." *Ibid*.

96. Cousteau's description of "our farewell to the upper layers of the sea." *Ibid*.

96. "To enter this great unknown medium must produce greater knowledge of the oceans and lead to assessment and exploitation of their natural resources." James Dugan, ed., *Jacques-Yves Cousteau's World Without Sun* (New York: Harper & Row, 1964).

96. Cousteau predicted the "conscious evolution of 'homo aquaticus' . . ." James Dugan, "Portrait of Homo Aquaticus," *New York Times*, June 21, 1963.

97. "What's wrong with science fiction as a presentiment of reality?" *Ibid*.

97. "There would be no serious reason to abandon all those things we love. . . ." *The Shark*.

98. Falco's complaint that Conshelf I was "too mechanized" reported in *The Living Sea*.

98. Falco and Wesly were to be the "first men to occupy the continental shelf. . . ." *Ibid*.

98. Cousteau describes Albert Falco as having "as much courage as anyone I have known." *Ibid*.

99. Falco's writings and comments—"I feel completely alone and isolated. . . . The water is beginning to come into our grasp. . . . Under the sea, everything is moral. . . . To walk"—also from *The Living Sea*.

100. A team member's complaint—"What on earth put this idea into your head?"—from *Jacques-Yves Cousteau's World Without Sun*.

100. Raymond Kientzy and André Portelatine's complaint that they "perspired like fountains." *Ibid*.

100. "To see what would happen to a group of average men during a month-long sojourn." *Ibid*.

101. Raymond Coll's description—"There were cables everywhere . . ."—from *Calypso Log* (June 1981).

103. The Captain toasted the "ever-enchanting realization that we are living inside the sea." *Jacques-Yves Cousteau's World Without Sun.*

104. *The New Yorker's* review from the January 2, 1965, issue.

104. Bosley Crowther's initial review from *New York Times,* December 23, 1964.

104. Cousteau's letter—"May I strongly state that we don't need tanks or studios"—*New York Times,* January 10, 1965.

105. Crowther's response—the final scene is "so trickily staged and so vaguely explained . . ."—*New York Times,* January 10, 1965.

105. Undersea habitations would "lead mankind to greater rewards than the space race." "Working for Weeks on the Sea Floor," *National Geographic* (April 1966).

106. Exchange between Simone Cousteau and a reporter. *Ibid.*

107. Albert Falco's remark—"On air, we find everything so beautiful. . . ."—*Ibid.*

VI. TELEVISION

109. "The only field in which I know I'm gifted is cinema." *TV/Radio & Cable Week* (June 23, 1985).

109. '[Cinema] encompasses many other art forms." *Calypso Log* (June 1985).

109. Louis Malle's praise—"For someone wanting to become a filmmaker . . ." —from *Jacques-Yves Cousteau: The First 75 Years.*

109. Philippe's comment—"[My father's television idea] ran up against the ingrained habits of Madison Avenue"—from *The Shark.*

110. "I love films, but television is for me the greatest reward there is." *New York Times,* September 10, 1972.

110. Jean-Michel's complaint—"The [French] government was very tough on us . . ."—from Gordon Chaplin, "Jacques-Yves Cousteau: Drowning in His Own Legend," *Washington Post Magazine,* January 11, 1981.

110. Wolper's advice—"Lookit, this is showbiz"—*Ibid.*

111. "You have to be attractive." *Ibid.*

111. "We are not documentary. We are adventure films. . . ." David Crook, "The Captain Won't Settle for Anything but Adventure," *Los Angeles Times,* June 15, 1986.

112. "I am like a child who does not quite know what he is strong enough to do and what he is too weak to attempt." Jacques-Yves Cousteau with Philippe Diolé, *Life and Death in a Coral Sea* (London: Cassell, 1971).

112. The shark "ranks among the most perfect. . . ." *The Shark.*

112. Facing his first shark, Cousteau is "uneasy with fear." *Silent World.*

112. "The camera demanded lively sharks." *Silent World.*

113. Cousteau admitted "a sense of danger came to our hearts." *Ibid.*

114. The shark's powerful tail "shook us up considerably." Jacques-Yves Cousteau and Philippe Cousteau, *The Shark.*

114. Shark seen as the "epitome of muscle power and streamlined design." *The Ocean World of Jacques Cousteau: Quest for Food.*

114. Cousteau suggests the shark is no more a killer than "the housewife who served bacon." *The Shark: Splendid Savage of the Sea.*

115. "The better acquainted we become with sharks, the less we know them. . . ." *Silent World*.

115. Reviews of Cousteau's first television segment summarized in promotional brochure prepared by Metromedia Producers Corporation.

115. Eugenie Clark's complaint—"Cousteau's films are misleading in a way . . ." —from *Washington Post Magazine*, January 11, 1981.

115. "Our films have only one ambition—to show the truth about nature and give people the wish to know more." *New York Times Magazine*, September 10, 1972.

116. The mirror "was smashed into a million fragments . . ." *Life and Death in a Coral Sea*.

117. Janice Sullivan Cousteau's comment—"I said yes before he could change his mind"—*Cousteau*.

117. Janice Cousteau's comments—"I lived in a world of fashion shows . . ." —from *Los Angeles Times*, June 26, 1977.

117. Janice Cousteau's remark about her mother—"She married too young . . ." —*Ibid*.

118. Philippe's description of the balloon—"the poor man's helicopter"—from *Life and Death in a Coral Sea*.

118. Philippe had "this belief that animals are focusing on him." *The Whale*.

118. Philippe's comment—"Perhaps [the whale] was even talking to me . . ." —*Ibid*.

119. Simone described Philippe as "the biggest playboy in town." *National Geographic* (March 1966).

119. Bosley Crowther's review—"The intimacy with the explorers, intelligently and humorously set up . . .—from *New York Times*, September 25, 1956.

120. Christopher Palmer's comment—"The Captain was the key pioneer in nature filmmaking . . ."—from his interview with the author.

120. "What is not apparent on the screen is the almost insurmountable difficulty of such an enterprise. . . ." *The Shark*.

121. "Unfortunately, we will now have to cut short our study of the furred sea lions." Jacques-Yves Cousteau and Philippe Diolé, *Diving Companions: Sea Lion, Elephant Seal, Walrus* (Garden City, N.Y.: Doubleday & Co., 1974).

121. "Experiments to befriend animals." *Ibid*.

121. Comments about the octopus from Jacques-Yves Cousteau and Philippe Diolé, *Octopus and Squid: The Soft Intelligence* (New York: A&W Visual Library, 1973).

122. Cousteau foresaw when "we will be in need of friends in the sea with whom we may begin to communicate." *Diving Companions*.

122. Cousteau's practice of tormenting creatures is described in *The Whale*.

122. He became "addicted to naming animals that we meet in and on the water. . . ." *Life and Death in the Coral Sea*.

123. Cousteau argues against the "idea of removing animals from their natural environment . . . it is useless to pretend that captivity in any form is less than cruel. . . . [Cousteau rejected] the idea of training and conditioning animals. . . ." *Diving Companions*.

123. Would the sea lions "follow our divers in the depths of the sea . . . ?" *Ibid*.

124. He acknowledged "their longing for freedom will very likely be stronger than any attachment they may feel for us." *Ibid.*

124. "Pepito and Christobald were subjected to a course of progressive training. . . ." *Ibid.*

124. "It has been impossible for anyone from *Calypso* to rent an auto in Puerto Rico." *Ibid.*

124. The scene denoted "the perfect understanding between man and animal. . . ." *Ibid.*

125. Christobald's "need for freedom was something that he shared with us. . . ." *Ibid.*

125. "I had been forewarned that I would have to use 'all my charm'. . . ." *Ibid.*

125. Cousteau concluded "it would be useless to continue our experiment. . . ." *Ibid.*

125. His film asserted that "two marine mammals were our willing companions in the sea." "The Unexpected Voyage of Pepito and Christobald," broadcast in January 1969.

125. The sea lions "had been free to come and go as they wished." Jacques-Yves Cousteau and Philippe Diole, *Three Adventures: Galápagos, Titicaca, The Blue Holes* (Garden City, N.Y.: Doubleday & Co., 1973).

126. The spectacle had been "an extraordinary experience in communal living." Jacques Cousteau and Alexis Sivirine, *Jacques Cousteau's Calypso* (New York: Harry N. Abrams, Inc., 1983).

126. "I am conscience-stricken. . . ." Jacques-Yves Cousteau and Philippe Diolé, *Diving for Sunken Treasure* (Garden City, N.Y.: Doubleday & Company, 1971).

126. Bernard Delemotte's comment—"I think I'll buy some land . . ."—*Ibid.*

127. "We carried out, for the first time, a systematic dig in a coral bank." *Ibid.*

127. "We have learned something very important. . . ." *Ibid.*

128. "For these people, trapped in a bleak and barren land. . . ." *Three Adventures.*

128. Cousteau was "ready for a new adventure." *Ibid.*

128. Whales "bear such a strong resemblance to man. . . ." *The Whale.*

129. "We were the first to seek them out in a spirit of friendship and curiosity, in the depths of the sea." *Ibid.*

129. Philippe's comments—"a mouth unlike any that I had ever seen before; . . . the whale and I had reached a perfect understanding; . . . I think that those were the most beautiful hours that I have ever spent in the water in my whole life"—*Ibid.*

130. Excerpts from Cousteau's March 1969 diary reprinted *Ibid.*

130. We inflict "a very superficial kind of wound. . . ." *Ibid.*

131. The emotional declaration by the professor (Ted Walker) *Ibid.*

131. "It seems somehow wrong to record the great emotion of this lover of animals." *Ibid.*

131. "We have seen great animals of the sea die before. . . ." *Ibid.*

131. "A sperm could be in a frenzy of rage for an hour. . . ." *Ibid.*

131. "We had all learned before to bend to the whims of the sea. . . ." *Octopus and Squid: The Soft Intelligence.*

132. "Today individual men are concerned with the choices that lead to war and peace, and with this new realization comes hope." "Lagoon of the Lost Ships," broadcast in January 1971.

132. The mosquitoes were "like a layer of coarse dust." *Diving Companions.*

133. Cousteau described the salmon's "majestical procession upstream." *Ibid.*

133. *Daily Variety*'s review—"emotionally gripping and poignant"—reprinted in promotional materials by Metromedia Producers Corporation.

134. The baby walrus "not only accepted man but became instantly and wildly attached to him." *Ibid.*

134. Cameraman Michel Deloire's comment—"When [the lobsters] move, they're like some incredible lawn mower"—*Ibid.*

134. "Despite all our technological gadgetry. . . ." *Ibid.*

135. Victor Hugo's "The Octopus, O horror! Inhales a man," from *Toilers of the Sea* (Paris: Garnier-Flammarian, 1980).

135. Cousteau admitted that "the myths on which we are born die hard." *Octopus and Squid: The Soft Intelligence.*

135. The clasp of the octopus's arm "is a strong thing, rather like that of a noose. . . ." *Ibid.*

136. "For television, what we needed was not merely an expert. . . ." *Ibid.*

136. "Joanne is very feminine. . . . Altogether, a James Bond heroine." *Ibid.*

136. He could explain that "by looking at the octopus's eyes, the diver has the sensation of lucidity. . . ." *Ibid.*

137. Cousteau concluded that "the most remarkable thing about the octopus is its ability to grasp a problem that is presented. . . ." *Ibid.*

138. The men "are rather expert at the conduct of these rituals." *Three Adventures.*

138. Darwin's description of iguanas quoted in *Three Adventures.*

139. The narrator's descriptions—"the iguana is free at last from its tormentors. Or is he really free?"—from the film "The Dragons of Galápagos," broadcast in February 1971.

139. Notes from Bernard Delemotte's diary also from *Three Adventures.*

140. Cousteau "did everything possible to insure that our investigations would prove valuable from a scientific standpoint." *Ibid.*

140. He described the "bizarre underwater ballet. . . ." *Ibid.*

141. It was "the most difficult exploration of my career." *Ibid.*

141. "We are the possessors of a secret shared by only a few divers." *Ibid.*

141. Dick Cavett's comment—"most people would rather meet Jacques Cousteau than anybody"—from *New York Times Magazine,* September 10, 1972.

141. Excerpts from Cousteau's 1968 log—"I have renounced my ambitions in all other areas. . . . For every pleasure that I have derived, I have had to scale a mountain of aversion. . . . There has always been a sense of being trapped. . . . I will remain alone on this little ship, bitter, with accusations of infidelity running through my mind"—from *Diving for Sunken Treasure.*

142. "It became obvious to me that all the support complex had to migrate from the surface. . . ." *Man Re-enters the Sea*.

142. He was to build "the ultimate in deep-diving equipment. . . ." *Ibid*.

143. "The concept remains above criticism, and the *Argyronete* family of steel water spiders will multiply in the future." *Ibid*.

143. Dolphins "seemed to me to be deformed and perverted by their captivity and their contact with man." *Dolphins*.

144. The tank was "sufficiently large for a dolphin to feel practically free." *Ibid*.

144. "We've spent the day waiting for our dolphin to 'talk.' " *Ibid*.

145. "The film that was taken by our dolphin cameramen was totally without interest." *Ibid*.

146. The homes of the Imragens were "windowless, and even smaller and more ill-smelling than one would think possible." *Ibid*.

146. "One dare not say that man and dolphin eventually became accustomed to one another's presence." *Ibid*.

146. Eskimos "are not a saving people. . . . there is not a single resident of the village who knew how to go about constructing an igloo." *Diving Companions*.

147. The team leader's comments about tourists—"None of us could say a word . . ."—from *Three Adventures*.

147. "Seeing tourists on the islands of Galápagos, I could not help believing that man has degenerated alarmingly." *Ibid*.

148. "It is a shame that we cannot extend to threatened human populations. . . ." "Life at the End of the World," broadcast in November 1974.

148. John O'Connor's review from "Jacques Cousteau Runs Aground," *New York Times*, November 24, 1974.

148. "[Antarctica is] the most beautiful place in the world." Mary-Ann Bendel, "A Cousteau's-Eye View of the World," *Vis à Vis*, April 1988.

149. "Today the penguins are protected from slaughter." "The Flight of Penguins," broadcast in January 1974.

150. "Surrounded by a majestic beauty that still haunts me today. . . ." "Beneath the Frozen World," broadcast in March 1974.

151. "Without exaggeration we were in grave danger of losing the ship and the crew." "Blizzard at Hope Bay," broadcast in March 1974.

151. Reviews from the *Los Angeles Herald Examiner* and other newspapers from promotional materials supplied by Metromedia Producers Corporation.

VII. SETBACKS

166. Richard Murphy's comment—Satellite mapping was "totally consistent with the Cousteau spirit of ocean exploration"—from *Calypso Log* (March 1987).

166. The network spokesman's comment that Cousteau specials had "slipped" from Lynn Simross, "New Undersea Worlds Await Capt. Cousteau," *Los Angeles Times*, August 6, 1976.

166. Cousteau argued that network executives had "systematically torpedoed his shows." *Ibid*.

167. "I think [the networks] underestimate the public." *Ibid*.

168. Jean-Michel: Project Ocean Search attracted "some college students. . . ." Steven Blout, "Exploring with Cousteau," *Esquire* (May 1982).

170. The PBS shows were "more difficult than those we did with the animals. . . ." *Los Angeles Times,* August 6, 1976.

170. "We're beginning another major undertaking." *Jacques Cousteau's Calypso.*

171. "Another handful of fragments have been returned to man's visible inheritance from the past. . . ." "Diving for Roman Plunder," broadcast in March 1978.

172. "The mystery that had shrouded the sinking of the *Britannic*. . . . " *Jacques Cousteau's Calypso.*

172. Plato's descriptions of Atlantis from *Critias* and *Timaeus.*

173. "The Minoan artists told us of a fragrant world of animals and flowering plants. . . ." "Calypso's Search for Atlantis," broadcast in May 1978.

173. "There is nothing whatsoever there to be found. . . . [Plato created] a fantasy of Atlantis. . . ." *Los Angeles Times,* November 23, 1978.

174. "Our descent into the void. . . ." "Calypso's Search for Atlantis."

174. John O'Connor's review of the Atlantis series from *New York Times,* May 1, 1978.

174. Arrangements analyzing the Mediterranean's marine environment "took all Cousteau's patience and diplomatic skill." *Jacques Cousteau's Calypso.*

174. "Like an underwater dust storm. . . ." *Calypso Log* (March 1979).

175. "Fish are caught systematically on their mating grounds. . . ." *Ibid.*

175. "Polluting agents had not yet created a real danger in most parts of the Mediterranean." *Jacques Cousteau's Calypso.*

176. "I am not an American citizen." *Calypso Log* (June 1983).

178. Janice Cousteau's comment—"With that injury . . ."—from Susan Schiefelbein, "The Cousteau Clan," *Dial* (July 1982).

178. Janice Cousteau's comment—"Philippe would have hooked wings on his back if he could"—from *Jacques-Yves Cousteau: The First 75 Years.*

179. Philippe Cousteau's conclusion—"Today, the Nile no longer goes its own way"—from "The Nile," broadcast in December 1979.

179. Cecil Smith's review of "The Nile" in *Los Angeles Times,* December 6, 1979.

179. *Daily Variety*'s review from the December 10, 1979, issue.

181. "Nothing is changed in our program. . . . What was a tragedy for my son was a miracle for his co-pilot." *Nice-Matin,* July 6, 1979.

181. Janice Cousteau's comment—"Cousteau lost his future when Philippe died"—from *Washington Post Magazine,* January 11, 1981.

181. Jean-Michel's comment—"It was very tempting to my father. . . ."—*Ibid.*

181. Jean-Michel's comment—"The moment I heard about Philippe . . ." —from *Dial* (July 1982).

181. Janice Cousteau's letter—"We shared 13 golden years together"—from *Calypso Log* (March 1980).

182. "Mon cher Philippe: I will always remember that day. . . ." Cousteau Society correspondence.

183. The *Los Angeles Times* review of "Clipperton" from the February 25, 1981, issue.

183. "My skin was attacked as if immersed in acid." *Calypso Log* (June 1980).

184. The Captain "thought of the comparable human tragedy that had happened in this very place." "Clipperton: The Island Time Forgot," broadcast in February 1981.

184. "Now his brother Michel . . . will join me. . . ." *Los Angeles Times,* December 6, 1979.

184. Jean-Michel's comment—"I started with the watchwords 'More for Less' . . ."—from *Washington Post Magazine,* January 11, 1981.

185. John Sears's comment—"The magnetism of the man is unbelievable"— from *Washington Post Magazine,* January 11, 1981.

185. Norfolk Mayor Thomas's comment—"very excited at the prospect of the headquarters being moved here"—from *Virginia Pilot,* June 4, 1979.

185. The water and sediment specimens would "provide months, if not years, of lab work for the Venezuelan scientific community." *Calypso Log* (December 1979).

186. Divers "risked their lives to save the life of a baby humpback whale. . . ." *St. Lawrence: Stairway to the Sea,* broadcast in October 1982.

188. The saltwater "attacked open relays and circuit breakers. . . ." *Calypso Log* (June 1981).

VIII. REDISCOVERY

189. "It was love at first sight." Bill King, Jacques Cousteau at 75, "TV Week," *Atlanta Constitution,* June 10, 1985.

190. "I'll tell you why we went to the Turner deal. . . ." *Christian Science Monitor,* October 16, 1981.

190. "Rivers that used to fertilize the sea with salts and nutrients. . . ." *Calypso Log* (December 1982).

191. He called it "the greatest and most difficult expedition I have ever undertaken. . . ." *The World of Cousteau: A Captain's Logbook,* a promotional booklet by the Turner Broadcasting Service.

192. Joseph Campanella's narration—"A single river carries one fifth of the fresh water flowing on earth"—from *Journey to a Thousand Rivers,* broadcast in March 1984.

193. The dolphin's beak "is abnormally long. . . ." Jacques-Yves Cousteau and Mose Richards, *Jacques Cousteau's Amazon Journey* (New York: Harry N. Abrams, 1984).

193. The pink dolphin "hunts through the woods with the dexterity of a jungle cat." *Ibid.*

194. The Cousteaus "endured endless danger and discomfort." *The World of Cousteau: A Captain's Logbook.*

194. The scientist's [Richard Murphy] comment—"This is great! . . ."—from *Jacques Cousteau's Amazon Journey.*

195. Jean-Michel's notes—"The scene below us staggered our imagination"— from *Jacques Cousteau's Amazon Journey.*

195. Notes of the Cousteau Society researcher (Paula DiPerna)—"The digging began . . ."—from *Calypso Log* (June 1984).

195. Jean-Michel's comment—miners appeared "like the largest crowd of extras ever assembled . . ."—from *Jacques Cousteau's Amazon Journey.*

197. "For people who are hungry. . . ." Warren Hoge, "20th Century Begins to Intrude on Sleepy Amazon," *New York Times,* May 14, 1983.

197. Jean-Michel's comment—"There will be films . . ."—from *Calypso Log* (June 1982).

198. Jean-Michel's comment—"I have learned perhaps more about leadership from this one man . . ."—from *Calypso Log* (March 1985).

199. Kukus's comment—"Wildlife has fled from our hunting grounds . . ." —from *Jacques Cousteau's Amazon Journey.*

200. Jean-Michel's comment—the meeting between Kukus and Belaunde was "a step in the right direction"—*Ibid.*

200. Jean-Michel's comment—Kukus's "identity was inextricable from the future of his people"—*Ibid.*

200. Review from *Hollywood Reporter*—"One expects a Cousteau documentary to be beautifully photographed. . . ."—reprinted in brochures by Turner Broadcasting System.

200. Simone Cousteau's comment—"I think it's the best one we did"—from *Washington Post,* March 22, 1987.

200. The natives had been turned into "circus performers in a freak show." *The New El Dorado,* broadcast in April 1984.

201. Three women were "castaways in time." *Ibid.*

201. Jean-Michel said cocaine caused "internal pollution of man." *The World of Cousteau: A Captain's Logbook.*

201. Jean-Michel had "developed into a true explorer. . . ." *Jacques-Yves Cousteau: The First 75 Years.*

203. Jean-Michel's comment—"We are with him. Good luck"—from *Snowstorm in the Jungle,* broadcast in January 1985.

203. Jean-Michel's comment—"virulence of the cocaine menace"—from *Jacques Cousteau's Amazon Journey.*

203. Drug trafficker's comment—"I do it to destroy the United States"—*Ibid.*

203. Guerrillas delivered "insidious chemical bombs made of white powder. . . ." *Ibid.*

203. The Captain warned "there are no pretty pictures of fish." Reuters News Service, January 5, 1985.

204. The Captain claimed "the Western world may decline." *Jacques Cousteau's Amazon Journey.*

204. *People* magazine's review—"The show begins to take on the tone of Reefer Madness . . ."—from June 22, 1985, issue.

204. "The story of the Mississippi is one of wildlife. . . ." *Calypso Log* (December 1983).

205. Jean-Michel's comment—"As I held the young bears . . ."—*Calypso Log* (June 1984).

205. Richard Murphy's comment—"The first such research covering the Mississippi's entire length . . ."—*Calypso Log* (December 1985).

205. Richard Murphy's comment—"Our brief survey . . ."—*Ibid.*

205. "The Mississippi River is not dead. . . ." *Cousteau/Mississippi: The Reluctant Ally,* broadcast in April 1985.

205. The promotional declaration—"an emotional, informative, and entertaining look at America's largest river"—from *The World of Cousteau: A Captain's Logbook.*

206. Cousteau's desire "to come up with a successor to our old exploration ship. . . ." *Calypso Log* (Summer 1983).

206. Cousteau "would not have those rotating drums on my ship. . . ." *Ibid.*

207. The Socialists' environmental policy is "terrible. . . . The minister is like a puppet. . . ." *Calypso Log* (Summer 1983).

208. "We have lost only the hardware. . . ." United Press International, November 17, 1983.

208. "This is not dream stuff. This is economic reality." *Sail* (February 1984).

208. Bertrand Charrier's comment—"Instead of an experimental platform on a catamaran . . ."—*Ibid.*

208. "You will understand how moved I am to be received here. . . ." Bruce Hager, "Cousteau Crosses Ocean with Penchiney Sail," *Los Angeles Times,* June 18, 1985.

209. Environmentalists "frequently find themselves saying no. . . ." *Calypso Log* (Summer 1983).

209. Turbosail "will transform world shipping." *Calypso Log* (September 1985).

210. "The Rediscovery series has little to do with the behavior of animals. . . ." *Calypso Log* (June 1986).

210. Cousteau planned "to take a fresh look at the planet man believes he already knows." Turner Broadcasting System's promotional brochures.

211. Complaints about the new diving equipment—from speech by David Brown.

211. "I do not make this tremendous change without misgivings. . . ." *Calypso Dispatch* (May 1985).

212. "I have never been there [Haiti] before." Turner Broadcasting System's promotional brochures.

213. Cousteau tried to record "the spirit of the Haitians themselves. . . ." *Calypso Log* (September 1985).

214. Staff description—"Celebrity and celebrant were the same . . ."—*Ibid.*

214. Cuba's aquatic system was "a sea brimming with wealth. . . ." Turner Program Services' promotional brochures.

214. The Cubans believed that "marine resources are assets rather than raw materials. . . ." *Calypso Log* (June 1986).

214. Comment of fisherman (Juan Ferrat Hernández)—"Even if I wanted to catch the small ones . . ."—*Ibid.*

215. "Absolutely *fantastique.* . . ." *Ibid.*

216. "I had hoped all along my journey through life. . . ." *Calypso Log* (June 1986).

216. "I am extremely happy to announce to you that you will soon be liberated." Letter to Lázaro Jordana, April 19, 1986. Cousteau sent a copy of the letter, also on Cousteau Society stationery, to Jordana's mother.

216. Lázaro Jordana's comment—"Cousteau saved my life . . ."—from his interview with Robert Spaulding.

217. Comment from the society writer (Mose Richards)—The Cape Horn expedition "evoked a sobering realization . . ."—from *Calypso Log* (June 1986).

218. The photographer's comment—"This is a dream come true for me"—from *Los Angeles Times,* June 15, 1986.

218. Comment from the reporter (David Crook)—"The Captain was part of the scenery . . ." *Ibid.*

219. *Calypso* possessed "the courage of new engines." *Calypso Dispatch* (March 1986).

219. "Rediscovery is an ambitious name." *Calypso Log* (September 1986).

220. Cousteau described "flames of stone in the sky. . . ." "Marquesas Islands: Mountains from the Sea," broadcast in May 1987.

220. "Because of delays at the shipyard. . . ." Phil McCombs, "South Pacific! The Passage to Papeete," *Washington Post,* March 22, 1987.

220. "There's a limit to what the viewer can assimilate." Phil McCombs, "Cousteau and the Capture of Paradise," *Washington Post,* March 15, 1987.

220. Narrator's comment—"In such an enchanted forest, witches and wizards could lurk"—from "New Zealand: The Land of the Long White Cloud," broadcast in January 1988.

220. "*Calypso* must glide carefully among the silent hazards." *Ibid.*

221. "People are happy or they go." *Washington Post,* March 15, 1987.

221. The diver's comment—Cousteau's "insatiable curiosity about everything concerning the sea . . ."—from *The Shark.*

221. The comment of the diver (James Dugan)—"expressions of [the crew's] joy in being young and water-borne . . ."—from *Calypso Log* (June 1981).

222. Mose Richards's comments—"beams creak with the stress of each forward lurch . . ."—from *Calypso Log* (March 1981).

222. Louis Prezelin's comment—"zillions of lobsters were clustered like bats" —from *Calypso Log* (December 1986).

223. The comment of the diver (Clay Wilcox)—"like watching a rare accident; you're not sure what just happened"—*Ibid.*

223. Jean-Michel's comment—"Native or whales—must there be only one choice?"—from *Calypso Log* (December 1987).

223. Papua New Guinea, is "an ecologist's Eden." *Calypso Log* (August 1988).

IX. THE ENVIRONMENTALIST

225. "We had grown so attached to the place [Aldabra] that it seemed like a threat to our own property." *The Living Sea.*

225. "The response gave me no illusions. . . ." *Ibid.*

226. Cousteau proposed to "manipulate the submarine environment. . . ." *Ibid.*

226. The account of Cousteau's campaign against nuclear dumping in the Mediterranean, including quotes from newspapers and bureaucrats, *Ibid.*

228. "It was one of the very rare victories against the nuclear lobby." *Christian Science Monitor,* October 16, 1981.

228. Stuart Udall's statements—"The swift ascendancy of technology . . ." from his book *The Quiet Crisis* (New York: Holt, Rinehart & Winston, 1963).

229. Rachel Carson's comments—calling her time "an age of poisons"—from her book *Silent Spring* (Boston: Houghton Mifflin, 1962).

230. Filling the Mediterranean gorge with toxic discharges provided "an unexpected scientific bonus." *The Living Sea.*

230. "We see for ourselves that the earth is a water planet. . . ." *Jacques-Yves Cousteau: The First 75 Years.*

231. "Both sciences [ecology and economics] have the same duty. . . ." *Calypso Log* (June 1981).

231. Space exploration is "midwife to the birth of a new global consciousness." Jacques-Yves Cousteau, *The Cousteau Almanac: An Inventory of Life on Our Water Planet* (Garden City, N.Y.: Doubleday & Company, 1980.

232. The Cousteau Society is dedicated "to the protection and improvement of the quality of life. . . ." Organizational brochures.

232. Cousteau boasted that his television shows reached more viewers than *Gone with the Wind. New York Times,* February 20, 1977.

232. "We are explorers. . . ." *Calypso Log* (December 1981).

232. "I am entering a new phase in my life. . . ." *Christian Science Monitor,* January 9, 1975.

232. "There is sufficient evidence that world leaders are systematically lying about environmental and energy matters." *Ibid.*

233. Cousteau proposed to go over the heads of the "conventional decision makers. . . ." *The Cousteau Almanac.*

234. "Because the money you give now may literally help to save the world." Organizational brochures.

234. The Cousteau Society's "Bill of Rights for Future Generations" outlined in *The Cousteau Almanac.*

234. Governor Jerry Brown's comment—"Let us not forget . . ."—from *Calypso Log* (December 1979).

235. "The majority of scientists see no hope." *Christian Science Monitor,* January 9, 1975.

235. "After diving extensively and taking hundreds of measurements. . . ." *National Geographic* (December 1981).

236. Cousteau called for "vastly increased monetary investment for nuclear research." *Calypso Log* (March 1980).

236. The Captain expressed concern about the "potential for dispersal of bomb-grade materials. . . ." *Calypso Log* (December 1981).

236. The society's conclusion—"The waters of the lagoon displayed only infinitesimal traces . . ."—from *Calypso Log* (February 1989).

236. An observer's description of Cousteau's Mururoa expedition as "a whitewash" from *Greenpeace* (March/April 1989).

236. Bengt Danielsson's comments—"A guided tour" and "You are out of your depth."—*Ibid.*

236. "Instead of simply being negative [environmental activists] need to offer constructive counterproposals. . . ." *Calypso Log* (Summer 1983).

237. Mose Richards's review of the Captain's lobbying approach from *Calypso Log* (October 1981).

237. Cousteau described his early spearfishing as a stupid act done "because I was baffled by the familiarity of the fish." *Los Angeles Times,* August 15, 1986.

237. The Captain calls recreational anglers "perverts." *Field and Stream* (February 1987).

237. Cousteau says hunters are "working to diminish the quality of the race." Mark Schwed, "A Farewell Voyage of Rediscovery," *Los Angeles Times,* August 15, 1986.

237. The Cousteau Society's comment—". . . the Society and most sport fishing groups have the same goal in mind . . ."—from *Calypso Log* (March 1981).

237. *Field and Stream*'s description of Cousteau as "egotistical . . ." from the June 1986 issue.

238. "The two ships consistantly pollute . . ." *Washington Post Magazine,* December 4, 1988.

238. Brice Lalonde's comment—"Cousteau wasn't comfortable with our approach."—from his interview with Robert Spaulding, September 12, 1988.

239. The Cousteau Society claim to have a "significant impact" on Congressional debates from *Calypso Log* (September 1982).

239. Cousteau boasted of creating "an abiding affection for the undersea world. . . ." *Calypso Log* (December 1982).

239. The Ohio State University survey and the Cousteau Society's response from *Calypso Log* (December 1982).

240. The review (by Peter Wood) of *Oasis in Space*—" 'Oasis' " indulges in no cosmeticizing."—from *New York Times,* February 20, 1977.

240. Philippe's comment—"Our earth stands alone . . ."—*Ibid.*

240. Philippe's comment—"We had counted on corporate sponsorship of the shows"—*Ibid.*

240. "[The *Oasis in Space* series] was that important." *Ibid.*

242. The Cousteau Society's boast that "valuable information can be collected. . . ." from *Calypso Log* (March 1984).

242. The United Nations' declaration reprinted in Marjorie Ann Browne, "The Law of the Sea Conference: A U.S. Perspective," Congressional Research Service Issue Brief Number IB81153.

242. Cousteau envisioned an "ocean constitution." *Calypso Log* (December 1980).

242. An international authority should "set safety, health, and general ecology guidelines. . . ." *Ibid.*

243. "What we are trying to do is to slightly modify the concept of exclusive economic zones into zones of responsibility." *Christian Science Monitor,* October 16, 1981.

243. Cousteau described his White House luncheon as "cordial and satisfying." *Calypso Log* (October 1981).

243. "The ending of the Law of the Sea negotiation process. . . ." *Calypso Log* (December 1982).

244. Jean-Michel's comment—"Television is the most superficial way of reaching people"—from *Washington Post,* January 11, 1981.

244. Norfolk's prediction that the Ocean Center would be a "mecca for sightseers . . ." from *New York Times,* June 10, 1979.

244. The *Times Advocate* editorial—"The Cousteau Caper is just another one of these frantic attempts . . ."—reprinted in *Washington Post,* January 11, 1981.

245. The Cousteau Society prediction that visitors would enjoy "a personal adventure . . ." from *Calypso Log* (September 1984).

245. The Cousteau Society's prediction that visitors would enjoy "a cycle of emotions . . ." from *Calypso Log* (June 1986).

245. The Norfolk mayor's comment—"If [Cousteau] is on television . . ." —from *Washington Post,* January 11, 1981.

245. The comment by the journalist (George Reiger)—"The attitude seems to have been that Norfolk was darned lucky . . ."—from *Field and Stream* (June 1986).

245. "I'm disappointed. [Norfolk officials] don't know what they're missing." *Washington Post,* May 30, 1986.

246. At the Cousteau Ocean Center in Paris, the Captain appeals for everyone to "protect what they love." *Calypso Log* (June 1987).

246. "We [must] defuse the threat of an atomic war. . . ." *Calypso Log* (December 1981).

246. "The interaction between people and the aquatic system. . . ." *Calypso Log* (December 1986).

247. Cousteau spoke of "a moral gateway that exploration has given to humanity." *Calypso Log* (March 1986).

247. "Protecting dolphins and whales would be of no avail. . . ." *Calypso Log* (March 1985).

X. THE POET

248. "I was playing when I invented the aqualung." *Dial* (July 1982).

248. "Well, I think it will work. . . ." James Dugan, "Portrait of Homo Aquaticus," *New York Times Magazine,* June 21, 1963.

249. The perfect life is for a man to be "pushed by his instincts, needs. . . ." Sara Davidson, "Cousteau Searches for His Whale," *New York Times Magazine,* September 10, 1972.

249. "From birth, man carries the weight of gravity on his shoulders." *Calypso Log* (June 1985).

249. Cousteau's description of his three philosophies from *New York Times Magazine,* September 10, 1972.

250. "[Bertrand Russell's] work for me is the fantastic combination. . . ." *Calypso Log* (June 1985).

250. Russell's writings summarized in *Bertrand Russell's Best* (New York: New American Library, 1961).

250. "When I reason . . ." *Calypso Log* (June 1985).

251. "I think the only usefulness of people today. . . ." *Ibid.*

251. Cousteau promised to "devote all of his remaining efforts" to a vast exchange of children. Speech at Mount Vernon, Virginia, June 1985.

251. Cousteau believes "people use [marriage] to avoid facing the fact that we are all solitary and perishable." *New York Times Magazine,* September 10, 1972.

251. Cousteau believes love is "a drug to blur the truth. . . ." *Ibid.*

251. "I find myself flirting with the morbid idea of lassitude." Cousteau Society brochure.

251. "[My personal life] is no one's business but my own." *Washington Post,* May 30, 1986.

251. "Are there beautiful women here?" *New York Times Magazine,* September 10, 1972.

252. "[Mountains are] oppressive things." *New York Times,* February 22, 1953.

252. "We can spend three months waiting on *Calypso*. . . ." *New York Times Magazine,* September 10, 1972.

252. Jan Cousteau's comment—"He always brought good weather."—from *New York Times Magazine,* September 10, 1972.

253. Sara Davidson's comment—"It is dark as night . . ."—from *New York Times Magazine,* September 10, 1972.

253. Cousteau credits his skill to "fantastic luck." *The Living Sea.*

253. Philippe's comment—"I have known highly skilled seamen . . ."—from *The Shark.*

253. Cousteau recalls that "water fascinated me. . . ." *Calypso Log* (June 1985).

254. "The spirituality of man cannot be completely separated from the physical." *Silent World.*

254. "Undersea exploration is not an end in itself. . . ." *Jacques-Yves Cousteau's World Without Sun.*

254. "Organic anesthetics can be extracted from marine animals. . . ." *The Ocean World of Jacques Cousteau: Quest for Food.*

254. Cousteau believes the undersea environment "is not ours." *Calypso Log* (June 1987).

255. "Bull! If you begin to believe in yourself. . . ." *Los Angeles Times,* June 15, 1986.

255. "We enrich our own souls when we reach out. . . ." *Calypso Log* (March 1980).

255. "The history of the *Calypso* is important to me. . . ." *Life and Death in a Coral Sea.*

255. "[My crew were] sensitive men, men who have not found happiness or peace in leading an ordinary life." *Ibid.*

256. "[The crew must withstand the] stress from too much to do. . . ." *Calypso Log* (February 1988).

256. "We lose about one person a year." *Ibid.*

256. Louis Malle's comment—"Cousteau was graceful enough to give me credit . . ."—from *Calypso Log* (June 1985).

256. "That's easy, it's because Armand made me the best cameras in the world." *Ibid.*

257. "When one person . . . has a chance to lead an exceptional life. . . ." Turner Broadcasting System's promotional brochures.

257. Philippe Cousteau's comment—"We were akin to those knights-errant . . ." —from *The Shark.*

257. "I'm not interested in achievements. . . ." *Atlanta Constitution,* June 23, 1985.

258. "I'm pretty good with presidents." *Christian Science Monitor,* October 16, 1981.
259. Jean-Michel's comment—"While the world looks at life . . ."—*Dial* (July 1982).
259. Not spiritual or religious, "but a life full of daily inspiration. . . ." *New York Times,* June 21, 1963.
259. "[The book] would be an almanac. . . ." *Calypso Log* (October 1981).
260. Mose Richards' comment—The almanac "is about the entire world"—from *The Cousteau Almanac.*
260. "[The almanac] is a monument of data on uncorrelated things." *Washington Post,* March 22, 1987.
260. "[The *Peace Almanac*] will not be what people think." *Ibid.*
260. Richard Murphy's comment—"Everybody just rolled up their eyes"—*Ibid.*
261. Susan Schiefelbein's comment—The book will be "a conversation about life . . ."—from interview with author.
261. "After all the dangers of the Bomb. . . ." *Washington Post,* March 22, 1987.

XI. THE LEGACY

264. Jean-Michel's comment—Environmental preservation "begins with the inglorious, day-after-day analytical toils of scientists"—from *Calypso Log* (June 1982).
264. Jean-Michel's comment—Cousteau films have "generated financial support for scientific research"—*Ibid.*
264. Jean-Michel's comment—"Without the documentaries . . ."—*Ibid.*
265. Simone's role was to do "everything the men cannot do. . . ." New York *Daily News,* December 17, 1964.
265. Jean-Michel's comment—"We are really considering changing our views about [women]"—from *Washington Post,* May 30, 1986.
265. Cousteau feels "much freer having practically no money for myself." *Calypso Log* (June 1985).
265. "We are completely self-supported. . . ." *Calypso Log* (June 1983).
266. Jean-Michel's advertisement—"Education is the only means by which to appreciate the true values embodied in the ocean"—from *Calypso Log* (February 1988).
267. The Cousteau Society's advertisement—"Because in works of art . . ." —from *Calypso Log* (March 1983).
267. *Calypso Log* editors' note—We "agonized at taking two full pages in the *Log* to offer merchandise items"—from *Calypso Log* (September 1986).
270. The society advertises that winners will "dive with either Jean-Michel or Captain Cousteau." *Calypso Log* (June 1988).
270. "[Jean-Michel] beats me in one thing—he's a good administrator." *Variety,* May 29, 1985.
270. Jean-Michel's comment—"With the death of Philippe we've lost a talent I don't have"—from *Dial* (July 1982).

271. Jean-Michel's comment—"My father has achieved almost everything"—from *USA Today,* June 7, 1985.

271. Jean-Michel's comment—"[The Captain] is my boss . . ."—from *Christian Science Monitor,* June 23, 1985.

271. Jean-Michel's comment—"I remember my father as a philosopher"—from *Calypso Log* (March 1985).

271. Jean-Michel's comment—"There's a sailor and a sub-sailor."—from *Washington Post Magazine,* December 4, 1988.

271. Jean-Michel's comment—"My commitment is to focus on management of our world ocean resources . . ."—from *Calypso Log* April 1988.

272. David Brown's comment—"Jean-Michel really grilled me."—from *Washington Post Magazine,* December 4, 1988.

272. A society staff member's comment—"Zheek is a poet."—*Ibid.*

272. Armand Davso's comment—"The Captain has taught me many things" —from *Calypso Log* (December 1982).

273. Raymond Coll's comment—"I continue to dive because of the beauty . . ." —from *Calypso Log* (June 1981).

273. Dominique Sumian "is an experienced professional diver. . . ." *Calypso Log* (June 1982).

273. Louis Prezelin's comment—"You have to join the action"—from *Calypso Log* (September 1985).

274. Jean-Michel's comment—Simone "has been *Calypso*'s guiding spirit" —made at the Captain's seventy-fifth birthday party.

275. The Cousteau Society's statement—"The woman is naked"—from *Calypso Log* (March 1985).

275. "Today, social problems swallow the world" *Calypso Log* (December 1986).

275. Jean-Michel's comment—A peace park "would be a buffer zone for nature . . ."—from *Calypso Log* (April 1988).

276. *Island of Peace* "introduced a people who have managed to establish peace. . . ." *Calypso Log* (April 1988).

276. Frédéric Dumas's comment—"When I met Cousteau . . ."—from *Calypso Log* (June 1985).

276. Louis Malle's comment—"I always loved working with Cousteau . . ." — *Ibid.*

276. Albert Falco's comment—"I am in my sixties"— *Ibid.*

276. Ruth Dugan's comment—"When I picture [Cousteau], I see him leaving great piles of paper everywhere"—from *Washington Post Magazine,* January 11, 1981.

277. Ellen Goodman's comment—"It isn't possible to be participant and recorder at the same moment"—from *Washington Post,* May 24, 1988.

277. "I live in my ivory tower. . . ." *Los Angeles Times,* June 15, 1986.

278. The Cousteau Society publicist's comment—Cousteau has "rescued countless endangered species . . ."—from *The World of Cousteau: A Captain's Logbook.*

278. Cousteau pledged to become "a fighter against the system when it is wrong." *Christian Science Monitor,* September 9, 1975.

278. Cousteau also pledged to "present the case of our Water Planet. . . ." The Cousteau Society's direct-mail appeals.

279. "I have made friends with death." *USA Today*, June 7, 1985.

279. "I have accepted death not only as inevitable but also as constructive." *Los Angeles Times*, June 13, 1985.

279. "I pray to God to be switched off in action." *USA Today*, June 7, 1985.

279. Cousteau admits his vertigo is "very disagreeable." Phil McCombs, "South Pacific! The Passage to Papeete," *Washington Post*, March 22, 1987.

280. "As a token of my deep solidarity, I wish to express my sincere desire to take part in one of the next shuttle flights." *Calypso Log* (March 1986).

281. "Maybe when you [Céline] have cut your hair properly. . . ." Comments made at seventy-fifth birthday party.

281. "The great absence tonight—Philippe." *Ibid.*

281. "I have a good wife and a good son. . . ." *Dial* (July 1982).

281. "From the very first, my sense of wonder at the sea has alternated with a sense of revulsion." *Diving for Sunken Treasure.*

281. "My motive in seeking out new sites to explore . . ." *Ibid.*

281. Cousteau takes "my pride from a wild love for life. . . ." *Calypso Log* (March 1987).

282. "When I finish a film, I never look at it again. . . ." *Atlanta Constitution*, June 10, 1985.

282. Jean-Michel's comment—"My job is to allow my father to be as efficient as possible . . ."—from *Washington Post Magazine*, January 11, 1981.

282. "You know, I think I'll do it all." *Calypso Log* (June 1985).

Index

307